23-38

ERRATA

〇〜〇〜〇

A Study in
BALKAN CIVILIZATION

BORZOI STUDIES

❧ IN HISTORY ❧

CONSULTING EDITOR:

EUGENE RICE

COLUMBIA UNIVERSITY

TRAIAN STOIANOVICH

RUTGERS UNIVERSITY

A Study in
BALKAN
CIVILIZATION

ALFRED·A·KNOPF   NEW YORK

TO MY MENTOR
FERNAND BRAUDEL
AND TO
MARCELLE, CHRISTIAN,
AND
DIANA

ACKNOWLEDGMENTS

Without the work of fellow historians, anthropologists, sociologists, psychologists, archeologists, economists, and geographers, this study would have been impossible. My special thanks go to Warren I. Susman, Professor of American History at Rutgers University, for his encouragement and understanding. My greatest intellectual debt —and, in a very real sense, a very personal debt—is to my friend and mentor, Fernand Braudel. In a less personal way, I am under deep obligation to the searching, probing, experimental method of *Annales (Economies, Sociétés, Civilisations)*. Finally, but not least, I am grateful to the Rutgers Research Council for the financial assistance that made possible the completion of my research.

PREFACE

✧○✧○✧

History is past, present, and future: lasting, changing, and becoming. Events are indeed the raw stuff of history, but history is more than mere events, either minute or "great." It is an art—the art of understanding men in time and across space; it is a science—the science of the sciences of man.

Needless to say, neither historians nor other scholars will accept this definition without query. This study in Balkan civilization is an answer to that query. It is therefore not a standard or conventional history, much less a conventional history of the Balkans. It seeks instead to be a "total history." In other words, my goal has been to perceive as many of the various avenues and categories of human experience—more precisely, of Balkan experience—as possible and to move in the direction of elaborating a science of the sciences of man.

An interdisciplinary study, the book makes use of anthropological and sociological theory and grapples with the problem of economic change. The subjects covered are very diverse: they range from folklore and climate to birth techniques, pedagogy, and demography; from the role of salt in neolithic cultures to the role of silver in the medieval world and of price and wage movements in the premodern era; from status groups to kinship, clanship, and men's societies; from millenarian movements to revolution (the "Western Revolution" of the Napoleonic and post-Napoleonic era and the Communist revolutions of our own time); from the "industrial devolution" of the seventeenth, eighteenth, and nineteenth centuries to modernization; from archaic to modern notions of work, time, and space.

The book differs from anthropological studies in that it deals with large regional subcultures—Balkan civilization in the plural—instead of confining itself to "little communities." It is also historical or diachronic, a study of social space-time relationships. It differs no less from historical studies of the traditional type; for example, it is not limited to the usual short period of historians—a decade or a century—but embraces eight or nine millennia. It is, moreover, not a history of empires, kingdoms, republics, or city-states, but a history of peoples.

I hope it can be a guide—but not a mold. It is daring. I dare hope that it is sound, a challenging synthesis of working hypotheses.

T. S.

NOVEMBER *1966*

CONTENTS

❦❧

MAPS and DIAGRAMS

A Study in

BALKAN CIVILIZATION

INTRODUCTION

The subjects of our study are the *Balkans* and *civilization*. Both require definition.

The term "Balkans" lacks precision. Derived through Turkish from two Persian words meaning "high house" or "mountain," it is applicable to the area in question precisely because the latter contains four or five different mountain systems: the Pindus and Dinaric Alps in the west, the Rhodope Mountains in the center and southeast, and the Carpatho-Transylvanian and Balkan Alps in the northeast. Four seas also bound the Balkans: the Adriatic and Ionian to the west, the Aegean to the south, and the Black to the east. As one approaches the sea, one leaves the Balkans. At the same time, certain Balkan aspects linger on in the Aegean and Adriatic islands. Similarly, upon confronting the steppe to the northeast, one bids the Balkans adieu. But a few typically Balkan cultural traits extend into the steppe, and steppic traits—geographic and cultural alike—are manifest in eastern Thrace and south of the Danube and Sava rivers, areas that virtually everyone recognizes as integral parts of the Balkans. Some scholars and laymen exclude Greece, Dalmatia, Transylvania, or Moldavia and Wallachia (Rumania) from the Balkans, often with considerable justification. Even fewer will admit to the inclusion of Hungary. Our own approach is more flexible. We assume there is a core area that no one may exclude: whatever is not sea or steppe between the four seas and the Sava and the Danube. But we shall often traverse these limits, for several Balkan cultures merge in fact with the sea and the steppe.

Before the term "Balkans" gained currency around the middle of the nineteenth century, the area to which it alludes lacked a general name. In classical antiquity, the western portion was known as Illyricum and the eastern as Thrace. Medieval European travelers, on the other hand, designated various Balkan regions as Romanie, and the Ottoman Turks identified the eastern and central portions as Rumelia. Both names are derived from the long history of the Balkans as part of the Roman Empire. In the eighteenth century, European travelers called most of the area Turkey-in-Europe, in obvious reference to its inclusion within the Ottoman Empire since the fourteenth, mid-fifteenth, or early sixteenth century. A narrow region along the Adriatic coast, however, remained Venetian from the Middle Ages to the time of Napoleon, and during the sixteenth, seventeenth, and eighteenth centuries a northwestern area became part of the Habsburg dominions, later known as the Dual Monarchy (Austria-Hungary).

Our second concern is with the problem of civilization. Of many possible definitions of civilization, two strike us as especially relevant. First, the statement of an anthropologist, who defines culture—a synonym for civilization—as "an open system in a state of stable but moving equilibrium." The system maintains a boundary and accepts inputs or innovations and discharges older traits at approximately equal rates. It changes continuously but gradually in terms of content but remains relatively constant in terms of structure or complexity of total arrangement.[1] A historian adds that civilization is "first of all a space, a 'cultural area,' a dwelling," filled with "a mass of

[1] Anthony F. C. Wallace, *Culture and Personality* (New York: Random House, 1961), p. 142.

very diverse 'goods' or cultural traits": the form and substance of a house and roof, tools and weapons, a dialect or group of dialects, culinary tastes, manners of belief, or ways of love. "The regular arrangement, the frequency of certain traits, their ubiquity in a precise area are the first signs of cultural cohesion. If to the spatial coherence there is added a temporal permanence, the total repertory, the set, is a civilization or culture." [2]

Geologists, archeologists, and psychiatrists are generally concerned with layers—strata and substrata of rocks, cultural objects, or thoughts and feelings. They will hardly accept as a maxim that the most exposed is what is most important. On the contrary, they hold to the view that what is buried deep is often what is most significant. Historians, on the other hand, tend to stress surface phenomena and, unlike gestalt psychologists, who study human behavior in terms of total configurations or structures, emphasize individual occurrences and what is unique.

Geological, archeological, and psychological principles enter into the very organization of our study. Each chapter is an entity in itself, but the chapters should in fact be read consecutively, for each is a view into a particular system of coherences, notably of the structure that must exist before the next structure can arise. The deepest structure relates to the earth and cosmos, above it is a biological layer, above the biological a technological, above the technological a social, above the social an economic stratum. The geographical and biological structures change most slowly, and only after the rise of an economic or pure-economic structure can there be human individuality or a personality culture. We therefore open our study with a chapter on earth culture and conclude it with a chapter on personality, the newest and most fragile of all systems of coherence.

2 Fernand Braudel, "L'Apport de l'histoire des civilisations," in *Encyclopédie Française*, XX, *Le Monde en Devenir (Histoire, Evolution, Prospective)* (Paris, 1959), p. 20.12–7. [Author's translation]

KEY

NEOLITHIC SITES		MEDIEVAL MINE SITES
(1) Nea Nikomedeia	(6) Tuzla	1 Brskovo
(2) Sesklo	(7) Butmir	2 Novo Brdo
(3) Vršnik	(8) Karanovo	3 Srebrenica
(4) Starčevo	(9) Hamangia	4 Kratovo
(5) Vinča		5 Siderocapsa

Figure 1. Balkan Geography

I

EARTH CULTURE

❦

In the lore of the Pelasgian pre-Greeks, black earth was the most fertile of soils, and by way of homeopathic logic the opaque or black acquired among them a wondrous quality. Among the Slavs, the words for magic and black (and red) exhibit an identical root, *čar(n)* or variations thereof, and possess a cognate in Latin *carmen* or English "charm." Anglo-American cultures refer to the black art and to black magic. Wicked from the viewpoint of the Christian church, the black art is awesome and uncanny in the world vision of pagans.

EARTH MOTHER

To the ancient Arcadians of the Peloponnesus, the Earth Mother was Melaina, the Black Divinity. A fitting title for the deity of fruitfulness and fullness and "mistress of the earth and sea": black like the black-earth ritualistic pottery of Lesbos. Wearing black robes and a horse's head, in order to achieve communion with the ocean of ancestors, the legendary Melaina—or Demeter—retires to a cave—the paleolithic temple—to mourn the disappearance of her daughter Persephone. The

7

fruits of the earth perish and famine threatens. But a miracle occurs. The god of the underworld restores Persephone to her earthly abode in exchange for her promise to rejoin him annually. Upon her return the earth dons a garment of green, fruits grow again, life is joy.

Under Roman rule, the peoples of Pannonia and Dalmatia (present-day Hungary and Yugoslavia) honored three goddesses: the "mothers of the Pannonians and Dalmatians" of Roman inscriptions, probable replicas of the Greek Moirai (the trinity of spinners of fate) or of the Celtic *Matres Deae*. A veiled memory of this tradition persists in Serbian riddles, in which the secret names for earth are *Mama,* girl friend (*druga*), mistress (*gospa*), bride (*neva*), or parent's sister (*tetka*).

The clay, bone, stone, and ivory female figurines of the Aurignacians suggest that the Earth-Mother cult goes back to the prenomadic Aurignacian mammoth hunters of Eurasia. Aurignacian figurines represent two goddess types: one short-legged, obese or pregnant, and broad-hipped; the other tall, long-legged, and slender. Both figurines drew attention to the areas of fertility, one depicting perhaps the Mother and the other Kore, daughter ready for initiation to womanhood. Or, they may have incorporated dissimilar esthetic principles, the round and the cylindrical.

The role of Aurignacian women was symbolic: to obtain by mimetic ritual an abundance of wild herds and so ensure the biological and cultural continuity of the band. However, in the postglacial period, with the rise of nomadism and the downgrading of the pseudoeconomic role of women, the cult of the Great Mother similarly declined. When it was revitalized after the introduction of hoe-farming by women, it gained an added significance: to secure by mimetic ritual an abundance of crops.

Little is known of Balkan paleolithic art (what we call art was then in fact a form of magic), but in the Balkans as elsewhere, neolithic art tended to shift from naturalism to symbolism and abstraction, even in representations of the Great Mother, now often portrayed as a stylized tree or cross. Participants acting ritually in behalf of an entire group sought to divest themselves of their individuality by putting on a mask, a device for achieving communion with the Prime Mother. Tattoos and painted designs on neolithic figurines discovered at Gradac in Serbia, Cucuteni in Moldavia, and Sesklo in Thessaly presumably proclaim their sacral character. Extant neolithic clay stamps suggest that magical designs were likewise applied to the human body. In any event, Thracians, Dacians, Agathyrsi, Sarmatians, Illyrians, and Celto-Illyrian Japodes practiced the magical art of puncturing or tattooing the body in the time of Cicero, Virgil, Pliny, and Strabo. In Bosnia, home of the ancient Illyrians, the custom of tattooing persisted among Roman Catholics of the Vrbas valley until the twentieth century. Tattoo patterns were known to them by various names: cross, ear of corn, twig, fir tree, circle, and ring fence, all symbols of regeneration and procreation, with an overlay of a later sun cult. They utilized, in effect, the supposedly archetypal mandala symbols of Jungian psychology.

KOUROS

Under a complex set of circumstances, including the appearance of bronze and iron technologies and of horse-breeding nomads, there was a shift of emphasis between 2500 and 1500 B.C. from an Earth Mother to a Sky Father. Although never complete, the shift was aided by the subsequent development of cities, by the growth of enlightenment, by the apparent displacement of totemism by anthropomorphic religion, and by the spread of Christianity and Islam.

The transformation came through the partial evolution of the totemic cults (tree, ivy, serpent, wolf, dog, deer, goat, bull, boar, bear, horse, etc.) into a cult of the reborn male youth or

Kouros: Dionysos of the tree, Dionysos Zagreus, the Thracian Sabazios, and Attis, Adonis, Osiris, and Hermes, or the rider of the "green horse" (*hippos chloros*), the three-headed Thracian cavalier, the three-headed "tsar" Trojan (or Trajan), and their Christian successors: St. George, St. Theodore, St. Martin, St. Michael, St. Nicholas, and St. Sava. The latter are all horsemen; St. Sava was reputed in Serbian legend to have as companions both a horse and hound, and St. George was known as the rider of the green horse Zelenko.

All the Kouroi were underworld demons who resettled in the skies. All were messengers of death and resurrection. All were culture heroes, inventors, teachers, saviors: the first of the prometheans, first to domesticate animals and give them different tasks, first to teach man to yoke oxen to the plow, first to practice the art of metallurgy, first of the millers and weavers, first to cultivate the vine and the olive. Inventions earlier credited to the Earth Mother were often reassigned to these males. They were especially venerated, however, for those inventions, like the hammer, axe, scythe, millstone, mill wheel, and implements of war, that aided the process of transition from an Earth Mother to a Sky Father cult.

The enactment of the mimetic death and resurrection of Dionysos and Osiris lived on in the Christian story of the resurrection of Christ. The Christ in effigy of the Easter holy days is in fact one of the few sculptured (hence, three-dimensional) figures retained in the Greek Orthodox church after the partial victory over iconoclasm in the ninth century by the partisans of the cult of icons. The Easter holidays occur indeed during the season of the Eleusinian mysteries, and both depict a period of awakening from the sleep of death. Greek peasants look upon the Easter festival, one of the few occasions on which they joyously get drunk, as conducive to the growth of their crops.

Many persons believe that wooden and other three-dimensional idols or images disappeared from the social and religious practices of Byzantium and the Greek world after the compromise between the image-breakers and the advocates of the cult of icons. In Athens, however, where paganism lingered longer than in almost any other part of the empire, wooden idols known as *xoana* were borne in processions conducted to ensure communal health and wealth even as late as the War of Greek Independence (1821). This was an obvious carry-over from the procession of the twelve *xoana* representing the Olympians of the east Parthenon frieze. These processions were regularly followed in Greek antiquity by a sacrifice and communal meal, similarly designed to ensure the health and prosperity of the city.

Rites of the death and resurrection of the male youth were enacted in Greek girls' spring initiation ceremonies until a half-century ago. In the Zagori district of Epirus, the Kouros was known as Zaphiris, and a girl normally played his part. Sometimes, however, he was a wooden doll (idol) or a bundle of leaves in the form of a cross. The ritual thus suggests an older rite of the death and resurrection of Kore, the Earth Daughter. Covering Zaphiris (girl, boy, idol, or cross) with leaves and flowers in a ceremony purporting to portray his death, a band of local adolescent girls would burst into a threnody bewailing his legacy: a house in ruins and a grieving bride (*kouremadia*) "with a belly [stretching] to the mouth." Of a sudden, however, Zaphiris would miraculously come to life.

GREEN GEORGE

The Balkan Slavs link growth and fertility rites with St. George's Day (April 23). In Macedonia and Bulgaria, young people celebrate the day by swaying on swings. Like dancing and jumping in the air and over fire, swaying symbolizes growth, vitality, virility, fertility. In Bulgaria, young men and maidens set up swings from tree branches and sing songs. In

one such song, the Sun's Mother instructs him how to win a
maiden "more radiant" than he:

> Coming are the sacred days,
> Will come also holy George's day.
> Lower then the hammocks from the sky,
> On that wondrous day, St. George's day.
> To swing and sway for their health,
> All the girls will come to play.
> Maid Dobrinka will also come!
> Lift then the hammock up, up, up,
> And raise the maiden to the skies![1]

In Croatia, a "Green George" leads a company of "Georges"
in a *kolo* or round dance from one village house to the next;
the dancers sing songs welcoming nature's rebirth and calling
for the fertility of the soil. In Slovenia, a "Green George" and
a company of goatskin-clad youths, or *koranti,* enact the struggle between winter and spring. Between the "Green George"
of the Balkans and the "Green One"—*al-Khudr*—of Muslim
Arabs, identified by Arab Christians of Syria with St. George
and regarded by members of both faiths as a spring deity, the
relationship is obvious. There may also be a connection between the Croatian Georges or Slovenian *koranti* and the
Phrygian *korybantes,* Cretan *kouretes,* and Roman *salii* of old.
The latter were youths who played the role of fertility demons
and possessed gear simultaneously musical and military: a
stretched skin to serve both as shield and timbrel, and a
cudgel, sword or spear that was also a drumstick.

St. George's Day was a day of fun and frolic, but the spring
festival also required precautionary measures to assure the fertility of cattle and crops. In certain parts of Serbia, until recent
years, it was the solemn duty of the master and mistress of each

---

[1] Boris A. Kremenliev, *Bulgarian-Macedonian Folk Music* (Berkeley and
Los Angeles: University of California Press, 1952), p. 131. The translation
is my own; it differs somewhat from Kremenliev's, although both transla-
tions convey the same essential meaning.

household to perform certain rites, either on the eve or morning of St. George's Day. They would place a small stone on each fruit tree to make it taboo to caterpillars, pass some milk through a hole in an oak bark to assure the family of cream (*kajmak*) thick as the bark for the rest of the year, make crosses of hazelnut branches and stick them in the fields in order to obtain a plentiful harvest, place a bucket of water in the cattle enclosure to entice each cow to yield an equivalent quantity of milk, rub the udders of milch-cows and sheep with nettle, and so on.

Serbians and Croatians thus designate St. George's Day as the "herdsman's holiday" or "feast of the herds." On this day they observe, or did until recently, the traditions of baking a ritual cake for the health of their cattle, ceremoniously milking their sheep and making their first cheese of the year, weaning the lambs born during the previous winter, and driving their herds and flocks from the lowlands to the pastures of the verdant mountain. St. George is known to them indeed as the shepherd, the lord of the forest, and, enigmatic as this may seem, the protector of wolves.

FIRE RITES

Until the last few decades, St. George's Day was also an occasion for the lighting of bonfires, as were St. John's or Midsummer's Eve (June 23/24, the summer solstice of the old Roman calendar), the feast of St. Vitus (June 28), the three days preceding and following the feast of St. Peter (July 12), the Bulgarian fire feasts or *goreštnici* (July 15, 16, and 17), and the three days before and after the feast of the prophet Elijah (July 20). The lighting of the fires was designed to purify, exalt, and kindle anew the forces of life. The rite was a general practice among all the peoples of the Old World.

Almost everywhere in the Balkans, the participants in fire rites shouted, sang, and leaped over the fire. Sometimes they danced or raced wildly through the woods and over the hills. Erotic in appearance, their behavior was essentially ritualistic, except as it degenerated through the process of secularization. The singing, dancing, hopping, turning, shouting, and gesticulating were intended to demonstrate the health, vigor, and virility or femininity of the actors and thus magically procure for them future health and vigor, a bride or husband, a long life, and even immortality.

The ritual fire was a special fire, variously known as the living, sacred, or divine fire. It was produced in several ways— basically, however, by the paleolithic method of rubbing two pieces of wood; in the Balkans, hazel, willow, oak, linden, or dogberry were traditionally used. The fire rites assumed different forms in different places, and the occasion for the ritual varied. In some places, the fire was made on a special day of each year in accordance with well-defined customs; in others, the building of a new house might be the occasion for a fire to symbolize the passage or transition from one residence to another. Or the occasion might be the occurrence of some other significant event, like an epidemic; this too required a rite of passage, one that was intended to leave behind a world of calamity and disease in order to enter a world of well-being. There have been fire rites even for cattle, such as the so-called shrine of the ox (*volovska bogomolja*). In the event of an epizootic, for example—and in some places at a fixed time of the year—Balkan-Slavic villagers passed their cattle, sheep, goats, pigs, and horses through a tunnel covered by a fire, or led them between two trees whose branches had been set ablaze—another rite of passage into a world of well-being.

The making of a living fire, or "needfire," was generally preceded by the quenching of the old fires and followed by the lighting of the hearths with the new fire. The practice prevailed in the nineteenth century among both the Balkan Slavs and the Albanians, but it was very old, having been known to all the ancient Mediterranean and Indo-European cultures.

The classical Greeks, for example, kept an ever-burning sacred fire in their Prytaneion, or civic hearth building, the ancestor of our town hall. Among the Romans and Hebrews of antiquity, as well as among the Greeks, the living fire was normally created by rubbing two pyrites. The Romans generally made the fire at the feast of the Paliliae (or Pariliae) on April 21, an occasion for confession, purification, and renewal, resembling in many ways the later paganlike pastoral and agricultural festival of St. George.

NEOLITHIC CULTURE

The culture of the Earth Mother, of Kouroi, Green Georges, and Thracian cavaliers, and of the rekindling of fires is a culture partly of paleolithic origin but so thoroughly remodeled that we may properly designate it as neolithic. Until the mid-nineteenth century, the folk culture of the Balkans was fundamentally an earth or a neolithic culture of this kind, a culture of survivals and anachronisms.

In a sense, all our preceding remarks constitute a description and definition of neolithic culture. Beyond this, however, that culture embodied a gradual but basic shift from food-gathering as a primary way of life to the cultivation of plants and domestication of animals, which in turn led to the formation of settled farming communities.

Until recently, archeologists placed the beginning of the Balkan neolithic period in the first half of the third millennium B.C. During the last decade or two, however, many of them have suggested that the period should be updated. They base their recommendations on the radiocarbon method of dating.

Devised at the close of World War II, the radiocarbon method is based on the hypothesis that radioactive carbon-14 atoms present in living matter are lost at a fixed rate when a plant or animal dies. By measuring the residual radioactivity in organic matter, scientists determine the approximate date at which the matter was part of a living plant or animal. What reduces the method's reliability, apart from a few technical problems that are yet to be resolved, is the fact that the radio-activity level has not always been constant. By and large, however, scientists consider radiocarbon dates for the neolithic period as trustworthy, more so in any event than dates for the paleolithic period and the period of the last two millennia.

Because the method has been applied sparingly to Balkan sites, our dates may have to be revised when more of them are available as checks. On the basis of current data, however, here is a chronological table of the earliest Balkan and Western Asiatic neolithic:

TABLE 1

Place	Location	Culture Complex	Date B.C.
Jarmo	Iraq		6750 ± 200
Jericho	Dead Sea valley		6480 ± 160
Nea Nikomedeia	Greek Macedonia		6220 ± 150
Belt Cave	Northern Iran		5840 ± 330
Khirokitia	Cyprus		5685 ± 100
Hacilar IX (deepest level)	Central Anatolia		5600
Gyálarét	Hungary	Körös	5332 ± 100
Vršnik III	Yugoslav Macedonia	Starčevo	4915 ± 85
Gornja Tuzla	Bosnia	Starčevo	4889 ± 75
Vinča	Serbian Danube	Vinča A	4426 ± 60
Hamangia	On the Danube west of Constanţa	Pontic-Anatolian-Cycladic	4106 ± 70
Csöszhalom	Hungary	Tisza	3647 ± 60
Hăbăşeşti	Moldavia	Cucuteni A	3539 ± 80

Many eminent scholars reject the notion that a neolithic farming culture developed independently in Europe. Vladimir J. Fewkes, for example, finds no acceptable sign of independent cultural evolution in the central Balkans and Danubian area and infers that a neolithic culture arose there only after peoples who had learned to farm in other regions had settled there. On the other hand, while accepting this hypothesis in part, the late V. Gordon Childe stressed that the neolithic culture of the middle Danube region contained not only cultural traits introduced from the south—cereals (one-corn wheat and millet), farming methods, clay seals, vase-painting techniques, and a preference for Spondylus shells—but a number of indigenous traits. Because it served the needs of the local inhabitants, this culture was preserved, with certain refinements and minor intracultural transformations, until the middle of the nineteenth century.

More extreme than Childe, Richard Pittioni rejects the notion that neolithic culture was carried to the Danube by immigrants from other regions and denies the likelihood that it arose through the spread of ideas from abroad (stimulus diffusion). Holding that the transmission of ideas requires and assumes prior relationships between peoples, Pittioni advances instead a theory of "historical convergences," which maintains that Danubian dwellers developed a neolithic culture when local conditions were sufficiently ripe to make them want it and to make them ready to borrow elements from other cultures and remold them to suit their own needs. A stimulus from abroad could thus occur only after a conscious or unconscious demand for stimulation by some members of a given culture.

SALT OF THE EARTH

Crucially pertinent to the theory of historical convergences is the fact that a neolithic culture could not arise in Europe until after the transformation of the cold climate into a moist temperate one and of tundra vegetation into deciduous forest. The forest became unsuitable for hunting in large bands, and people were thus impelled to settle along river and lake banks and marshes, where shells, fish, and aquatic plants like the water chestnut and yellow nenuphar were abundantly available as food.

The earliest Balkan neolithic communities thus huddled close to rivers and lakes (see Figure 1). Nea Nikomedeia emerged near the mouth of the Haliakmon and Axios (Vardar), at the edge of the former Yiannitsa Lake. Otzaki, Tsani, and Magoulitza arose in the valleys of several small Thessalian streams to the south, and Sesklo appeared to the southeast, near a lake and close to the sea. Vršnik sprang up near the Bregalnica; Vinča, Starčevo, Kličevac, and Žuto Brdo near the confluence of the Danube and the Sava or the Danube and the Morava; Gornja Tuzla near the two Tuzla rivers. Moreover, several networks of cultures—Körös (Criş), Tisza, and Maros (Mureş)—are named appropriately after rivers.

After an initial existence as food gatherers around lakes, marshes, and rivers, the people of Nea Nikomedeia, Sesklo, Vršnik, Starčevo, and Tuzla learned to domesticate both plants and animals. According to Robert J. Rodden, the Nea Nikomedeia dwellers domesticated, or were on the verge of domesticating, sheep, goats, pigs, and cows some 9,000 years ago; during this period they also engaged in spinning and weaving, grew wheat, barley, lentils, and peas, fished, and gathered pistachio nuts and acorns in the surrounding forests. In addition, they made pottery and statuettes of fertility goddesses. The earliest Starčevo levels show similar evidence of fishing, domestication of plants and animals, pottery-making, and spinning and weaving.

Following the innovation of hoe-farming and the taming of one or more animals, men gradually altered their food habits. Hunters had generally roasted their meat—for man had known the use of fire in the paleolithic period—or had eaten it raw. In either case, they had obtained the salts needed by their bodies without adding sodium chloride. Neolithic men, on the other hand, were obliged to add salt to their foods after they adopted a new culinary method: boiling their vegetables, cereals, and meats. They likewise required salt for their animals and for the preservation of their meats, fish, and vegetables from season to season. A vegetable they learned to preserve quite early was the cabbage, from which they may have made a kind of sauerkraut similar to the *kiselo zele* of the later Bulgarians, which requires six kilograms of salt to a hundred heads of cabbage. The storage and boiling of foods created in turn a need for containers and may have been a significant stimulus to the making of pottery, that is, of pots for neolithic man's soups and cereals and for other food that had to be cooked in a pot.

A few human societies started to add salt to their foods about 10,000 years ago, but the cultural traits suggesting a need for sodium chloride—farming, domesticated animals, and pottery—became manifest in the Balkans between 9,000 and, 5,000 years ago. The fact that so many of the words for salt in Indo-European languages are cognates would indicate that most Indo-Europeans were familiar with it at least 4,000 years ago, before the migrations of the second millennium B.C.

Because they required salt in their daily diet, the earliest farmers had to settle in an area where they could easily procure it, or they had to produce or otherwise obtain surpluses for use in exchange for gifts of salt. Indeed, the earliest neolithic communities were generally located close to salt supplies. We may at least infer this from current place names around neolithic sites. Haliakmon, river site of Nea Nikomedeia, thus contains the Greek word for salt (*hals*) and was presumably so named because of the salt present at its mouth. Similarly, the first syllable of Tuzla, a center of salt works for many centuries, is the Turkish name for salt, and the Illyrian term *bos,* from which is derived the name for the province of Bosnia, in like manner signified salt. Bosnia is thus literally "the salt country." In addition, the dwellers of the areas of the former Starčevo and Körös cultures have secured much of their salt during the last two millennia from the mines of neighboring Wallachia, from salt works such as those of Slănic and Doftana in Muntenia or Ocnele Mari in Oltenia. Is it unreasonable, then, to conjecture that the older Starčevo and Körös peoples did likewise? Or, they may have got their supplies from the mines of adjacent Transylvania. The salt of the mines of Moldavia, Bukovina, and Galicia doubtless catered to the needs of the Cucuteni and later Tripolye culture, which occupied the steppic region from the Siret River and Danube delta in the west and south to the Dnieper in the east.

In historical times, marine salt was gathered at the mouth of the Hebrus (Marica) in the northern Aegean, along the eastern Adriatic coast and its Mediterranean continuation—at Trieste, at Piran, Koper, and Milje in maritime Slovenia, at Pag and Šibenik, at the mouth of the Neretva (ancient Narenta), at Gruž or Gravosa (in the territory of Ragusa or Dubrovnik), at Novi (Castelnuovo) and Kotor (Cattaro), at Durrës (Dyrrachium), at Corfu, Santa Maura, and Zante, in the Gulf of Arta, and at Clarenza and Patras—in the Gulf of Smyrna, at Naxos, Phocaea, and Mitylene (Lesbos), at Burgas (ancient Anchialos), and at Cyprus.

An English traveler, John Locke, relates his impressions of the Cypriot salt lagoons in the year 1553:

> . . . we hired horses to ride from Arnacho to Salina, which is a good mile. The salt pit is very neere two miles in compasse, very plaine and levell, into the which they let runne at the time of raine a quantitie of water comming from the mountaines, which water is let in until the pit be full to a certaine marke, which when it is full, the rest is conveyed by a trench into the sea. This water is let runne in about October, or sooner or later, as the time of the yeere doth afforde. There they let it remaine until the ende of July or the middest of August, out of which pits at that time, in stead of water that they let in they gather very faire white salt, without any further art or labour, for it is only done by the great heate of the sunne. . . . The most part of all the salt they have in Venice commeth from these Salines,

and they have it so plentifull, that they are not able, never a yeere to gather the one halfe, for they onely gather in July, August, and September, and not fully these three monethes. Yet notwithstanding the abundance that the shippes carie away yeerely, there remaine heapes like hilles, some heapes able to lade nine or tenne shippes, and there are heapes of two yeeres gathering, some of three and some of nine or tenne yeeres making, to the value of a great summe of golde. . . . This salt as it lyeth in the pit is like so much ice, and it is sixe inches thicke: they digge it with axes, and cause their slaves to cary it to the heapes.[2]

Locke was describing the salt lagoons of the plain of Larnaca. A similar lake, with a poorer grade of salt, was situated to the west of Limassol.

In the first century A.D., the Romans appear to have regarded the salt of Cyprus as the best of all marine salts. We can infer from this that salt was probably also known to the neolithic folk of Khirokitia. The location of their settlement, halfway between the lagoons of Limassol and Larnaca, would suggest that this was not unlikely.

Like the Western Asiatic sites of Jericho and Jarmo, the Balkan and Aegean neolithic sites were invariably situated close to salt marshes or mines, or in a place to which salt could be brought to them by boat and later by cart or horse. When more thoroughly untangled, the story of salt should clarify once and for all the still uncertain relationship between the process of cultural diffusion and the process of historical convergences; that is, whether the act of transmitting ideas and goods is more significant than a community's objective and subjective readiness to receive them. Nevertheless, we can guess

[2] Richard Hakluyt (ed.), *Principal Navigations, Voyages, Traffiques and Discoveries of the English Nation,* Vol. II, Part 2 (London: George Bishop, Alfred Newberie, and Robert Barker, 1599), p. 108. For more recent editions of the above, under the same title, see Vol. V (1904), pp. 93–94, published by James MacLehose and Son (successor, Jackson Son & Co., Ltd.) of Glasgow, or Vol. III (1927), pp. 26–27 of the Everyman's Library edition, published by J. M. Dent & Sons, Ltd., of London and Toronto, and E. P. Dutton and Co. of New York.

even now that communities near but not actually at a salt site were prodded into producing surpluses in order to exchange their surplus commodities for salt. Later, the salt gatherers themselves were inspired to produce goods that imitated those they had acquired in this way. Finally, gift exchange evolved into economic exchange, a business of professional traders. Neolithic culture spread in these ways from one community to another. The process of cultural diffusion was inextricably entangled with the process of historical convergences.

PERMANENCE OF CULTURE AREAS

To the concept of historical convergences, let us add the concept of the spatial continuity of cultures, or "permanence" of culture areas. Despite ethnic migrations, despite the modification of techniques, despite the appearance of new elite cultures, the creation of empires, and the disappearance of old and the appearance of new tongues, the total number of culture areas remained approximately the same from the creation and diffusion of the neolithic way of life to the close of the eighteenth century. Furthermore, culture areas have tended to remain as distinct entities, with only slightly shifting frontiers, even when the total culture of an area was altered through the influx of new ethnic groups or the intrusion of other cultures.

As intimated in our introduction, culture is an organized and partly integrated way of life, a system of learned or conditioned human behavior and the processes and patterns of communicating basic system values to succeeding generations. All persons sharing a common system of behavior and a common language or other forms of communication are thus members of a separate and unique culture. But culture is also bipolar, at once catholic and parochial. Its catholicity finds expression in an ecumenical world vision, in knowledge, things, and symbols that can be easily transmitted from one society to another through the medium of culture-bearers in both. Its parochial or folk configuration derives from its ethnocentric vision of the world. On the one hand, it is for export. On the other, it can belong to no other people.

What is exported, moreover, is never an entire culture, only individual culture traits. When a people moves from one area to another, it has to divest itself of many of its old traits, and it acquires in the new area many new ones. Each culture area thus tends to continue as an entity even though the culture it lodges may be changed substantially or even replaced by an altogether different one.

Similarly, culture areas tend to preserve their distinctiveness through the constant need of the societies they lodge to make decisions. But decisions can be crucial: A society may have a choice of several courses of development, but once a decision is made and the society starts off on one particular course, it is extremely difficult to turn back and start off on another one. The choices objectively open to a society are theoretically very large. In practice, however, they are limited by the experiences that each particular society has already had, and especially by those decisions that constitute a "psychohistorical focus"—the choices that foster a distinctive emotional pattern, a specific complex of cultural values, a precise way of organizing a particular environment; in short, the choices that allow the society to assert its basic identity even as it changes in detail.

Examples of a psychohistorical focus are the "Greek Miracle," the Renaissance, Calvinism, the French Revolution, the Russian Revolution, and now the Relativity Revolution or age of data-gathering and processing devices, of probing into the subconscious and manipulating the mind, and of mobilizing alternately promising and frightening nuclear sources of power. Of all the above, the last is probably the most crucial. Only one psychohistorical focus approaches it in importance, the neolithic view of the world.

A psychohistorical focus is a special vision of the world, a special way of occupying and manipulating space, a special complex of attitudes toward the earth and the cosmos. Among elite groups, it changes more frequently than at the folk level, but in either case we confront what Fernand Braudel aptly calls *la longue durée,* for it can last hundreds and thousands of years and "exceed in longevity all other collective realities." [3]

A folk psychohistorical focus that has lasted until our own time came into being in the central Balkans during the fifth and fourth millennia. In general outline, this folk culture was everywhere alike, a culture of fisherfolk and farmers, free of the culture of cities, which hardly existed until the first millennium B.C. After the rise of the cities, the folk culture became a peasant culture, different from the folk culture in that it was dominated from without. The new peasant culture retained, however, the basic psychohistorical focus of the older folk culture.

The neolithic folk culture of the Balkans constituted in some respects a single civilization, but it was also in the neolithic period that the Balkans split into several culture areas and subareas. We can identify five of these areas with a fair degree of assurance: a central folk culture—Starčevo—in what is today Serbia, Macedonia, and western Bulgaria; a northern complex of Danubian cultures—Körös, Maros, Tisza—in Hungary and Transylvania; an eastern culture of the steppes—Cucuteni in Moldavia, Hamangia and Boian along the lower Danube, and Tripolye in the western Ukraine; a southern Aegean culture; and a northwestern culture—Butmir—in Bosnia. The steppic culture extended southward from the Danube across eastern Bulgaria and Thrace into Thessaly. The central or Morava-Vardar culture (in its Vinča forms) ran from northeastern Bosnia or from the Serbian Drina in the west to Troy and western Anatolia in the east and to Macedonia and Thessaly in the south. Eastern Bulgaria was thus a zone of encoun-

---

[3] Fernand Braudel, "L'Apport de l'histoire des civilisations," in *Encyclopédie Française,* XX, *Le Monde en Devenir (Histoire, Evolution, Prospective)* (Paris, 1959), pp. 20.12–10 to 11. [Author's translation]

ter between the central Balkan and the Moldavian or steppic culture, while Thessaly was a zone of encounter of three culture areas: central, Moldavian, and Aegean.

The steppic complex of cultures revealed a preference for obese female figurines, painted pottery, and spiral design; later it embraced a zoomorphic art. In the Danubian cultures, painted pottery was rarer, incised or banded ware (with textile and basketry motifs) was more frequent, and spirals occurred in repetition patterns. The central Balkan cultures displayed a preference for incised pottery, finger-impressed designs in white paint, and spirals, but not for repetition patterns. Moreover, their female figurines were more slender. The Butmir culture of central Bosnia was like the Danubian and central Balkan in its appreciation of incised spiral designs, like the Danubian in its choice of repetition patterns, and like the Anatolian in its predilection for black-earth statuettes of Hittite-like physical type. Aegean neolithic culture possessed its own set of distinctive characteristics.

In terms of content and detail, the above cultures have been modified across the centuries in a variety of ways. But they have retained their individuality as culture areas despite a multiplicity of political experiences and an *apparent* lack of linguistic continuity.

SOIL, FOREST, AND CLIMATE

More important in the shaping of cultures than cultural anthropologists will normally admit is geography. But once a psychohistorical focus has been chosen and the culture of an area becomes established, minor changes in the relations between fauna, flora, and the works of man and nature will not significantly alter the culture unless other factors—technology, sociology, and economics—also intervene. We shall attempt to demonstrate the correctness of this view by a brief discourse on Balkan soils, forests, and climates.

In the Cambrian period of the Paleozoic era, several hundred million years ago, the Balkans constituted an uninterrupted continental land mass with Asia Minor, but during the Silurian period a vast inland ocean extending from Sumatra to the Atlantic moved in to usurp most of the area. Geological folding during the Carboniferous period produced the Carpatho-Balkan mountain system and caused a partial recession of the sea. Subsequently, during the Tertiary period, the Carpatho-Balkan system and the Slovenian, Dinaric, and Pindus Alps were uplifted, and the Cambrian core, or Rhodope Massif, was altered. These upheavals culminated during the Tertiary and Pleistocene in the formation of the Adriatic and Aegean seas and in the submersion of Pannonia and adjacent areas in a revived but shallow inland sea. As the continental glaciers withdrew, the sea was slowly drained off by the Danube, which cut a gorge (Iron Gate) through the Carpatho-Balkan system, thus dividing it into two parts, a Carpatho-Transylvanian system to the north and a Balkan system to the south.

The Balkans began to acquire their present physical appearance only in Pleistocene times and just prior to the neolithic. Residues of the former inland sea remained, however, as lakes or lake basins, such as the now drained and tilled Lake Copais of Boeotia (first drained in Minoan times and then again at the close of the nineteenth century), the Vardar-Morava and Marica depressions, which were once lake basins, and many Macedonian lakes. Until a hundred years ago, remnants of the old sea were also evident in the Hungarian Plain, a portion of which, including stretches of the Danube and a zone east of the Tisza, from the Bega to the Njírség, lay under water for more than eight months of the year.

Also formed in interglacial times and after the final withdrawal of the continental glaciers (8000 B.C.), just before the neolithic, were the loess soils of Pannonia and of the eastern Balkans and the Ukraine. (Loess is now rare in the western and southern Balkans, either because the area was widely forested during the Pleistocene and loess was never deposited there, or because the loess has since been carried away by erosion.) Loess comprises fine, porous particles of mud which dried up after the glacial retreat and were blown by winds to various foothills or dropped in relatively treeless steppe areas.

Generally rich in humus, loess soils are very fertile, but several conditions must be met before they support a long-lasting forest cover: they must occur at a fairly great depth (more than the usual ten feet common in Pannonia), the water table in the area should not be too low, and rainfall should be fairly abundant. Aware of many of these needs, an intelligent British observer of a century ago noticed an important distinction between the forest-bearing and alluvial soils of central Serbia and the loess of the Banat:

> The soil at Požarevac is remarkably rich, the greasy humus being from twenty to twenty-five feet thick, and consequently able to nourish the noblest forest trees. In the Banat, which is the granary of the Austrian empire, trees grow well for fifteen, twenty, or twenty-five years, and then die away. The cause of this is that the earth, although rich, is only from three to six feet thick, with sand or clay below; thus as soon as the roots descend to the substrata, in which they find no nourishment, rottenness appears on the top branches, and generally descends.[4]

Indeed, during the eighteenth and part of the nineteenth century, sand and clay soils gained ground in Hungary to the detriment of loess, as trees were felled and marshes drained to further the growth of a cereal economy and fulfill the requirements of new colonists and of a generally expanding population.

For a fine study of Mediterranean forests between the sev-

---

[4] Andrew Archibald Paton, *Servia, the Youngest Member of the European Family: or, A Residence in Belgrade, and Travels in the Highlands and Woodlands of the Interior, during the Years 1843 and 1844* (London: Longman, Brown, Green, and Longmans, 1845), pp. 255–56.

enth and eleventh centuries, one may turn to Maurice Lombard.[5] Unfortunately, Lombard errs in regard to the central Balkans and western Greece, where forests were far more widespread than indicated on his map. For example, during the First Crusade (1096), the troops of Walter Sans-Avoir and his uncle Walter of Poissy took eight days to traverse the densely wooded *silvae Bulgarorum*—so named for their location in an area once forming part of the Bulgarian Empire—between Belgrade and Niš. These forests are curiously missing from Lombard's map.

In 1433, another traveler from Western Europe, Bertrandon de la Broquière, councillor of Philippe le Bon of Burgundy, was less impressed by the magnitude of Serbia's forests—the *silvae Bulgarorum*—than by her allure as "a very pretty and well inhabited country," with a "great profusion of villages and good foods and especially good wines."[6] A tremendous colonization effort had transformed the Mačva plain, Morava valley, and right bank of the middle Danube into one of the most densely settled areas of the Balkans.

Three centuries later, the same area was perhaps more sparsely settled than any other Balkan land. Where there had once been people there were again forests. The wife of the English ambassador to the Porte, Lady Mary Wortley Montagu, accordingly spent seven days in 1717 passing through the thick woods between Belgrade and Niš.

In 1830, Serbian forests were slightly thinner, in consequence of the recolonization undertaken after 1750, but an English major, George Keppel, received a letter from a friend

[5] Maurice Lombard, "Un problème cartographié: Le bois dans la Méditerranée musulmane (VIIe–XIe siècles)," *Annales (Economies, Sociétés, Civilisations*), XIV (April–June 1959), 234–54 and map at end of periodical.

[6] Charles Schefer (ed.), *Le voyage de Bertrandon de la Broquière, écuyer tranchant et conseiller de Philippe le Bon, Duc de Bourgogne* (Paris: Ernest Leroux, 1892), pp. 203–11. [Author's translation]

describing the area between Niš and Belgrade in terms very similar to Lady Montagu's. Trees became more frequent as one moved northward from Niš, low oak brushwood lay on each side of the road for many miles, and "immense oak forests" covered "the face of the whole country" between Jagodina (Svetozarevo) and Belgrade. "The vast quantity of timber which lay felled on the side of this road to rot" grieved him: "If we had but all these useless trees in England!" But signs of the imminent decline of Serbian forests were already at hand: "We repeatedly saw the finest oak trees in blaze: a hole is cut near the bottom, and a fire lighted in it. This is the easiest way of clearing the ground." [7]

More lyrical in his enthusiasm for the Serbian woods after his trip of 1833 from Niš to Belgrade was the French poet and politician Alphonse Marie Louis de Lamartine. Traversing an "ocean" of "virgin forests," Lamartine traveled for six days through "magnificent and perpetual umbrages with no other spectacle than the endless colonnades of enormous and lofty trunks of beech, the waves of foliage swayed by the winds, [and] the avenues of hills and mountains in the uniform garb of their secular oaks." Upon orders of the government of the new principality, however, the people were cutting roads, a sight that made him feel as if "in the midst of the forests of North America, at the moment of the birth of a people or the founding of a new colony." [8]

The proud woods of the *silvae Bulgarorum,* of Šumadija, or Serbian Sylvania, are no more. In place of forests of oak and beech now stand patches of *šibljak,* deciduous brushwood.

[7] George Keppel, *Narrative of a Journey across the Balcan, by the Two Passes of Selimno and Pravadi; Also of a Visit to Azani, and Other Newly Discovered Ruins in Asia Minor, in the Years 1829–30,* 2 vols. (London: Henry Colburn and Richard Bentley, 1831), Vol. I, pp. 456–58.

[8] Alphonse Marie Louis de Lamartine, *Voyage en Orient: Souvenirs, impressions, pensées et paysages pendant un voyage en Orient, 1832–1833,* Vol. II (Paris: Hachette et Cie, 1911), pp. 257, 264. [Author's translation]

Southward, šibljak yields to pseudomacchie or evergreen brushwoods and then to hard-leaved evergreen shrubs, or macchie, and low, shrubby phrygana.

We cannot estimate, with any degree of precision, the extent of the deforestation that occurred before 1830. Moreover, even for the period since then, information is scarce and sometimes unreliable; for some regions, there is no information on the deforestation that took place before the end of the nineteenth century. It is therefore with some reservation that we present the data in Table 2 showing the decline of Balkan forests between 1830 and 1950 and the partly successful effort in Serbia and Bulgaria during our own century to revive them. Since, moreover, we possess two sets of Bulgarian figures, we may conclude either that deforestation continued in Bulgaria until the mid-1920's or that it was stopped between 1910 and 1920. The forest coverage of Greece seems twice as extensive in 1920 as in 1910, but the increase is illusory, being solely a reflection of the annexation to Greece in 1912 of the more widely forested areas of southern Macedonia and Epirus. In the Serbian case, several estimates depict a less sharp decline of forests during the nineteenth century than is shown in the table and therefore reveal a less notable recovery in the twentieth. Part of the problem stems from the insuperable difficulty of arriving at a precise and universally satisfactory definition of a forest.

A human problem since the neolithic period, since the taming of the sheep, goat, and pig, and since man's use of slash-and-burn methods to clear the ground of trees, deforestation has sometimes also been an opportunity, as in the case of Attica, where, according to Arnold J. Toynbee, it was the challenge that inspired Athens to become the mentor of Hellas:

> When the pastures of Attica dried up and her ploughlands wasted away, her people turned from the common pursuits of stock-breeding and grain-growing to devices that were all their own: olive-cultivation [actually learned from the inhabitants of southwestern Asia] and the exploitation of the subsoil. The

TABLE 2

Territorial Extent of Forests in Various Balkan Areas
1830–1950

(Percentage of total area)

Area	Year											
	1830	1850	1870	1890	1900	1910	1920	1930	1940	1950
Bosnia-Hercegovina	—	—	—	—	—	50.0	48.0	45.5	43.5	41–45.9
Bulgaria	—	—	—	—	31.0	29.0	23.5	—	—	—
(Alternate statistics)	—	—	—	—	32.0	28.0	27.0	28.0	32.0	—
Croatia-Slavonia	60.0	—	—	—	—	—	34.0	33.5	33.0	32.4
Greece										
Pre-1912	—	—	—	12.0	11.0	9.5	—	—	—	—
Post-1912	—	—	—	—	—	—	19.0	18.0	17.0	14.5–16.5

(Table 2 continued)

Area	\multicolumn{10}{c}{Year}									
	1830	1850	1870	1890	1900	1910	1920	1930	1940	1950
Montenegro	—	—	—	—	—	—	52.5	—	—	28.9
Moldo-Wallachia	—	—	—	—	21.0	—	19.0	—	18.0	—
Serbia	65.0	50.0	35.0	22.5	19.0	15.0	18.0	20.5	23.0	25.8
Vojvodina	—	—	—	—	—	—	5.1	—	5.0	5.0

SOURCES: For some of the sources on which this table is based and for an overall view of the problem of forests and deforestation in the Balkans, readers may refer to Emile [Jacques Yvon Marie, Baron] de Borchgrave, *La Serbie administrative, économique et commerciale* (Brussels: P. Weissenbruch; Belgrade: P. Tchourtchitch, 1883), pp. 126–31; Pierre George, *L'Europe Centrale*, II, *Les états* (Paris: Presses Universitaires de France, 1954), map on p. 724; Auguste François Victor Jardé, *The Formation of the Greek People*, translated from the French by M. R. Dobie (New York: Knopf, 1926), pp. 25–29; Branislav Jovanović, "O sumama Srbije početkom XIX veka," in Fasc. 32 of the Serbian Geographic Society (Srpsko Geografsko Drustvo), *Geografski lik Srbije u doba Prvog ustanka* (Belgrade, 1954), pp. 17–35; George Clenton Logio, *Bulgaria Past and Present* (Manchester, Eng.: Sherratt and Hughes, 1936), pp. 169–77; Werner Markert (ed.), *Osteuropa-Handbuch: Jugoslawien* (Köln/Graz: Böhlau-Verlag, 1954), p. 246; Emmanuel de Martonne, *La Valachie. Essai de monographie géographique* (Paris: Armand Colin, 1902), pp. 295–98; Alfred Philippson, *Das Mittelmeergebiet: Seine geographische und kulturelle Eigenart*, 3rd ed. (Leipzig and Berlin: B. G. Teubner, 1914), pp. 147–55; Alfred Stead (ed.), *Servia by the Servians* (London: William Heinemann, 1909), pp. 255–59; Peter F. Sugar, *Industrialization of Bosnia-Hercegovina, 1878–1918* (Seattle: University of Washington Press, 1963), pp. 129–38, 160–61, 211–12; Bickham Sweet-Escott, *Greece: A Political and Economic Survey* (London and New York: Royal Institute of International Affairs, 1954), pp. 94, 124, 178; William Bertram Turrill, *The Plant Life of the Balkan Peninsula: A Phytogeographical Study* (Oxford: Clarendon Press, 1929), pp. 135–216; Slavtcho D. Zagoroff, Jenö Végh, and Alexander D. Bilimovich, *The Agricultural Economy of the Danubian Countries, 1935–45* (Stanford, Calif.: Stanford University Press, 1955), p. 239.

gracious tree of Athena not only keeps alive but flourishes on the bare rock. Yet Man cannot live by olive-oil alone. To make a living from the olive-groves, the Athenian must exchange Attic oil for Scythian grain. To place his oil on the Scythian market, he must pack it in jars and ship it overseas—necessities which called into existence the Attic potteries, and the Attic merchant marine, and also the Attic silver-mines, since international trade demands a money economy and thus stimulates an exploration of the subsoil for precious metals as well as for potter's earth. Finally, all these things together—exports, industries, merchant ships, and money—required the protection and defrayed the upkeep of a navy. Thus the denudation of their soil in Attica stimulated the Athenians to acquire the command of the sea from one end of the Aegean to the other, and beyond; and therewith the riches which they had lost were recovered a hundredfold. [Furthermore], the extinction of the Attic forests compelled Athenian architects to translate their work from the medium of timber into the medium of stone and so led them on to create the Parthenon instead of resting content with the commonplace log-house which Man has always built in every place where tall trees grow.[9]

Numerous factors have made for deforestation: accidental and naturally provoked fires; the building of houses and navies; the burning of limestone and charcoal; the smelting of gold, silver, lead, and iron; the collection of resin to make pitch; the building of roads; the drainage of marshes and consequent lowering of the water table; the kindling of forest fires to catch brigands or enemy troops; the exportation of timber and fuel wood; the ravages of sheep, pigs, and goats; and slash-and-burn farming and forestry. Behind some of these factors loom economic development and population growth. But a factor still missing from our analysis is climate. Was climatic change, we now inquire, the result of deforestation and afforestation, or were the latter occurrences themselves manifestations of climatic change?

[9] Arnold J. Toynbee, *A Study of History*, Vol. II (Published under the auspices of the Royal Institute for International Affairs by Oxford University Press, London, 1934), pp. 39–41.

Balkanologists have devoted less attention to climate as a factor of historical change than have scholars of Scandinavian, North American, and Alpine studies. In his monumental *Méditerranée,* however, Fernand Braudel points to a number of facts that may signify a deterioration of Mediterranean climate during the latter part of the sixteenth century. More unreservedly, Scandinavian scholars hold that there was a climatic deterioration in Scandinavia, and one of them—Gustaf Utterström—supposes a simultaneous improvement of climate in an intermediate zone extending from England to the southern Baltic. Utterström further links the growing need for grain in the Mediterranean toward the close of the century to climatic impairment, and the ability of the Baltic countries to place grains in Mediterranean markets after 1580 to climatic improvement in the Anglo-Baltic zone. Data on the Balkan climate are very meager, but our own research, mostly in French consular archives, reveals a few suggestive details (see Table 3).

Inconclusive though they are, available facts for the Balkans and adjacent areas tend to support the view of a more humid and cooler Balkan climate from the close of the sixteenth to the end of the eighteenth century, indeed almost to the mid-nineteenth century in Hungary and Serbia. Until about 1840, observers continued to describe Serbia as a land of bogs and swamps, some of which never dried, notably in the Sava, Drina, Kolubara, and Morava lowlands. Its later transformation was achieved in part by private and public reclamation projects. In a more profound sense, however, it may have been more properly the result of the contraction of the Alpine glaciers, which began in earnest around 1840.

By 1850, the cold humid phase came to an end, yielding to a warm dry phase. Since that time, the average yearly temperature has increased everywhere in the Balkans except in peninsular Greece by half a degree Centigrade every fifty years. In Attica and peninsular Greece, a slight cooling of the climate may have occurred.

TABLE 3

Date	Area	Information
June 1601	Balkans	Torrential rains ruined crops and, says Braudel, made people fear "a corruption of the air."
1580, 1589, 1594–1602, 1608–10, 1640–44, 1664, 1676–79, 1700–3	Alps	Gap in data on Balkans, but Alpine glaciers steadily expanded and continued to do so until 1720. Not unlikely that this helped produce cooler and wetter springs and summers in Balkans, as it did in France and Central Europe.
December 10, 1631	Salonika	Rain of ashes fell on Salonika for 24 hours. Probably resulted from eruption of Mt. Vesuvius that day. During same month, similar rain fell on Istanbul.
Summer 1694	Northern Balkans	Notation in prayer book found in Valjevo district (Serbia) in 1820's: "So the Turk came to Varadin but ran away again because of the heavy rain; rain fell for forty days in the summer of 1694."
December 1695	Levant, Egypt, Asia Minor	Drought prevented germination of wheat in the Levant and Aegean. In Asia Minor, rats ate wheat reserves, threatening Anatolia with famine. In Cairo, 800 persons died of starvation daily.
Autumn and winter 1713–14	Aegean Macedonia	Drought and cold.
February 1714	Athens and Aegean	Rain for last 10 months.
June 2, 1714	Aegean Macedonia	Drought continued; wheat prices soared.
Winter 1725	Istanbul	Wet, cold, stormy winter, worst in years. May have been worse than in the Baltic.

(Table 3 continued)

Date	Area	Information
September and October 1729	Banat	Continual rains and storms. In late September, "terrible" hail storm caused damage valued at several million florins to public buildings in Timişoara (Temesvar).
Winter 1730	Istanbul and Thrace	Rude winter. So much snow that Bosporus was transformed into "glacial sea."
April 11, 1739	Aegean Macedonia	Snow fell; frost destroyed fruit and vegetable crops but apparently not cereal crops. Snowfall preceded and followed by period of dry weather.
April 22, 1739	Salonika	Turks began public prayers for rain.
May 17, 1739	Salonika	Still no rain.
May 21–28, 1739	Salonika	Rained for an entire week.
Summer 1743	Aegean Macedonia	Rain interrupted a drought sometime before August 17.
December 24–25, 1754	Alexandria (Egypt)	Eighteen French and more than twenty other boats destroyed in storm nearby.
Winter 1755	Istanbul	Hard winter.
Spring 1755	Balkans and Anatolia	Drought. Public prayers for rain.
July to September 1772	Istanbul	North wind continued to blow without interruption.
Spring 1789 to spring 1790	Levant and Dardanelles	Repeated storms destroyed "prodigious quantity" of merchant ships.
October 1829 to April 1830	Moldavia	Winter of "unheard-of rigor." At one place temperature fell below $-30°R$ ($-35.5°F$, $-37.5°C$) on December 12, 1829.

If typical, the changes in the average yearly temperatures of the following Balkan and fringe-Balkan towns would imply a trend toward a warmer climate in the northern bulk of the peninsula and an unaltered or slightly cooler climate in the extreme south:

TABLE 4

Town	Base Years	Average Temp.*	Base Years	Average Temp.	Increase or Decrease
Ljubljana	1851–1900	9.06°C	1901–1950	9.50°C	+0.44°C
Zagreb	1872–1908	10.9°	1909–1945	11.5°	+0.6°
Belgrade	1888–1916	11.1°	1917–1950	11.8°	+0.7°
Athens	1858–1903	17.6°	1894–1929	17.4°	−0.2°

* Temperatures in degrees Centigrade.

Temperatures in Sofia have followed the pattern set at Belgrade, Zagreb, and Ljubljana, and at distant Kazan in the USSR, where the average yearly temperature rose between 1828 and 1934 by 1.5 degrees. In fact, the Balkan climatic trend reflects a world-wide tendency toward a warmer climate.

Many scholars ascribe the warmer and drier Balkan climate since 1850 to deforestation and urbanization. But in Attica and peninsular Greece, where urbanization was speedier and more intense than in the rest of the Balkans and where deforestation has continued despite the government's efforts to infuse in the people a rational "love and respect" for trees (differing from the old tree worship), the already warm climate has not become warmer. Deforestation and reforestation may indeed result in local alterations of climate, but the "causes" of general climatic change are of extrahuman origin.

Important as they were to daily life, the periodic climatic changes and the shifts in the total acreage of forests to which we have referred have produced no significant alteration in the frontiers of Balkan *culture areas*. Correctly analyzed, our data would favor the theory of the "permanence" of culture areas:

one may thus lay much stress on geography without espousing a theory of "geographic determinism."

SPACE: MANA AND TABOO

Man's vision and organization of space change in accordance with fluctuations in his notions of the cosmos. But since neolithic times, man's conception of the cosmos has been almost everywhere basically identical, steeped in the principle of the sacred or mythical space, the system of symbolically if not always geometrically concentric zones, Mircea Eliade's "architectonic symbolism of the Center."

In the neolithic period the house arose around or beside a symbolic familiar center such as the hearth. Around each house was maintained a space needed to ensure the psychological tranquillity and biological survival of household members. Apart from the temple-cave of paleolithic times, temples do not appear to have evolved in the Balkans until the second millennium, and at first they assumed the form of a sacred place with the sky as a roof, as on the island of Crete or at the hill settlement of Sultan in Bulgaria and at Paraćin and Rudnik in Serbia. Whether with a natural sky-roof or with the man-made sky of the later buildings, the new temple was both a special place of congregation and a special time of communion. It was in fact a spatial expression of the temporal and cosmic outlook of a special group that was so large (relatively) that it could not be brought together in an ordinary house and so separated physically that it could be easily assembled only at special (normally seasonal or vegetative life-cycle) intervals.

Perhaps a survival of the prehistoric temple is the South Slavic institution of the *zapis*. A sign of the cross carved in a holy communal or ancestral tree, usually a linden, the *zapis* existed in almost every Serbian rural community, among many Bulgarians, and among some Rumanians. In Serbian villages where settlers originated from widely different areas, there was a *zapis* for each group considering itself bound by its own specific traditions.

The fruit of a *zapis* tree was normally sacred or taboo, and climbing the holy tree was forbidden. As the residence of an underworld demon, it was the place of resort for the satisfaction of collective or communal needs, the holy place at which members of a community gathered at harvest time (a seventeenth-century source defines the times as every Sunday of the ninth month). There the community joined in a procession led by an Orthodox priest: the members circled the tree three times, performed a sacrifice, and ate a common meal. Rarely a geographical center, the *zapis* was always a symbolic center: the *sacral* center of the community, its only rivals were the graveyard and the church.

In early historical and probably in prehistoric times, a community was defined essentially in two ways, in terms of its inner hallowed space and in terms of its outer boundaries. In fact, from the latter notion grew the Greek, Latin, Celtic, Germanic, and Slavic terms for community: the Greek *polis;* the Common Germanic *tûn* (English *town,* German *Zaun,* and Dutch *tuin*); the Celtic *dunum, dun,* or *dum;* and the Slavic *grad* and *ograda.* All of these terms originally referred to a physically or symbolically fortified ring-fence or hedge. In Kievan Rus, the word customarily denoting commune—*verv'*—alludes perhaps to the ritual wreaths or strings attached to special trees or posts defining the outer limits of a given community. The expression lives on indeed in the South Slavic *vrvca,* which ordinarily designates a string but also signifies a wreath or marker. The Polish word for commune—*opole*—may be a cognate of the Greek *polis,* while the South Slavic *okolina,* like the Latin *orbis* and *urbs,* denotes a circle, the outer ring of a community. *Okolina,* however, may contain not only the sense of circle—*kolo*—but also an earlier sense of stake. From this point of view, an *okolina* was the network of posts (or trees), the outposts identifying the outer limits of an organized human collectivity. If not accompanied by special propitiatory rites, penetration by outsiders into the zone protected by the *okolina* was tantamount to an invasion of the outermost ring of the sacred space.

The hearth, the *zapis,* the prytaneion, the cemetery, and the temple, church, or mosque were the sacral centers. Around one or more of the sacral centers later grew civic and commercial centers. Beyond the religious, civic, and commercial nuclei arose the residential quarters, and beyond these quarters extended the limits of the city. But these limits were a succession of boundaries, ending only when the outermost boundary, the *okolina,* was reached.

Possessing similar focuses of sacral and social attention, rural communities were especially concerned with the delimitation of properties. To mark the boundary between the fields of two or more farmers, the ancient Greeks made use of many diverse objects and natural phenomena—statues, wayside altars, sanctuaries, watersheds, watercourses, and confluences of rivers. But the customary markers of places sacred and taboo were posts erected at regular intervals. Known to the Greeks as an *omphalos* and to the Romans as a *mundus,* the post, pillar, column, or obelisk was usually set above or beside the gravemound of an underworld demon or an ancestor, and was often ringed at the top with a wreath (resembling the Serbian *vrvca*). It was in fact a symbolic tree, characteristically a fruit tree. Believed to be the possessor of mana, or generalized impersonal supernatural power, it was always a focus of collective emotion and sacral fervor.

In Albania, at least until World War II, the designation of clan, family, and village boundaries required the participation of village or tribal elders and the performance of a precise ritual in which the persons charged with the erection of limits had to lay a curse upon themselves as assurance that their acts would conform to local precepts of justice. Albanian markers consisted of small stones, rocks, and boulders, small "witness" stones buried beside a larger stone, big stones with charcoal buried beneath them, deep holes, old trees, trees with notches, roads, and irrigation canals. In some parts of the country, the younger members of a family were ceremoniously shown the traditional markers at the spring festival of "Summer's Day." Boundary disputes were frequent and sometimes settled by the shedding of blood, for no group could honorably permit the loss of land consecrated by an ancestor.

North of the Danube, boundary markers no less sacred than those dividing families, villages, and clans separated territorial states. The Imperial (Austrian) consul to Bucharest, for example, describes the frontiers of Transylvania, Wallachia, and Moldavia in the 1780's as follows:

> The sources that spring from the summits of the Carpathians form the natural limits of Transylvania. Those to the south belong to the two principalities [Wallachia and Moldavia] while the transmontane sources belong to Transylvania. The latter plants an [image of its] eagle and the former plant a large wooden cross to mark their boundaries.[10]

The wooden boundary cross of the Rumanians was in all probability a symbol of an underworld spirit, like the *omphalos* of the ancient Greeks. It was indeed a special form of the *omphalos* and of the memorial marker known to the South Slavs as *potka*.

Embracing three distinct meanings—marker, taboo, and penalty—the *potka* spells out to preliterate folk:

> I am the ancestral demon of this community or family. If you are not of my community or family, do not go and do not allow your animals to go beyond the point where I stand because I have the magical power to inflict evil and harm upon those who do not heed the sacred taboo. The community in turn will impose a penalty or fine upon anyone who offends me or disregards my inviolate instructions.

10 J. [Stephen Ignatius] Raicevich, *Osservazioni storiche naturali, e politiche intorno: La Valachie, e Moldavia* (Naples: G. Raimondi, 1788), pp. 33–34. [Author's translation]

The *potka* is doubtless an ancient South Slavic institution, and an explicit reference to it occurs in the mid-fourteenth century code of Emperor Stephen Dušan, where it possesses the sense of fine or penalty.

The material from which a *potka* is made and the form it assumes vary in time and space. A tree, branches (especially of the hazelnut) stuck in a heap of earth, a post, or a mere heap of earth are the most common materials in the zone of central Balkan culture—Serbia, western Bulgaria, Macedonia, and adjacent territories in Albania, Montenegro, and Vojvodina. This is also the zone where the most common term for boundary marker is *potka,* whereas in some parts of Bulgaria it is *počka, bočka,* and *botka,* and in Dalmatia it is *cilj.* In most areas the *potka* assumes several forms, but one form generally prevails in each region. The dominant form of *potka* in the Morava area of southern Serbia, for example, is a post or pillar with a cross carved on it; in Timok near the Rumanian frontier in eastern Serbia, it is a post with a wreath of grass tied near the top; in Srem or western Vojvodina, it may be a post, stake, or pillar, and attached to it is a wreath (as in many parts of Europe), a sheaf of straw, or a board with a cross carved on it; in Kosovo and in the Skoplje area of Macedonia, the *potka* assumes the form of a mound of earth; and in Dalmatia and Montenegro, it is a mound of stones with a cross either erected over it or carved on one of the stones.

Geographic and topographic variations probably account for the different forms, with trees and posts prevailing in the middle forest zone, imported boards in the steppe area (Vojvodina), mounds of earth in deforested plains areas, and mounds of stones or individual stones in the Dinaric-Mediterranean karst region.

Since the nineteenth century the *potka* has been modified in two ways. First, the carved or erected cross has tended to vanish from the markers of Dalmatia, Montenegro, and Vojvodina, and perhaps of Macedonia (where the disappearance may have begun earlier, perhaps under the impact of Islam). Then, in Vojvodina, the board on which a cross was formerly carved started to bear the inscription—and several decades before the advent of communism—*ZABRANJENO* (FORBIDDEN).

The primitive purpose of the *omphalos* or *potka* was doubtless magical: to procure abundance and fertility and to ward off alien and evil spirits. In the early phases of the neolithic period, however, the institution probably began to acquire a protoeconomic significance—to keep strangers and their herds off the meadows and fields of some given human group. But the magico-religious and economic functions were so intricately intertwined that the purely economic role of the *potka* failed to be appreciated in a notable way until the nineteenth century, when it started to lose its magical role by being desacralized, secularized, rationalized.

The *potka* thus reflects the premodern vision of the world of the Balkan peoples. That vision also embraced, however, the concept of a holy or cosmic mountain (or mountains) as a link between heaven and earth. Vestigial beliefs current among Serbians until a half-century ago indicate that their ancestors once (but not in "earliest" times) had imagined the earth and sky as being joined together by hooks reaching out from four cosmic mountains lying at the four corners of the earth. Montenegrins believed that Mount Durmitor was one of the mountains that held up the sky, while Dalmatians ascribed a similar function to Mount Otres. Furthermore, Serbian poetry suggests a liaison between earth and sky by way of the mythical "iron mountain" (*gvozdena planina*), and Serbian mythology creates a vision of a "mountain of naiads" (*vilina gora*), which presumably reaches up from the earth to the moon.

In their notion of a cosmic mountain, premodern Serbians participated in a common premodern Mediterranean, Asiatic, and European, perhaps even all-human, view of the universe. Their Durmitor and Otres, their iron mountain and mountain of nymphs have parallels if not equivalents in the Mount Sumeru of Uralo-Altaics, in the pyramids of the Pharaohs, in the ziggurat and holy mount of Sumerian history and mythology, in Mounts Olympus and Parnassus, and in the Delphi of the Greeks, in Mounts Sinai and Zion of the Jews, and Rila and Pirin of the Bulgarians and eastern Macedonian Slavs, and in the sacred Christian Mounts Tabor, Athos, and Golgotha.

Although the conception of a sacred or necessary space is common to all peoples, the fourfold view of the world—four holy mountains, four heavenly rivers, four seas (northern, southern, eastern, and western), four suns, four points of the compass, four seasons of the year, four city quarters, four factions (the Blues, Greens, Reds, and Whites in Byzantium), and four tribes—is predominantly an Oriental notion. In Europe, Africa, and America, the prevalent world view was in terms of the number three. Indo-Europeans thus counted the passage of time in terms of nights and of the three crowings of the cock and divided the day (daylight) into morning, noon, and evening. This European numerical notion pervaded the thought of the ancient Hellenes until they came into contact with the Asiatic world of the Aegean, whereupon the European and Asiatic notions were drawn into a synthesis or allowed to exist symbiotically, or one prevailed over the other. For example, the Aegean-influenced Achaeans came to regard themselves as divided into four tribes and grouped their ships in multiples of four. The Dorian communities of later Hellenic invaders, on the other hand, were less influenced by Aegean culture and consequently conceived of themselves as members of three tribes and grouped their ships in multiples of three. The Balkan Slavs ultimately incorporated into their culture—the date of occurrence remains unknown—the presumably Asiatic image of four cosmic mountains.

Balkan man, we have observed, was until recently an earth man, like the other men of the world, a product of neolithic cultures, bound religiously, psychologically, and economically to the soil and space around him. The elite cultures that arose in the classical era of antiquity, in Roman, Byzantine, and Ottoman times, and in consequence of the teachings of Christianity, Judaism, and Islam, affected him and forced him to modify the folk culture. But not until the eighteenth and nineteenth centuries, indeed not until our own time, would an elite culture appear that would cause a radical transformation, seemingly an obliteration, of the old neolithic culture. Submerged, however, as it now is, the old folk culture still profoundly conditions the deepest thoughts and feelings of peasants, workers, writers, and thinkers, and of men of action and politics—in short, of Balkan man in general.

II

BIOTECHNICS and
SOCIAL BIOLOGY

◦⟨⟩◦◦⟨⟩◦

Balkan man's view of space offers an insight into his world view in general. We can refine and sharpen this insight by examining his manner of perception and determining the relative importance of the various senses and the significance of different parts of the body and of different bodily techniques and gestures in the expression of that world view. What we know about his manner of perception, gesture, and movement is derived from studies of classical antiquity and the medieval era and from relatively recent cultural anthropology, but the world vision and human condition they reveal doubtless date from a considerably more archaic way of life.

Man relates his environment to his own biological need for comparatively unbroken activity, or mobility, and for group life. Except theoretically, therefore, one can hardly discuss biotechnics—the manner of mobilizing the various parts of the body to cope with the environment—without some reference to sociology and technology, for group life requires the formalization of techniques, while the need for mobility, given the character of man's brain and hand, results in technical activity. Even when highly formalized, however, biotechnical acts probably retain some of their biological foundations. But technology is more than mere biotechnics. For these reasons, and because gestures are a mode of psychophysical communication more important sometimes than verbalization, we shall turn now to the subject of biotechnics. In so doing, we shall also probe into some aspects of the ill-defined discipline that lies at the frontiers of biology and sociology and is closely related to social psychology and dynamic sociology.

THE ILLUSTRIOUS OR THE TARNISHED FACE

Three dominant personality value orientations have characterized Balkan society for several thousand years: shame, guilt, and courage. As shown in Table 5 (p. 48), each of these value orientations is bipolar. The negative pole is sometimes the feminine pole, and thus some of the negative qualities are becoming in or "natural" to a woman. By and large, however, males are expected to behave—although they often fail to do so—in terms of the positive pole. Each value is identified by an abstraction in current use, of which we cite only the Greek and Serbian forms.

The customary expression in Serbo-Croatian and Bulgarian for the honor-shame value orientation, the most widely prevalent of the three value systems, is *obraz,* a term closely related to the Latin *imago* or Greek εἰκών, and to the Latin *persona* and Greek πρόσωπον. The Latin *imago,* we know, was the mask of wax molded on the face of a deceased ancestor and deferentially treasured in the family home. The *persona,* deriving perhaps from the Etruscan *farsu* and less immediately from the Greek *prosopon,* similarly defined a ritual or ancestral mask. The various meanings of *obraz* (as inferred from medieval Slavic documents)—form, image, character, person, symbol, face, figure, statue, idol, guise, and mask—suggest a history not unlike that of *imago* and *persona.* Its etymology—"cut-about" or "carving-around"—hints on the one hand at an

TABLE 5

Positive Pole	Greek	Serbian	Negative Pole	Greek	Serbian
Honor and glory, honor and esteem	*kleos* and *time*, *philotimia*, *philotimo*	*čast i slava* or *čast i poštenje*	Shame, modesty, humility	*entrope*	*sramota*
Philanthropy, good deeds, benevolence, pious donation	*philanthropia* and *eusebia*	*dobro delo* or *sevap*	Ritual inadequacy, pollution, sin, guilt	*hamartia* or *miasma*	*grehota*
Manliness, virility, nobility, courage in terms of the needs of patriarchal society and "humanity"	*arete* or *andreia*	*čojstvo*	Wanton violence, overbearing pride, use of power without moderation, "inhumanity" or self-assertion	*hybris*	*ljutina* or *nečoveštvo*

image or idol, perhaps of an ancestral deity, and points on the other to χαρακτήρ, the Greek term for carving tool, which was subsequently extended to the image shaped by the tool and ultimately acquired the meaning of "character."

Two expressions—*svetao obraz* and *crn obraz*—recur constantly in Serbian epic or heroic poetry, the chief vehicle of the courage culture, to denote, respectively, a face of illustrious reputation or a tarnished face. Indeed, from the Middle Ages —and, we suspect, for thousands of years before that—to the end of the eighteenth, and even well into the nineteenth, century, Slavic and non-Slavic inhabitants alike regarded the face as "the focus of honor." Even until the opening of the twentieth century, Serbian peasants traditionally raised their right hand or middle and index fingers to their face to seal a pledge. The focus of a person's honor if he and his family were honorable, the "face" became the focus of his shame if he or his family betrayed a trust or violated the folk culture. In the latter instance, he became a *nečovek* or "non-man," a man "without a face": *bezobrazan*.

The precedence of the honor-shame over the philanthropy-guilt orientation is amply demonstrated by an enumeration of sins in the peasant's system of values: disrespect for one's elders or older brothers; beating or striking one's parents; incest; desecration of the prescribed forms of behavior toward one's godparent, godchild, and foster brother or sister; neglecting to make a ritual visit to the home of a newly married daughter or sister; the commission of almost any act injurious to the existing family system; a transgression against any firmly rooted family, village, or clan way of life; niggardliness in the exchange of gifts; and killing the lead ram of a flock. The last was regarded as sinful because it frequently led to the dispersion of an entire flock and to economic loss or disaster for one or more families. Even the sinful was what was shameful, while the shameful included all human thought and action that was a threat to the existing social values.

THE REASONABLE EAR, THE WILLFUL EYE, AND THE RIGHTEOUS HAND

Through an appreciation of popular attitudes toward the face, and primarily toward the ear and eye, we may extend our knowledge of Balkan folk cultures. The French literary critic Paul Valéry appropriately observes in one of his verses:

Dans le poète:
L'oreille parle,
La bouche écoute. . . .[1]

This description of poetic culture may apply with equal validity to the cultures of preliterate peoples and of peoples in the early stages of literary evolution. Modifying Valéry's formula, we produce a verse more directly pertinent to our study:

In the Balkans:
The ear converses,
The mouth hearkens. . . .

On the other hand, in his *La Jeunesse de la Science grecque,* Abel Rey describes the Greek imagination as "remarkably visual." [2] This visualism is a structural characteristic of the maritime and insular peoples of Aegean culture, and we may distinguish indeed between the cultures of the maritime fringes, where the history of visualism goes back to the seventh and sixth centuries B.C., and the cultures of the Balkan interior (often very close to the sea), where visualism is of much more recent origin.

The emergence in ancient Greece of individuals who consciously or unconsciously set a higher value upon the visual function than upon the other senses, a partial consequence perhaps of the quality of the Aegean light, led a portion of Greek society to perceive each object as an independent or clearly differentiated plastic unit and allowed it to create a discipline (or several disciplines) of philosophy and to develop the sciences of mathematics, physics, biology, history and politics, and a rudimentary form of anthropology. But the mass of Greeks remained faithful to their beliefs in the gruesome sisterhood of Cholera, Plague (Panoukla), and Smallpox (Vlogia), in the ubiquity of capricious and sometimes cruel nymphs and nereids, in dryads or maiden inhabitants of fruit-

---

[1] Paul Valéry, *Tel quel,* I (Paris: Editions Gallimard, © 1941), 142.
[2] Abel Rey, *La Jeunesse de la Science grecque* (Paris: La Renaissance du Livre, 1933), pp. 27–28.

bearing trees, in Sir Boreas (the North Wind), in the "Bad Hour" (noontime), in half-human and half-animal centaurs (*kallikantzaroi*) who, like Chiron of old, effected cures with potions and incantations.

The Greek centaur occasionally assumed the guise of a wolf or *lykokantzaros* (and *vrykolakas*), a creature like the werewolf or wolf-haired man (*vukodlak*) of the Serbians, who was reputed to thirst for the blood of young maidens and was said to be the mate of a fire-winged gnome called *v(j)eštica* (literally, "the wise one," related to the ancient British *wica*). Outbreaks of lycanthropy, a form of madness in which the sufferer imagined himself to be a wolf or some other beast, were in fact very frequent in Western and Eastern Europe alike during the Middle Ages, and it was commonly held among the South Slavs that a werewolf in life became a vampire at death.

Still widely current among the Slavic, Greek, and other peasantries of the Balkans at the beginning of the twentieth century, these beliefs were, to be sure, the consequence of long tradition, but even more fundamentally they derived from a specific kind of mental structure: from the dominance in their societies of the nonvisual senses—hearing, smell, taste, and touch—which normally give rise to a diffuse, fluid, indeterminate, intuitive conception of subjects, and to an oral tradition, exemplified by Homeric and post-Homeric oral poetry (800–500 B.C.), by the Akritan epic cycle of ninth- and tenth-century Byzantium, and by the epic cycles of Serbian poetry (1400–1850).

The Balkan peasant was "visually backward," but this does not mean that he lacked good vision. For example, nineteenth-century Montenegrins apparently enjoyed a vision rarely marred by myopia. For all that, they were hardly visual-minded, for like other Balkan peoples and like pre-Enlightenment Europeans in general, they perceived visually not only—nor even primarily—the objects that were there, but the zoomorphized and personified things that supposedly lay behind the "objective" things: pure and impure spirits, fortune and misfortune, nymphs and werewolves, the echo and the nightmare, the guardians of marshes, caverns, and cemeteries (that is, the vivid images evoked by phosphorescent sparks), and a host of other subjective phenomena.

Distinctions are sometimes made between the visual Greeks and the auditory-minded Hebrews, who were made aware of God's presence by the clap of thunder and the blast of trumpets. Among the Greeks too, however, visual-mindedness remained essentially a minority phenomenon. Particularly in the village, the sense of vision, as a cultural device, failed to achieve an appreciable superiority over the other senses. An anthropologist thus properly identifies the basic mental structure of a contemporary Boeotian village by a reference not to its visualism but to its sense of smell:

> A sprig of basil is a common offering to a guest, with the admonition, necessary only for non-Greeks, to rub a bit of it between the fingers to release its aroma. Indeed, the sense of smell is a far more frequently functioning mode of perception in [the Boeotian village of] Vasilika than in America. The villagers investigate unrecognized substances by smelling them, the quality and freshness of food is tested partly by smell, the decision as to when food is properly seasoned or as to when it is cooked sufficiently is partially determined in the same way.[3]

But of all the nonvisual senses, the most significant in the previsual era and in societies with a previsual or antivisual orientation is the sense of hearing. The members of such societies frequently believe that "reason" or even the source of life itself is localized in the ear. Hesiod, for example, relates that the medicine man Melampous gained his prophetic knowledge by allowing snakes to lick his ears. The Albanian Ghegs of a much later era reduce the snake to the size of a worm and contend that this vital worm, lodged in the ear, is the agent of life and that the individual dies when the worm dies. In the

[3] Ernestine Friedl, *Vasilika: A Village in Modern Greece* (New York:

Middle Ages, a Latin hymn to the Virgin promulgated the idea of the immaculate conception in the ear, and almost universally people have worn earrings to protect the ear against the Evil Eye.

In Serbian society, the practice long prevailed in schools—almost to our own time—of "pulling children by the ear." During the nineteenth century, for example, teachers customarily ordered a pupil correctly answering a question to pull the ear of schoolmates who had previously given a wrong answer. As this custom was sometimes practiced, it mirrored the personal inadequacies of the teachers themselves, who were largely divorced from the ancient civilization of the folk but insufficiently immersed in the ways of modern civilization. The original intent of the pulling of the ear, however, was not to exhibit sheer cruelty, nor to demonstrate where power and authority lay, nor even to be appropriately harsh toward mental indolence, but rather to fortify the power of memory and reasoning of those pupils who displayed a deficiency in that respect through the extension of the hand of the more industrious, more gifted, or craftier student to the ear of the less industrious, less gifted, less crafty, or otherwise less fortunate. Moreover, when the future Serbian grammarian and folklorist Vuk Karadžić attended primary school in Loznica in 1796, it was still common practice for teachers to impose on pupils a ritual beating every Saturday—*subota: djačka bubota*. This beating, from which no pupil escaped, was administered with a hazelwood rod, for the hazelnut was regarded by Serbians as the "tree for knowing good and evil." The function of the hazelwood rod was to transfer to pupils a feeling of responsibility.

Two words served to designate a witness in medieval Serbia: *svedok* and *posluh*. The first identified an individual who knows something about a given event or person (like the English term itself) and the second referred to a person providing hearsay evidence. Neither term clearly designated an observer, for the best evidence was generally considered to be hearsay evidence and data concerning the reputation of a person or of his family. On the other hand, an early nineteenth-century Serbian proverb contends that "it is better to believe the eyes than the ears." But other proverbs then current, and seemingly of older origin, held that the eyes are "deceivers," that they "see everything but themselves," or that "they are [deceptive as] water." Contrarily, a good reputation is "better than a golden belt," and the word went out to the young: "Marry with your ears, not with your eyes."

In the 1840's, when Serbian art was just beginning to develop along Western European lines, an English observer visiting a house in Šabac that contained paintings of contemporary Serbian political figures was much amused by an oil painting of Prince Miloš:

> It was altogether without *chiaro scuro;* but his decorations, button holes, and even a large mole on his cheek, were done with the most painful minuteness. In his left hand he held a scroll, on which was inscribed *Ustav,* or Constitution, his right hand was partly doubled *à la* finger post; it pointed significantly to the said scroll, the fore-finger being adorned with a large diamond ring.[4]

From the point of view of Renaissance canons of art, founded on the principle of a single source of light illuminating a scene and one immobile eye looking at that light and so giving an apparent depth to the scene, the picture was "primitive." More exactly, it was based not on visual perception but on the reputation and status of the person being portrayed. "Byzantine" and "Slavo-Byzantine" ecclesiastical art of the eighteenth and first half of the nineteenth century differed from the secular art of the Balkans in medium and subject matter, but the two converged in their baroque or rural-seigniorial style and in their symbolic conceptions of nature.

4 Andrew Archibald Paton, *Servia, the Youngest Member of the European Family: or, A Residence in Belgrade, and Travels in the Highlands and Woodlands of the Interior, during the Years 1843 and 1844* (London: Longman, Brown, Green, and Longmans, 1845), pp. 114–15.

It is wrong to suppose, however, that the Balkan peoples minimized the importance of the eye. Indeed, they may have agreed with the conclusions of modern research that the dilation of the pupil of the eye not only reflects changes in light intensity, but measures the interest and emotional involvement and attitudes of the viewer. Like many other peoples, they have been intuitively aware for thousands of years of the power of the "fascinating eye": the βασκανία or ὀφθαλμός βάσκανος of the ancient Greeks, the *fascinatio* of the Romans, the κακὸ μάτι of Greek peasants of more recent times, or the *urokljivi oči* of the Serbians. In classical antiquity, the "fascinating eye" was sometimes attributed to entire communities and ethnic groups, notably to Cretans, Thebans, Cypriots, Illyrians, and Triballi.

Localizing human reason in the ear, South Slavic peasants associated will and pathos with the eye, the principal nonoral agent for the expression of anger, surprise, interest, contentment, indolence, mockery, disdain, deceit, humility, coquetry or desire. In other words, the eye is a mirror of the human emotions and passions, and it was commonly believed that a *zloočnik* or possessor of the Evil Eye could inflict misfortune and distress upon a pretty maid or strong or handsome youth, bring on an epizootic, or cause a small child to fall ill or even die. Thus, when a person admired a child, he was expected, in virtually all rural areas, to spit in the direction of its face or make a pretense of doing so. The mother or other protector of the child would frequently retort with the formula: "The fascination back to your eyes!" Until a century or half-century ago, South Slavic girls were in the habit of wearing a pendant or necklace of phallic, fertility, and power symbols, including images of such objects as cowrie shells, crosses, trees, hands, steps, cocks, tools, and weapons, as a means of warding off the Evil Eye.

One of the most effective symbols against the Evil Eye, according to popular tradition, is the right hand with the palm facing outward in the direction of the foreign eye, and fingers and thumb retained in their natural position. This gesture is often found on the tombstones or funereal and ancestral monuments (*stećaks*) of the western Balkans, sometimes represented as expressions of the religion and art of the Bogomil or Cathari heresy of medieval Bosnia, but doubtless of earlier origin.

Being an instrument and symbol of protection, the right hand is sacred. Pious Balkan Muslims and their coreligionists in other areas rarely use a knife or fork for eating, but when they do they invariably employ the right hand, dropping one tool to take the other, for Muslim tradition forbids them to take food with the left hand, just as they may not touch certain portions of their body with the right.

The right hand is similarly a symbol of justice and contract. A sale or purchase was thus often sealed in rural Serbian areas, even at the beginning of the present century, with a ritual handshake or clasping of right hands. Slavic nuptial rites also required a handshake between the contracting parties (the families concerned), and it is not without significance that the South Slavic terms for engagement (*poroka, zaruke,* etc.) and for an order of goods (*poruka*) both contain the root "hand."

The hand protects and binds. It also counts and measures. In the Homeric era, for example, the Greeks made use of their fingers in varying positions to express numbers mounting to the thousands. The Romans likewise employed the art of manual enumeration. In Serbian, there is a special word for the weight that a person can carry on his back (*zametica*), for the quantity of wood he can transport in the same manner (*breme*), or for the quantity of wood he can bear on his shoulder (*naramak*), but measures of length or quantity easily translatable into units of the body are expressed primarily in terms of the hand, arm, or foot. For example, *nokat* represents the length of a fingernail; *prst,* a finger's length; *dlaka,* a palm's length; *palac,* a thumb's length; *rastegljaj,* an elbow's length; *stopa,* a foot or step; *korak,* a pace; *pedalj,* the distance from the end of the thumb to the end of the middle finger when extended; *čeperak,* the distance from the end of the thumb to the end of the index finger when extended; *šaka,* a handful; and *pregršt,* a quantity that can be held in both arms. The same or similar words exist in Bulgarian, but such expressions are not confined to any specific ethnic group but rather reflect a general pattern in archaic cultures (of which vestiges remain in modern civilizations): a tendency to relate units of measure to the body and, above all, to the just or righteous hand.

GESTURES, TECHNICS, AND CIVILIZATION

Peoples with approximately the same language sometimes misunderstand and distrust each other. A different alphabet may be one source of such misunderstanding, as in the case of the Serbians, Bosnians, and Croatians, the first with a tradition of Cyrillic characters; the second with a mixed tradition of "Bosnian," Latin, Cyrillic, and Arabic scripts; and the third with a tradition of Glagolitic (a script somewhat older than the Cyrillic, now largely restricted to the liturgical books of a few Dalmatian communities) and Latin. But another source of discord is a wholly different set of gestures. An early nineteenth-century traveler and one-time chaplain to the British Embassy in Istanbul, Rev. Robert Walsh, clearly perceived the importance of gestures in distinguishing Ottoman from European civilization:

> The Turkish barber pushed the razor from him—ours draws it to him; the carpenter, on the contrary, drew the saw to him, for all the teeth are set in—ours pushes it from him, for all the teeth are set out; the mason sat while he laid the stones—ours always stands; the scribe wrote on his hand, and from right to

left—ours always writes on a desk or table, and from left to right. . . .[5]

The source of such differences may be technological. But once tools adapted in a certain way to the hand or to other parts of the body are widely diffused within a society, a psychological predisposition is created in their favor which makes it difficult for members of the society to accept tools requiring a different form of manipulation.

Some gestures have no direct relationship to technology but are such an essential part of intracultural communication that they will be altered only with the greatest reluctance and only in periods of tremendous cultural stress. Such gestures include the manner of saying "yes" and "no." The classical Greeks, who possessed a highly developed art of gesture, brought the head down to indicate acknowledgment and turned it sideways to show disapproval. Later, under various Oriental influences, they modified their gestures.

At the close of the period of Ottoman expansion in the latter part of the sixteenth century, the Balkans were divided into three broad cultural areas: (1) a northwestern zone, where the old gestures were preserved, as in most of the rest of Europe; (2) a southern and southeastern zone, in which Greeks and Orthodox Albanians brought their head down to say "yes" and threw it back to indicate "no"; and (3) a central and eastern zone, in which Serbians, Bulgarians, and some of their immediate neighbors shook their head to show affirmation and nodded to demonstrate negation.

Since the Enlightenment of the eighteenth century, and especially since the Serbian and Greek revolutions, the eastern and southern modes of expression have receded before the northwestern, particularly in the cities. Around 1900, the zone of eastern gesture was limited to the area north of Greece, as

[5] Rev. Robert Walsh, *Narrative of a Journey from Constantinople to England* (Philadelphia: Carey, Lea, and Carey, 1828), p. 95.

that country was then constituted, and east and south of a line running along the Morava River to Ćuprija and then turning southwestward to Bar (Antivari) on the Adriatic. To the east of this line, however, was an expanding frontier territory in which the gestures of the urban male youth were "Western" and those of the old folk and of women were "Eastern." During the past half-century, the "Eastern" gestures have continued to decline in importance. The southern or southeastern gestures of the Greeks (and indeed of many Turks) have been somewhat more tenacious.

EMOTIONAL STATES

Like the peoples of other European premodern societies, Balkan man was impulsive and much inclined to violence. A nineteenth-century Serbian statesman, Ilija Garašanin, could thus call upon God to "slay" his enemies, the Orthodox Church of Greece could invoke against Eleutherios Venizelos for his espousal of the Allied cause during the First World War "the ulcers of Job, the whale of Jonah, the leprosy of Naaman, the bite of death, the shuddering of the dying, the thunderbolt of Hell, and the malediction of God and man." [6] Montenegrins, who—like the Turks, Albanians, and Bocchese, or inhabitants of Boka Kotorska on the Adriatic—engaged in headhunting when at war, until their government took steps to put a stop to the custom in 1862, are known to have torn Muslims to shreds with their teeth in hand-to-hand combat on the waters of Lake Scutari (Shkodër, Skadar).

Even more than violence, however, what characterizes the Balkan peoples is their impulsiveness and especially the ease with which they can pass from one emotion to its opposite, even in our own time. Joy gives way to tears and lamentations,

[6] Mary Edith Durham, *Some Tribal Origins, Laws, and Customs of the Balkans* (London: George Allen & Unwin Ltd., 1928), p. 281.

the tearing of hair, and the beating of breasts, and tears and lamentations yield to rejoicing, as at the wake of Attila the Hun in 453 A.D.:

> After having grievously mourned him, they [his subjects] proceeded to regale in banquetry, performing over his tomb the ritual that they call *strava*. Freely coupling opposite extremes of feeling, they passed from moments of funereal sorrow to moments of gaudy joy.[7]

Culturally, such joy is religious-magical—intended to animate the dead. The cultural response, however, is doubtless an expression of a psychological need: great grief must yield to joy, even hysterical joy, or else there is no more life. To paraphrase the French historian Lucien Febvre, every human feeling is at once itself and its contrary, while a given culture and the play of personal attitudes determine, at any specific moment, whether hate prevails over love or pity over cruelty. These contrasting states are unified, however, for one of them cannot manifest itself without engendering its opposite, at least at a latent level.

Certain cultures discourage the expression of the opposite poles of man's emotional states. The Puritan tradition provides one example of such a culture, but other traditions have likewise attempted to unify opposites in a middle way, or to free man from opposites: the Chinese *tao,* the Hindu *nirvana,* the Greek *sophrosyne,* the European Enlightenment. We shall deal with the attempts to create a middle way in the Balkans in our final chapter. Suffice it to say here that the dominant way of the Balkans was not the middle way, but the polar way: the way of honor and shame, ritual inadequacy and philanthropy, humanity and inhumanity.

A French doctor, Gabriel Frilley, who served at the court of

---

[7] Iordanis, "De origine actibusque Getarum," in Theodor Mommsen (ed.), *Monumenta Germaniae Historica: Auctorum Antiquissimorum,* Vol. V (Berlin: Weidmann, 1882), p. 124; Iordanis, *De origine actibusque Getarum,* Alfred Holder (ed.) (Freiburg i. B. and Tübingen: J. C. B. Mohr, 1882), pp. 58–59. [Author's translation]

Prince Nikola of Montenegro from 1870 to 1880, has left a re-markable medical portrait of the mental state of Montene-grins, which, in modified form, might be said to hold true also for other Balkan peoples:

> Neuroses appear to dominate the pathology of Montenegrins: neuroses of the understanding [the French term is "intelligence"] in considerable proportions for such a small population; neu-roses of the sensibilities, and especially of the head, [such as] migraine [and] the most varied kinds of neuralgia; add to this infantile paralysis, hysteria among at least a third of the women-folk, troubles of the nervous system among many men, [and] nervous beatings of the aorta, almost universal in both sexes.[8]

So prevalent among women in ancient Hellas that the Greeks associated it with a stoppage of the womb, hysteria often assumed the form of a mass phenomenon. George Thom-son relates, for example, that "cases of mass hysteria are re-corded from Sparta and Lokroi Epizephyrioi, and in both the victims were women. At Sparta they were cured by the medi-cine-man Bakis under instructions from the Delphic Oracle. At Lokroi they would be sitting quietly at their meal, when sud-denly, as though in answer to a supernatural voice, they would leap in a frenzy and run out of the town. They were cured by singing paeans to Apollo." [9] Cases of neurasthenia and hyste-ria might, moreover, have been even more numerous had it not been for the Dionysiac ritual of "mountain dancing" at regular times of the year, which provided a ritual outlet for irrational impulses.

Evidence of such "mountain dancing," particularly in the areas which did not come under the influence of the "middle way" of Greek antiquity—notably in Thrace, where the cult of Sabazios and Semele is transformed into the cult of St. Con-

[8] Dr. Gabriel Frilley and Jovan Wlahovitj [or, more properly, Vlahović, a Montenegrin by birth and a captain in the Serbian army], *Le Monténé-gro contemporain* (Paris: E. Plon et Cie, 1876), p. 417. [Author's translation]
[9] George Thomson, *Studies in Ancient Greek Society: The Prehistoric Aegean* (London: Lawrence & Wishart Ltd., 1949), p. 227.

stantine and St. Helen, and in the Scythian steppe—persists into modern times, to the opening of the twentieth century. In several Thracian villages, for example, between the night of May 2 and the week of May 21 (the feast of St. Constantine and St. Helen), the inhabitants, especially the women and girls, would engage in public dancing and singing and, on the night of May 20–21, barefoot medicine men (and women) [*nestenaria*] would enter into an orgiastic dance over hot embers. Reminiscent of the Gaelic May Day festival of Beltane, the Thracian fire dance was followed by a cathartic week of fun, frolic, festivity, and frenzy, the chief aim of which was ritual purification or renewal.

As the ritual outlets for the expression of irrational impulses were slowly removed through the spread of rationalism and what is sometimes called "Westernization" during the nineteenth century, there may have been an increase in manifestations of hysteria. In any event, the anthropologist Mary Edith Durham describes a curious form of neurasthenia among the women of Macedonia and Montenegro, often psychologically exhausted by their unenviable lot of childbearing, lactation, and toil:

> It begins as a hiccough, and becomes more and more intense until it is a violent and fast-recurring spasm of the diaphragm. The hiccoughs become louder and louder till they are an uninterrupted crowing like that of a hoarse rooster. So quick are they that the patient cannot breathe. Just as she appears to be in danger of choking, she suddenly pulls herself together, draws a long breath, gives a gasp or two, and recovers in a few minutes. At intervals the attacks may go on all day; nor, when the habit is acquired, is it easy to cure. To a certain extent it is under the patient's control; but not entirely.[10]

It was a form of protest, culturally permissible because the patriarchal society, then under attack from abroad and from the youth and "intelligentsia" in its midst, failed to realize how

[10] Durham, *op. cit.,* p. 273.

much the emotional behavior of its women could similarly constitute a threat to its continued existence.

CHILDBIRTH AND PEDAGOGY

Since childbearing and lactation constituted such an important part of the functions of the Balkan woman, an investigation of these subjects may be in order. Unfortunately, the data at our disposal are very meager. We know, however, that the basic birth technique in many ancient civilizations is exemplified by the birth of Buddha to Maya while she stood upright, holding to a tree branch. With certain modifications, this technique of childbirth persisted in many rural areas of the Balkans until the latter part of the nineteenth century and, sporadically, for a half-century longer. Women, especially in Montenegro and in some rural districts of Macedonia, often gave birth while working in the fields. During the 1860's, the usual technique in Montenegro, when the woman was at home, was to give birth while standing up, her legs spread apart and her arms resting on some piece of furniture, the domestic "tree branch." Another practice, reported a half-century later, was childbirth with the assistance of old women reputed to be midwives. The old women would walk the mother endlessly up and down the hut, supporting her under the armpits if she was too weak to go on but refusing to let her sit or lie down lest the child fail to drop out. If the floor of the hut was of stone, they spread straw over it to prevent the cracking of the child's head. The day after giving birth, or on the second day, Montenegrin women resumed their customary occupations. In other regions, they returned to their tasks a day or two later.

In some parts of the Balkans, as in southern Macedonia, along the present-day frontier between Greece and Yugoslavia, the pregnant woman enjoyed a relatively privileged life, if data accumulated during the past half-century are reliable for other periods. She owed these privileges to the desire of her family and community to improve her chances of bearing a healthy child. Efforts were thus made to exempt her from hard work, spare her certain unpleasant sights, and gratify her sense of taste. The most careful attention was given to this last point, for it was believed that a pregnant woman's culinary cravings were in reality expressions of the preferences and needs of the fetus or unborn child.

Almost everywhere in the Balkans the infant was swaddled, lightly in Albania, round and round in Macedonia. After forty days or after its first smile, it was allowed to have one hand free. In some districts of Albania infants were strapped to a board until their baptism or, in Muslim families, for the first forty days of their existence.

The naturalist Pierre Belon du Mans offers an invaluable short description of the child-rearing practices of the Turks, presumably in the towns, in the early part of the sixteenth century. After comparing Turkish and "Latin" (Western European) methods of pedagogy, Belon concludes that Turkish children are "never so stinky" nor so difficult to raise as the children of the "Latins." In effect, he relates, Turkish mothers breast-fed their children until the latter were at least ten months old, refraining from giving them cereals or milk from any nonhuman source until that time, whereas in Western Europe cereals and the milk of domestic animals were given to infants much earlier. Instead of featherbeds, Turkish infants had cradles of taut leather with a round opening over which were placed their nude bottoms. Below the opening was set a large pot, and a hollow pipelike tube of boxwood less than an inch thick and almost six inches long, with a round or elongated hook at one end depending on the sex of the infant, was joined to the urinary member of the child, with the straight end of the pipe being passed between its legs into the opening of the cradle. Keeping their infants cradled until they were able to control their physiological needs, the Turks avoided the soiling of their carpets, so essential a part of the Turkish home, diminished their need for linens, and were able, according to Belon, to keep their infants relatively clean, comfortable, and contented.

In Macedonia, children were not weaned until they began to teethe and very often not until their third or fourth year. During the first two or three years their upbringing was basically the task of the mother. The earliest experiences of children born in this area appear to have been relatively happy, for their mother normally changed them as soon as they wet themselves, fondled or tapped them playfully, tickled them around their lips to give them oral pleasure, and told them stories. A happy early childhood may account for the esteem in which Balkan men generally hold mothers and sisters, even when their attitude toward women in general is ambivalent or negative.

As the child grew older, and especially after the weaning, other authorities, more specifically cultural or social and less biological, began to prevail, and this may account for the reluctance of some Balkan women to wean their children. Normally, however, the mother herself began the process of accustoming the child to the acceptance of other authorities and the learning of principles essential to the preservation of the community, namely: (1) to be economical and, more especially, "not to drop crumbs when it eats"; (2) to honor its elders and cultivate a consciousness of age categories, give priority to the advice of elders, sit down at table in accordance with age (and sometimes in accordance with sex), and express conventional wishes of good luck to everyone (especially members of its own family and community) that it met or found at work; (3) to be diligent in terms of the needs of the family and larger community. This last requirement took the form in certain other Balkan societies, especially in Albania and Montenegro, of being provident in warfare or in thievery.

MOBILITY

Hunger was an ever-present problem. To cope with this bane, the Slavic and Albanian peasantry of the western provinces developed the custom of sending younger family members to winter or to be fed during winter in a more fertile region or with a more prosperous branch of the family; in spring these migrants would return to their primary homes. In the more fertile central and eastern areas, on the other hand, migratory peasant workers (*argati*) left their homes in spring to work on farms or estates in need of extra hands and rejoined their homes in late autumn.

Such population movements were more or less regularized, occurring at stipulated times of the year. In his epochal study of the Mediterranean, Braudel sketches a remarkable portrait of the role of St. George's Day (April 23, Old Style) and St. Demetrius' Day (October 26, O.S.) as the terminal dates of the winter and summer seasons throughout the eastern Mediterranean and the zone of Byzantine and Ottoman civilization. As St. Demetrius' Day drew near, the Turks brought their campaigns to a close. From then until St. George's Day, navigation almost ceased, epidemics were appeased, war yielded to diplomatic negotiation and correspondence, rumors abounded. Between St. George's Day and St. Demetrius' Day, commerce and agriculture were reactivated, war was resumed, and epidemics threatened again, while rents and debts became payable on one or both of the two holidays. Apprentices quit their homes on one of the two occasions to enter the service of a master craftsman, and village craftsmen departed from their homes at the time of the spring festival to offer their services in distant towns and provinces, generally returning for the autumn festival. Farmhands hired out their labor on St. George's Day and turned homeward for St. Demetrius' Day. Shepherds and shepherd folk abandoned their mountain pastures at the autumn festival to winter with their flocks in the plains, often many hundreds of miles distant, and returned to their mountains on St. George's Day. The two feasts, along with the feast of the Assumption (August 15), were also the chief occasions for group marriages. A Serbian proverb attests, moreover, to their importance in the life of the outlaw (*hajduk*), so characteristic a feature of Balkan society between the mid-sixteenth and the mid-nineteenth centuries:

> On St. Demetrius' *hajduks* disband,
> On St. George's *hajduks* together band.[11]

War, shepherds' migrations, agriculture, commerce, and marriage were thus endowed with a regular rhythm. Bandits, marriageable girls, farmhands, craftsmen, apprentices, shepherds, and warriors moved from one home, from one community, from one kind of activity to another on the occasion of the two feasts. The Balkan peoples of the premodern era were extraordinarily mobile.

In addition to this seasonally regulated mobility, there was a mobility provoked by fiscal and seigniorial pressures, by the looting and personal affronts of armies, by famine, and by plagues and other epidemics. But even this type of mobility was characterized by regularity, for the crises recurred every second or third year, often continuing for two or three years in succession. In the mountainous areas hunger was a graver threat than plague, in the lowlands and maritime regions plague, often preceded and accompanied by hunger, was a constant menace. Provinces along the routes of war, such as Thrace, Macedonia, and Serbia, were areas where plague was able to spread from one region to another, but in some places, both rural and urban, plague was endemic.

The prevalence of plague in most of the Balkans until the mid-nineteenth century had a detrimental effect on the rural

11 M.[ilan] Dj.[uro] Milićević, *Život Srba seljaka*, 2nd ed., revised and enlarged (Belgrade: Srpska Kraljevska Akademija, 1894), p. 144; Edmund Schneeweis, *Serbokroatische Volkskunde*, Vol. I, *Volksglaube und Volksbrauch* (Berlin: Walter de Gruyter, 1961), p. 137. [Author's translation]

and urban economy alike. In the cities, where the plague almost always wiped out a large percentage of the population, peasants without urban traditions and techniques replaced the older residents, while in the lowland villages, shepherd peoples from the highlands, without a complex agricultural tradition, replaced the agriculturalists.

There were also other categories of wanderers: migrant teachers and monks, moving periodically from one community to another, and migrant beggars, prophets, and healers. In years of economic and political crisis, moreover, tens and hundreds of thousands of peasants and unemployed artisans from smaller towns flocked to the capital and the larger cities. The Ottoman government reacted to this concentration of "useless and unemployed people" in Istanbul, the former Constantinople or Byzantium, by murdering or summarily executing several thousands of persons and deporting tens of thousands to the Asian shores of the Bosporus or to the European provinces. The periodic exportation of trouble from the capital, however, created trouble for the provincial towns, which reacted in like manner. The "useless and unemployed people"— adventurers, brigands, homeless vagabonds, unemployed or impoverished artisans and farmhands—then took to roaming the countryside, seizing land and other properties, offering "protection" to frightened peasants in return for a portion of their crop. Wanderers who succeeded in the latter form of enterprise, generally with the complaisance of a provincial governor or of local authorities or notables, were primarily of the Muslim faith, but a few were Christians.

In 1788, while the Ottoman Empire was at war with Russia and Austria, the Turkish soldiery so thoroughly terrified the inhabitants of Bulgaria that many of them took flight to the mountains of Macedonia, just as many thousands of Orthodox Serbians and Macedonians and Roman Catholic Bulgarians and Albanians sought refuge north of the Sava and Danube during the Austro-Turkish war of the closing decades of the seventeenth century. In the Morea, Muslim landowners dispatched so much of their grains to Istanbul, Trieste, and western Mediterranean ports following the abundant harvest of 1788 that there was famine in the province during the winter and spring of 1789. Greek peasants coped with the problem by deserting their old villages for new lands of promise.

Such desertions were often followed by a return to the old community, although rural settlements were sometimes totally abandoned. But more significant than the actual fact of abandonment is the act of moving forward and backward, outward and inward, from the country to the town or to other countrysides, from the low country to the mountain, from the mountain to the low country, from the forest and cave to the plain and then back to the forest or cave.

To this history of flights (and sometimes of returns) characteristic of the premodern era, we might add the Serbian emigrations of World War I, so poignantly described by Dragoljub Jovanović:

> The most vivid picture left by the War in the memory of the Serbs is not of a cemetery or a blood-stained battlefield, although Serbia had given a formidable number of victims and had been the scene of the fiercest fighting. The most clear-cut impression of the Serbian campaign is the motley, pitiful spectacle of the *bežanija,* that endless, disorderly flight of fugitives muffled to the eyes, old women, children, on foot or in wooden carts patiently drawn by emaciated and exhausted oxen, driving in front of them some cattle and carrying on their backs or under their arms some chattels, the number and importance of which grew less with every stage of this removal which was always beginning again and never coming to an end. In short, the outstanding event of the Serbian war is not a great battle, such as Verdun, but the Great Retreat, that retreat which led the Serbs into exile through Albania—the last after so many others following on each advance of the enemy.[12]

12 Dragolioub Yovanovitch [Dragoljub Jovanović], *Les effets économiques et sociaux de la Guerre en Serbie,* Histoire Economique et Sociale de la Guerre Mondiale, Série Serbe (Paris: Presses Universitaires de France; New Haven: Yale University Press, 1930), p. 28; translated in David Mit-

Freed from the political picture, Yugoslavia's participation in World War II is similarly an account of retreats, of operations shifting from one part of the country to another, of the expulsion and repeated migration of peoples, of starvation and disease. In the Greek Civil War (1946–1949), poor villagers from the plains defected to the guerrillas in the hills, while prosperous and conservative villagers from the hills fled to the towns and villages of the plains in search of the protection of the army and gendarmerie.

The focus of our attention in this chapter has centered around the problems of psychological polarity and physical mobility. The face, ear, eye, and hand, and certain bodily techniques, have received special consideration because they provide us with an insight into the emotional states, as well as the cultural values, of the Balkan peoples. We have further probed into the traditional, seasonal, and critical situations that give rise to, or encourage, the physical mobility of Balkan man, for this duplicates and reinforces his psychological mobility, or polarity.

Let us not jump, however, to any erroneous conclusions: Balkan man is not inevitably more physically or psychologically mobile than his neighbors. Indeed, studies of deserted villages, of migrations, of urbanization, of colonization, of decolonization, and of historical psychology tend to show that man in general is mobile, at least under certain conditions. The only generalization now permissible in regard to Balkan man is that, like his fellow men, he was, throughout the premodern era and under the premodern type of situations created by war, collectively very mobile.

---

rany, *The Effect of the War in Southeastern Europe,* Economic and Social History of the World War, General Series (New Haven: Yale University Press; London: Oxford University Press, published for the Carnegie Endowment for International Peace, Division of Economics and History, 1936), p. 243.

III

TECHNOLOGY

❦

Marcel Mauss defines a technique as a traditional act or combination of acts designed to achieve a certain mechanical, chemical, or physical effect. Although the range of possible techniques is very wide, Jean Cazeneuve has divided them into two broad categories: techniques based on the principle of taking things as nature offers them and those based on the principle of organizing nature to suit the needs of man. To move from the first type of technique to the second requires a new time orientation, notably a sacrifice of current advantages to the goal of some future advantage. In this chapter, we shall deal with the second type of technique, that is, with the fact of technology.

Much is known about ancient Greek, Roman, and even Byzantine technology, but comparatively little about the technology of the Balkan peoples in the areas lying beyond the great urban centers. We shall therefore focus our attention on the rural sector. At the same time, we shall try to determine how and why the Balkans, once one of the most advanced regions of the world technologically, became a technologically backward area. Finally, we shall review the ceaseless efforts made since

the nineteenth century by the new Balkan nation-states to reduce or eliminate their technological backwardness.

METALLURGY

One of the earliest significant modifications of the neolithic
culture occurred through the invention of metallurgy, or of
techniques for fashioning ornamentations, tools, and weapons
of metal. As in the Near East, the first metal so employed was
copper, apparently by the peoples of the pre-Cucuteni, Boian,
Vinča A, and Tisza cultures, hence already in the fourth millennium. Some of the copper objects of these cultures were
doubtless imports, but others were probably made by metallurgical artisans and prospectors of unknown origin—perhaps
from the Caucasus—who had come to exploit the copper resources of the Carpatho-Transylvanian Alps and later of the
Balkan, Rhodope, and Dinaric mountain chains. The neolithic peoples of the Balkans may have acquired copper objects
from the metallurgists through gift exchange and subsequently
made use of them as symbols of social distinction and for the
purpose of facilitating ceremonial and other forms of gift exchange. Early copper products, including massive hatchet-
coins, were of minor practical value as tools and weapons.

The neolithic cultures failed to create efficient metal tools
and weapons until the invention of bronze, a much harder
metal, through the fusion of tin, antimony or arsenic, and native copper or reduced copper ores. Around 2000 B.C., several
centuries after bronze tools and weapons began to be known in
the Caucasus and Near East, a bronze technology spread to the
Balkans from three directions: from Minoan Crete and Anatolia to the southern Balkan periphery and from the north and
northeast to the Danube and northern Balkan regions. Bringing a bronze culture into the north and northeast were two
groups of nomadic peoples, known, respectively, as the chalice
pottery folk and the red ochre or corded pottery folk. Although

the origins of the chalice pottery people, who installed themselves in the Pannonian plain and adjacent mountain regions,
are obscure, the red ochre and corded pottery folk seem to have
originated in the vast steppes of southeastern Europe and
along the Caucasus-Mesopotamian frontiers. In addition to
their bronze technology, the latter brought with them the ox-
drawn cart and the horse, which had been domesticated along
the confines of Mesopotamia a millennium or so earlier.

The diffusion to the Balkans of a yet newer metallurgical
technique, iron manufacture, was similarly tridirectional.
Thraco-Cimmerian horsemen, for example, ushered it into the
northeastern zone (Moldavia and Wallachia) during the tenth
century B.C., at approximately the same time as its entry into
the Aegean area, whence it ultimately expanded into the
southern and central Balkan regions. In the northwestern
areas (Dalmatia and Bosnia), iron objects, notably pins, pend-
ants, brooches, bracelets, and razors, appeared shortly before
800 B.C. as imports from Italy. Soon thereafter, local iron manufactures were developed in that zone, as they had been in the
south and northeast.

The mining of copper, iron, lead, silver, and gold became
increasingly important in the succeeding centuries, and the
precious metals and other mineral products of the Balkans
drew the Romans ever deeper into the peninsula from the second century B.C. onward. The process of Roman imperial
expansion was very complex, however, and Rome would periodically pursue a policy of excluding the "barbarians" instead
of conquering and "civilizing" them. The "barbarians," however, refused to be excluded. As the Romans unearthed new
sources of wealth after each undertaking against "barbarism,"
they pressed forward to the Danube and beyond. The booty in
objects of gold and silver accruing to Emperor Trajan from the
conquest of Dacia (Rumania) at the opening of the second
century A.D. may have amounted to 165,500 kilograms of gold
(twenty times the annual gold production of Bosnia during

the same period) and 331,000 kilograms of silver, treasures that allowed him to remedy temporarily the precarious condition of Roman finances.

The Gothic, Hunnic, Avaro-Slavic, and Bulgar invasions (from the fourth to the seventh century) may have discouraged the continued operation of some Balkan mines, while other mining enterprises may have ceased or diminished in importance as a result of the spread of epidemics and the occurrence of a notable decline in the population of the eastern Mediterranean area during the second half of the sixth century. Indeed, one of the decisive factors behind the manifestation of iconoclasm in Byzantium during the seventh and eighth centuries may have been the loss of minerals to the triumphant Arabs in Asia and to the conquering Slavs in the Balkans, whence the need of Byzantine emperors to salvage the gold and silver of the holy ikons and their consequent determination to wage a systematic campaign against the use of images in religious worship. But mining was never wholly interrupted in the Balkans, and at the start of the thirteenth century new incentives arose that caused the mining of gold, silver, and other metals to be intensified.

The growth of the European population and European economic expansion in the eleventh, twelfth, and thirteenth centuries had stimulated mining activity in Bohemia, Hungary, Transylvania, Carinthia, Carniola, and the Germanies. This in turn led to the development of silver mines and the employment of new mining techniques in Serbia and Bosnia. The first mine explicitly mentioned in medieval Serbian documents is that of Brskovo, which was put into operation in the 1250's by Saxon miners drawn from Transylvania or Hungary. In Bosnia, mining as an activity of specialists appears to have been resumed around 1330. Silver mining grew most rapidly in the Balkans (Macedonia, Serbia, western Bulgaria, and Bosnia) during the fourteenth and fifteenth centuries, thus coinciding with the decline of the Central European silver mines during the Hundred Years' and Hussite wars. This decline resulted in a rising demand for Balkan silver in Ragusa (Dubrovnik), Venice, Alexándria, and Florence, and in the cities of southern Italy and Sicily.

At the moment of Europe's greatest need for the silver of Macedonia, Serbia, and Bosnia, however, the mines of these provinces fell one after another into the hands of the Ottoman Turks. In fact, Ottoman rulers and commanders consciously pursued a brilliant three-step program of conquering the roads leading to the gold, silver, lead, copper, and iron mines of the medieval Balkan states, then seizing the mines themselves, and finally reducing the centers of political opposition after they had been deprived of the economic basis of their power. Following the seizure of the mines of Kratovo in northern Macedonia at the close of the fourteenth century, further Ottoman expansion was temporarily halted by Tamerlane's victory in 1402 at Ankara. A decade later, however, the Ottoman commander Evrenos initiated a plan, subsequently pursued by his son Ishakbeg and his grandson Isabeg, to acquire the site of the most important silver mines in all of Europe: Novo Brdo. Finally, in 1454 and 1455, Mehmed the Conqueror's troops captured not only Novo Brdo but a series of other Serbian mining sites: Rudnik, Plana, Zaplanina, Trepča, and Janjevo. The Despot (title of the ruler) of Serbia sadly informed his Hungarian allies that the loss of Novo Brdo, "the nerve center of war on account of its mines," was tantamount to the loss of the country's very "head." A few years later the Turks similarly occupied most of the Bosnian mining sites.

Several of the Balkan mines declined during the second half of the fifteenth and early part of the sixteenth century. For example, the yearly revenues accruing to the state (or to the personal treasury of the sovereign) from the mines of Novo Brdo fell from more than 200,000 gold ducats in 1432 to

120,000 in 1520 and 40,000 in 1661. On the whole, however, the Turks seem to have maintained silver production at a high level. In compensation for the decline of Novo Brdo and certain other mining centers, they pushed the exploitation of the silver mines of Siderocapsa, presumably the former Chrysitis of Philip of Macedon. Located in the Chalcidice peninsula in the district later known as "the mining communities" (Mademochoria), the mines of Siderocapsa rapidly extended operations, especially after 1530, and reached a very high level of production during the 1540's, when they brought in monthly revenues to the Ottoman state of 9,000 to 30,000 ducats, or more than 200,000 ducats annually.

When the French mineralogist Pierre Belon du Mans visited Siderocapsa in 1547 at the order of his king, Francis I, the 6,000 miners and prospectors working in the area—mostly Bulgarians and Serbians but including some Greeks and Jews—used Spanish, recently introduced there by Jews expelled from Spain, as the language of trade. The technical vocabulary of the miners, on the other hand, was a Slavicized form of Saxon. Some of the miners may have been descendants of the Saxon immigrants who had gone to Serbia, Bosnia, northern Macedonia, and Bulgaria during the thirteenth and fourteenth centuries.

An unidentified Christian Armenian had taught the miners to separate gold from silver and lead with aquafortis (nitric acid), but in other respects their mining technology was Central European. A century earlier, Cardinal Bessarion, a Greek scholar from Trebizond who supported the idea of union between the Roman Catholic and Orthodox churches, had tried to persuade Constantine Palaeologus, Despot of the autonomous Byzantine province of Morea (Peloponnesus), to duplicate the technological strides then being made in Italy, particularly the technique of smelting by means of water-driven "leather bellows which are distended and relaxed untouched by any hand, and separate the metal from the useless and earthy matter that may be present." [1] Noted in France as early as 1340 (but apparently employed there even earlier) and adopted widely in Italy before or during Bessarion's time, water-driven leather bellows were in use at Siderocapsa at the time of Belon's visit. Under what circumstances the technique had developed there remains unclear. It may well have constituted part of the heritage of the Slavo-Saxons, although leather bellows by themselves are an innovation traditionally credited to the Scythian philosopher Anacharsis, contemporary of Solon.

The Siderocapsa bellows were operated by eight-spoked waterwheels turned by the water of seven mountain streams beside which were erected the five hundred or more charcoal blast furnaces of the miners. The heat created in the furnaces by the bellows was sufficient to melt and refine metals so well that they did not require subsequent hammering. One of the consequences of this process was the production of cast iron on a much larger scale.

On the other hand, iron-casting techniques may have reached the Balkans from two directions: not only from Western Europe by way of the north but also by way of the south and east through the agency of Turkic and of Indic peoples, such as the Gypsies. The Chinese may have produced cast iron as early as the second century B.C., during the reign of Emperor Wu. Several centuries later, the Sarmatians, who overran the southeastern European steppe from the east, were known to employ corselets of cast iron as part of their armament, and cast-iron manufacturing techniques probably quickly spread from them to the neighboring Turkic peoples. In any event, the term for cast iron in Russian and Bulgarian is *čugun*, derived perhaps from the Osmanli *çöygen* or from some other Turkic variant for cast iron. The period of acculturation of Eastern cast-iron manufacturing techniques in the Balkans is

[1] A. G. Keller, "A Byzantine Admirer of 'Western' Progress: Cardinal Bessarion," *Cambridge Historical Journal*, XI (1955), 346.

very uncertain, however: Did it occur in the fourteenth century? earlier? or later?

Taken as a geographic unit, the Balkans were not a technologically backward area in the fifteenth century and were not to become so until the closing decades of the sixteenth. Balkan mining was quite as important during the 1540's and 1550's as it had been a century earlier. Not until the last decades of the century was there a perceptible decline. This decline was slow between 1580 and 1640 (there may even have been a minor recovery during the reign of Murad IV, 1623–1640) and precipitous thereafter. As a consequence, the annual mining revenues of the Ottoman Empire (which were mostly of Balkan origin) thus declined from 600,000 ducats in 1546 to 500,000 ducats in 1590 and then to 100,000 ducats by the early eighteenth century.

The arrival in Europe after 1540 of enormous quantities of cheaply produced American silver made unprofitable the continued extraction of undiminished quantities of silver from the mines of Central Europe (revived between 1460 and 1540). The Germanies consequently lost their role of leadership in heavy industry to England. As German and Central European investments were diverted from industry to agriculture, landlords increased the amount of labor required of peasant cultivators in order to create surpluses for export to the more commercial and industrial states. In this manner, there emerged in the eastern portions of Central Europe what is often described as "the second serfdom." In the Balkans, the advent of cheap American silver produced a similar effect. To compete with the Indian slave labor of the Hispano-American mines, the Ottomans resorted to the use of forced labor in their own enterprises. The latter practice, however, induced skilled miners to run away and even become leaders of insurrection. With the decline of the material foundations of Balkan heavy industry, a "second serfdom" made strides in the Balkans, as it had in Central Europe. Since other factors also play a key role in its emergence, however, we shall return to this subject in our chapter on the economy of the Balkans.

The final revival of mining in the Balkans began around the middle of the nineteenth century. In the long interval of industrial stagnation and contraction, tales of lost or buried treasures were widely diffused, and itinerant Greek vendors were not averse to selling maps and "ancient letters" showing the supposed location of various treasures. With or without such maps and letters, hundreds of persons set forth each year in search of precious "relics." Only after the mid-nineteenth century would the hunters of metallic "relics" slowly yield to engineers, who would introduce the Balkans to the new era of steam.

HOE, ARD, AND PLOW

Before the age of steam, however, came the long era of the ard and plow and of the still older hoe and spade. In the course of thousands of years, the hoe and spade were modified and other tools were invented, so that by the classical era Greek peasants employed at least six different implements for penetrating the soil, turning it over, breaking up soils of different types, and removing weeds.

The ard and the plow are both plowing implements but differ from each other in several notable respects: An ard possesses a long beam, a plow a short beam. An ard plows symmetrically, pushing the earth aside in both directions; a plow functions unsymmetrically, turning the earth over to one side. An ard is a light instrument, normally not requiring more than a pair of oxen for traction; a plow is a heavier instrument, requiring two or more pairs of oxen and often using the power of horses rather than of oxen or asses. An ard scratches the surface of the earth, a plow penetrates more deeply. The ard is a more suitable instrument for contour plowing, for in hilly regions and in areas where the soil is not deep, the momentum of the plow brings into cultivation both fertile and infertile soils. Generally situated in hill country, fields under ard cultivation tend to be irregular, rounded, or rectangular. More common in the plains, those under plow cultivation generally assume the form of long strips.

It is not clear whether the earliest ard invented by man was an altogether new tool or whether it evolved directly from the spade in some regions and from the hoe in others. The early history of Balkan ards is similarly obscure. However, it is known that ards were being used in the Balkans at the time of Hesiod (around 800 B.C.). During the period of Roman rule, four different types of ard were in use in the Balkans, and each of these is still employed there in one or another district.

In the Sava and Morava basins and in northwestern Bulgaria, an instrument is used that possesses some ard and a few plow characteristics. The implement in question is symmetrical, but like a plow, it is furnished with a moldboard and can therefore plow unsymmetrically. In other words, it functions like the plow in pushing the earth to one side but like the ard in that it does not turn the soil over.

Although the question has been debated by scholars for a century or more, the origin of the plow is nevertheless open to less dispute than that of the ard. A growing body of evidence supports the thesis that the iron-rich Alpine regions, notably Rhaetia, are where the plow and plowshare first came into use, perhaps around 400 B.C., concurrently with the invention of the iron horseshoe by the Alpine Celts. By the first century A.D., the plow was widely known in the northern Roman provinces and was soon transmitted by the Romanized Celts to their Germanic neighbors, who subsequently passed it on to the Western Slavs.

The Southern Slavs may have acquired it in several different periods and from at least three different donors: the Celto-Illyrians, the Germanic peoples (including perhaps the Goths), and Byzantium. But the Balkan plow zone was confined, until the middle of the nineteenth century, to a few lake, river, and coastal basins in the south and east and to the Pannonian regions in the north, extending occasionally south of the Sava and Danube rivers and then withdrawing again. During the past century, on the other hand, the plow has penetrated into the peninsula from north, south, east, and west. Its initial expansion in this period was based in large measure on the importation of modern agricultural machinery from Hungary or from Western and Germanic Central Europe. Poor roads and inadequate vehicles, however, impeded the delivery of heavy machines to districts situated beyond the main highways of commerce. Thus, as late as 1882, when the Serbian government granted a subsidy to the firm of Vasić and Maksimović to enable it to establish a factory at Kraljevo geared to the manufacture of farm machines, Serbia customarily imported each year no more than 400 or 500 plows of modern make. Nowhere in the Balkans were modern machines coming into use very fast, and almost everywhere the growth of a cereal economy led after 1830 to a rapid contraction in the per capita distribution of horses, bovines, sheep, goats, mules, and asses. In other words, the per capita distribution of old sources of energy—animal power—declined before the growth of new sources of energy.

ANIMAL AND ROTARY POWER

Known in Sumer since the beginning of the fourth millennium, the wheeled vehicle arrived in Europe by two routes during the early part of the second millennium: from Asia Minor to the Aegean and from across the steppes of Southeastern Europe to Pannonia and the northern Balkans. The cart that arrived in the highlands of the south was two-wheeled, whereas both two- and four-wheeled vehicles were introduced from the steppes. Both were presumably of the pole or perch type. In other words, draft animals were hitched to the cart by means of a pole extending forward from the middle of the axle-tree.

For almost four millennia the four-wheeled vehicle prevailed only in the region north of the Danube and Sava. To the south of these rivers and east of the Morava and Vardar basins was a mixed zone in which the two-wheeled cart was dominant but the four-wheeled wagon did appear, particularly in fertile lowland areas. It appeared again, but rarely, in the region extending almost to the Drina River, but the area between the Morava in the east and the province of Hercegovina in the west was essentially a zone of the two-wheeled cart. West of Serbia, there were almost no four-wheeled vehicles until 1850, and in the Dinaric provinces of Hercegovina and Montenegro, as in the Peloponnesus, carts of any kind were extremely rare until the mid-nineteenth century. In Serbia, the number of bullock carts per 100 persons fell from 9.3 in 1866 to 7.1 in 1893; the number of horse-drawn carts decreased from 1.2 to 1.1 per 100 persons. The quality of the carts, however, was probably significantly better in 1893.

To a casual observer all Balkan carts were more or less alike, but important differences did exist. The greatest variety prevailed in the eastern and southeastern regions: two-wheeled and four-wheeled; covered and uncovered; long and short; drawn by buffaloes, bullocks or horses. Moreover, although the two-wheeled carts that an Italian witness noted in the plain of Salonika in 1591 resembled those of the Macedonian and Albanian highlands to the west in having spokeless wheels, they differed from them in being more solidly built, and particularly in having iron parts. In Serbia, on the other hand, most carts lacked even a single piece of iron until the 1860's, and iron parts continued to be absent from Albanian carts until half a century ago. At that time, the customary vehicle in the Albanian lowlands was a creaking, springless cart with two wheels, which were more than six feet in diameter in order to cope with the proverbial mud of the plains. In Epirus, around Arta, the carts in circulation in 1731 were somewhat different: short and of weak construction, consisting merely of three planks set upon an exletree and moved by two very small one-piece wheels without springs. As in many other Balkan areas, they were drawn by buffaloes.

In most of the Balkans, the prevailing carts continued to resemble their most ancient prototypes until the middle or end of the nineteenth century. Along the northern fringes, however, a few vehicles of a new type appeared during the seventeenth and eighteenth centuries, if not in the sixteenth. The new vehicle was the Hungarian *kocsi,* named perhaps after the village of Kocs in the vicinity of Buda (one of the twin cities which later formed Budapest), where craftsmen engaged in the manufacture of coaches at least as early as the first decades of the sixteenth century. But coaches may have been invented even earlier, for it appears that the ambassador of the king of Hungary and Bohemia presented the king of France in 1457 with a gift that aroused much amazement in Paris: a vehicle that may have been built with a suspension carriage. In Germany, moreover, the common name for a covered vehicle in the time of Charles V was "Hungarian carriage," and the usual German term for coach—*kotzschi* or *gutschi*—was presumably derived from *kocsi.* The Hungarian *kocsi* was at that time a coach drawn by three horses running abreast of each other and able to carry, in addition to the driver, four passengers and their baggage. It spread not only to Germany but also to the southern Pannonian areas. In any case, Ottoman sources of the mid-seventeenth century refer to the use in the region between the Sava and Drava rivers of a *serem araba* or "Syrmian vehicle," which may have been either a *kocsi* or a covered wagon with springs. The Serbians of the Niš area continued to call this type of vehicle a *srem* until the latter part of the nineteenth century. By 1800, moreover, the Serbians of the forests discerned in the marshy Mačva lowlands just south of the Sava a vehicle to which they gave the name "Mačva coach" (*mačvanska kočija*). A few such coaches may have been in use in Mačva province earlier in the century.

Sensing the superiority of Central European over Spanish and Italian roads and vehicles, Philip II of Spain ordered that the roads between Ascoli and the province of Apulia be repaired and improved so that grains could be delivered to their destination (Naples) with greater ease, *"como se hace en Alemania y otras partes"*—"as is done in Germany and other parts."[2] One of these other parts was the Pannonian basin, which was politically Ottoman during the greater part of the sixteenth and seventeenth centuries. In other words, the portion of the Ottoman Empire directly confronting Germany (or Austria) was precisely the portion with the best vehicles; it also may have been the zone from which, before its conquest by the Turks, one new type of vehicle at least had spread to Germany itself. The Ottoman Empire may consequently have felt no urgent need to continue doing in Pannonia or in the Buda area what was being done without let or hindrance in Germany.

But why were the *kocsi* and *serem araba* not widely diffused to the Balkans proper, south of the Sava and Danube, until very late? The answer may lie in the fact that the Balkans were endowed with a road system, inherited from Rome, that was more than suitable for all but the most extraordinary purposes. It had straight, unswerving tracks of heavy flagstone two and a half or three feet wide, appropriate for horses—the Roman *veredae*—in single file. To the right and left of the flagstones the earth was beaten down by herds, soldiers, and ordinary foot travelers, to form a path the total width of which was thirty feet or more. Moreover, the imperial roads were more or less adequately maintained during the sixteenth century. Central Europe, on the other hand, possessed a less important her-

---

[2] Fernand Braudel, *La Méditerranée et le monde méditerranéen à l'époque de Philippe II* (Paris: Armand Colin, 1949), p. 244. A revised edition of this valuable study, now in two volumes, appeared in 1966.

itage of Roman roads and therefore began to build paved roads suitable for haulage in the Middle Ages.

Furthermore, the Byzantine Empire, the medieval Balkan states, and the Ottoman Empire could be largely content with the roads that they found because the Balkans probably held an advantage in draft-animal power not only over Western and Central Europe but over the western Mediterranean as well. We refer in particular to the camel, Asiatic buffalo, mule, and donkey. Especially in mountainous regions, where even the best vehicles were of doubtful value until the advent of motor transport, the donkey was present in large numbers. Its very name—*gomari* in Greek and *magare* or *magarac* in South Slavic—signifies "beast of burden." In addition, early in the Middle Ages, the Asiatic buffalo was introduced into Byzantium and Bulgaria and later spread to the southern Serbian lands. With the advent of the Ottoman Turks, more buffalo entered the Balkans. Found at present in Thrace, Dobruja, and parts of Macedonia, the buffalo in the period between 1500 and 1850 was both more numerous and distributed over a larger territory, including Epirus, Thessaly, many parts of Bulgaria, Kosovo, and even Serbia proper. Less numerous than the buffalo but none the less important after the Ottoman conquest was the camel. Camels provisioned the armies of Suleiman the Magnificent during the siege of Vienna in 1529, camel caravans regularly visited Buda as long as it remained under Ottoman control, and camel caravans continued to come to Belgrade as late as 1848. Finally, let us note the feeling of the foremost authority on the Mediterranean, Fernand Braudel, that the use of mules as draft animals—perhaps even their distribution on a per capita basis (but alas such statistics are fragmentary or unavailable)—increased during the sixteenth century throughout the Mediterranean, including the Balkans. At the same time, Pannonia and the northern Balkans retained their reputation in Western Europe as a source of horses, especially for reconnaissance cavalry.

A historian of the horse and of antique and medieval technology, Lefebvre des Noëttes, contrasts the material civilization of Byzantium and the medieval West: In the ninth and tenth centuries, Western Europe adopted the iron horseshoe (for this invention of the Celts does not appear to have been widely diffused during Roman rule), the file arrangement for carriage horses, and the shoulder collar for the horse. (The latter had been known to the Chinese since the second century and to certain Eastern Europeans at least as early as the eighth.) Together, the three innovations allowed the horse to draw heavier loads and transport goods more rapidly over longer distances without injury to itself. Along with the improved roads of a later period, they helped create an incentive for the ultimate building of better carts and carriages. Similar innovations were achieved in ninth-century Byzantium: the iron horseshoe and an improved breastband for the horse. But it was not until the close of the fifteenth century, according to Lefebvre des Noëttes, that the Greeks adopted the shoulder collar, in spite of the fact that their neighbors, the Serbians, had employed it since the thirteenth century. Furthermore, he maintains, Byzantium did not apply the iron shoe to oxen, and although Byzantine carts were lengthened in the tenth century to give more elasticity to the perch and thus soften the effect of jolting, the weights that a horse or an ox could pull were not augmented by the change. The normal draft power of a pair of oxen remained at or below half a ton in addition to the weight of a cart.[3]

One may challenge Lefebvre des Noëttes' reasoning on several grounds, although his contributions are none the less exceedingly important and instructive. In the first place, he himself acknowledges that Byzantium did achieve certain improvements. Second, his data are largely derived from medieval art.

[3] Richard Lefebvre des Noëttes, *L'Attelage: Le cheval de selle à travers les âges, contribution à l'histoire de l'esclavage,* 2 vols. (Paris: A. Picard, 1931).

But while Western European, Serbian, and provincial Greek art was open to "naturalism" and folk expression, the Byzantine art form subject to Lefebvre des Noëttes' scrutiny, essentially the art of Constantinople, retained throughout its existence an impressive formalism. The art of Constantinople may consequently have refrained from depicting the horse with a modern collar in spite of the fact that such a collar may have been employed. Finally, and here as elsewhere much more research is necessary, Byzantium and the other Balkan states enjoyed perhaps a numerical superiority in draft animals to compensate for their technological inferiority in vehicles, if there really was such inferiority.

It is a mistake in any case to conclude that the medieval Balkan states crumbled and fell because of technological backwardness. On the other hand, the Ottoman Empire was victorious in the fifteenth and sixteenth centuries partly because its total technological equipment was not significantly inferior to that of Western Europe, particularly if compensating factors are taken into account, such as a probable superiority in animal power. The latter factor ceased to be compensating to the same degree after 1600 and ceased to be a compensating factor at all after 1700, for by that time European technology was in fact vastly superior.

THE INDUSTRIAL DEVOLUTION

Compared to the energy base of Western and Central Europe, the Balkan energy resources that were capable of being mobilized were hopelessly inadequate throughout the nineteenth century. In one sphere after another, Balkan industry faltered before the onslaught of European technology (and society). One of the first sectors to feel the impact of Western, notably English, superiority was the cotton industry, forced into competition with the most "progressive" sector of English production. In the last few decades of the eighteenth century, the cotton yarn industry had metamorphosed miniscule Thessalian Ambelakia into a hamlet with the prosperous air of "a borough of Holland." By 1801, however, residents of Ambelakia complained to the British traveler Edward Daniel Clarke that they had begun to "feel the effect of the preference given to English cotton thread in the German markets." Clarke himself comments that the grievance was doubtless directed against "the improvement adopted in Great Britain of spinning cotton thread in mills, by means of engines that are worked by steam, which has caused such a considerable reduction in its price;— all the thread made at Ambelakia being spun by manual labour." [4] Following the Napoleonic wars, the Ambelakiot cotton industry rapidly deteriorated. Having lost its former German markets, Ambelakia sank again into oblivion. In adjacent Tyrnavos,[5] the number of hand-loom establishments for the weaving of muslins declined from 2,000 in 1812 to 200 in 1830. In Albanian Scutari, the number of hand looms fell from 600 in 1812 to 40 in 1821.

A Balkan province in which textile manufactures, especially of coarse woolens, seemed to prosper after 1830 was Bulgaria. The reasons for its relative well-being are fairly clear: Bulgaria was a great sheep-raising and consequently wool-producing land. Since it was also geographically closer to Istanbul than were the other Balkan territories of Turkey and since it had been less successful than Serbia and Greece in giving its rebellions a political aspect, it found favor with the Ottoman government. Ottoman administrators thus readily entrusted gov-

[4] Edward Daniel Clarke, *Travels in Various Countries of Europe, Asia, and Africa* (London: T. Cadell and W. Davies, 1810–1816), Part II, Sec. 3, Vol. IV, pp. 281–87. See also Traian Stoianovich, "The Conquering Balkan Orthodox Merchant," *Journal of Economic History*, XX (June 1960), 257.

[5] André Andréadès, "L'Administration financière de la Grèce sous la domination turque," *Revue des Etudes grecques*, XXIII (March–June 1910), 154–55. Andréadès gives the name of the town as Tournovo. This may be either Thessalian Tyrnavos or Bulgarian Tărnovo, where there were silk manufactures. It is probably the former, since Thessaly and Macedonia, rather than Bulgaria, were the important areas of cotton cultivation.

ernmental orders for woolen cloth and military uniforms to wool merchants in Bulgaria who were engaged in the domestic or putting-out system; that is, in furnishing villages with supplies of wool to be woven into cloth by Bulgarian peasant women. After it was woven, the cloth was returned to the wool merchants, who used it to make the uniforms. Inspired by the regularity of the official demand for their products, several of the wool merchants established modern textile mills. The first woolen factory, founded in Sliven in 1834, was soon followed by others in Plovdiv (Philippopolis), Stara Zagora, Gabrovo, Samokov, Kotel, and other communities.

The continued inclusion of Bulgaria (until 1878) within the political and economic confines of the still territorially vast Ottoman Empire—in other words, the absence of revolution and political autonomy—aided the development of a modest Bulgarian textile industry. The Serbian revolution (1788–1815), on the other hand, provoked a further impairment of the long-deteriorating Serbian urban economy by causing skilled labor, capital, and capitalists to leave the area.

Other deterrents to Serbian industrial development were the abundance of fuel wood, which removed any incentive for discovering and developing other types of fuel; the ample supply of meat and other foods, ample at least in terms of the prevailing style of life; and the wealth of fertile land in proportion to the total population of the country. Shortages of fuel wood and land began to be felt around 1860, but attempts to industrialize encountered serious obstacles because they coincided with a local economic crisis which started in the late 1860's and merged with the world-wide economic crisis of 1873–1896. But as population density increased four times between 1815 and the end of the century, as the forests declined to one-third of their former size, and as the per capita distribution of meat and milk animals and beasts of burden fell by 1905 to one-third of what it had been in 1859, a real need arose for industrialization.

An industrialization program, however, had to await the

creation of a social foundation that would allow the pursuit of an industrial policy: a situation of law and order; the founding of primary, secondary, and higher schools; the improvement of roads; the establishment of pharmacies and hospitals; and the inauguration of relatively efficient agencies for the collection, evaluation, and dissemination of economic data. An industrialization policy also required the prior creation of an economic foundation: monetary and fiscal facilities, and public utilities. But whereas in Greece a national bank was founded in 1841, banking was largely delayed in Serbia until the 1870's or 1880's. The achievement of an adequate social and economic foundation was itself contingent upon the development of town life, that is, of centers where diverse talents were concentrated. But as late as 1866, Serbia possessed only one town (Belgrade) with a population of more than 25,000 and only four others with more than 5,000. The situation was still essentially the same in 1874. Only after the 1870's was a more dependable urban base laid that would favor the establishment of industry. Until 1880, Serbian capitalists reinvested their profits in commerce, land, and occasionally in institutions with a social purpose, such as schools.

Thus the principality of Serbia had only a single factory in 1847: a small glassworks near Jagodina (later Svetozarevo) founded by the Serbian Minister of Foreign Affairs, Avram Petronijević. The first steam engine, which was brought from Liège in 1849, was apparently not put into operation until the 1850's. As late as 1888, apart from its smelting establishments in the mines, a number of sawmills operated by hydraulic wheels, several flour mills, and its munitions and armaments works, Serbia possessed only twelve factories: 7 breweries, 1 distillery, 1 wax factory, 1 "fine soap" factory, 1 glass factory, and 1 textile mill. As late as 1898, only 17 Serbian enterprises made use of steam power, and in 1908 the number was still only 78.

Many Serbians had at first been hostile to steam power, not because of a repugnance to technological innovation but rather out of fear that the diffusion of steam to Serbia would undermine still further the ability of existing Serbian industry (mostly crafts, many of recent origin) to compete with the more highly industrialized countries of the world. Prince Miloš was opposed to the deepening of the Iron Gate (Danubian gorge at the Serbo-Rumanian frontier) and hostile to the introduction of steam navigation on the Danube on the ground that these acts would hurt or destroy Serbian commerce and industry. At the time, Serbian, Greek, and other Balkan boats and barges could negotiate the Iron Gate with relative ease. But if steam navigation were introduced or if the Iron Gate were deepened, virtually all the advantages would accrue to territorially larger, economically more viable, and technologically more advanced Austria (and Hungary).

Following the Serbian revolution, the ownership of boats operating along the Serbian and lower Danube had shifted from predominantly Turkish into Greek, Jewish, and Serbian hands. Moreover, the ports of Belgrade, Vidin, and Ruščuk (Ruse) had been rapidly transformed into shipbuilding centers that made small seagoing vessels with an initial maximum displacement of 128 tons, usually without precise plan or symmetry but commercially adequate. Between 1832 and 1834, the entrepreneur Nikola Kefala built in the yards of Smederevo, at the request of the Serbian government, a brig (the *Srbija*) with a displacement of 250 tons. Employing German, Turkish, Serbian, Greek, and perhaps English craftsmen, Kefala also constructed other boats on commission from the government. By 1834, about two hundred small Serbian craft plied along the Sava and Danube, going sometimes to Istanbul. Shipbuilding activity continued to flourish during the 1830's, and in 1840–1842 the brothers German(os) of Belgrade built a seagoing ship (the *Prince Michael*) at Brza Palanka with a displacement of 384 tons.

But hardly had the program of building a Serbian merchant marine got under way than it was confronted with the competition of steam. In 1831, the Austrian government granted the newly created Danube Steamship Navigation Company a long-term monopoly of navigation on the Danube, on condition that it extend its activities to the lower Danube and the Black Sea. Putting a first steamboat into operation along the course between Belgrade and the Iron Gate in 1834, the DSNC added a second in 1836. In 1844, a DSNC steamboat inaugurated service on the Serbian Sava, and in 1847 four DSNC steamboats were charged with passenger and freight service along the lower Danube. When, soon thereafter, Serbia announced its intention to open its own steamship service, DSNC competition immediately nullified its aim. By the middle of the century, there was no longer a Serbian merchant marine.

In the grotesquely unequal struggle for markets and commercial supremacy, not only was the existing Serbian merchant marine doomed to extinction, but no other could be built in its stead unless Serbia ceased to be economically subservient, notably by ceasing to be a landlocked state. Thus, when the Polish émigré statesman Prince Adam Czartoryski and his Paris-centered Polish Agency counseled Serbian "Constitutionalist" leaders in 1843 to embrace a program of expansion to the Adriatic, the Serbian Minister Ilija Garašanin promptly took heed. The following year he prepared a secret project (*Načertanie*), one of the goals of which was to make the Serbian economy independent of Austria. Other goals, and the means to the realization of the previous one, were the acquisition of an Adriatic port, the construction of a good road linking Belgrade to this port, the procurement of international guarantees of freedom of trade along the designated road, and as soon as feasible, the direct annexation to Serbia both of this road and of adjacent territories. Beyond this lay the vision of a great South Slavic state stretching from the Adriatic to the Black Sea.

But as Serbia was weak, Garašanin's project had to be postponed. At the turn of the century, however, following the redoubling of Austrian efforts to thwart Serbian economic independence by frustrating a Serbo-Bulgarian customs union, by imposing a virtual embargo on Serbian pigs, and by annexing Bosnia-Hercegovina, the Serbian bourgeoisie and intelligentsia openly espoused a policy of expansion to the sea. On the eve of World War I, the British Minister to Belgrade complained to his government that the Serbians were "quite off their heads" in their "visions of blue seas and Servian ships in the offing bringing home the wealth of the Indies." [6]

As well as frustrating Serbian navigation on the Danube, Austrian steam similarly removed the possibility of any other strong Balkan merchant marine on the river. By 1854, the DSNC was operating 7 steamboats and 29 tugs on the lower Danube (between the Iron Gate and Sulina); by 1864 this number grew to 29 steamboats and 102 tugs. Moreover, at the close of 1863, the company owned a total of 130 steamboats, with a displacement of 12,268 tons, and 492 barges, with a displacement of 98,176 tons.

Simultaneously, Austrian shipping penetrated the Black Sea from Trieste by means of the Austrian Lloyd Lines, which inaugurated regular service in 1839 between the mouth of the Danube and the Black Sea ports of Odessa and Trebizond. In 1846, six Austrian ships visited the Bulgarian port of Varna, as against 79 Turkish, 70 Greek, and 28 Russian ships. In 1849, it was 81 Austrian as against 76 Turkish, 49 Greek, 52 Russian, and 8 British ships. In 1851, 116 Austrian ships arrived at Varna. On the other hand, French and Russian companies failed to establish regular service on the lower Danube until the 1880's.

Far freer in the commercial sphere, precisely because it was situated along a relatively open sea, was Greece. The Greek

---

[6] George Peabody Gooch and Harold Temperley (eds.), with the assistance of Lillian M. Penson, *British Documents on the Origins of the War, 1898–1914*, Vol. IX, Part 2 (Printed and published by His Majesty's Stationery Office, London, 1934), p. 234, No. 313, letter dated Belgrade, November 30, 1912.

merchant marine thus grew dramatically from 61,000 tons at the outbreak of the war of Greek independence to a million tons at the time of World War I.

Everywhere in the Balkans except Greece, however, the effect of steam navigation was long detrimental to local ship-building, and the introduction of steam was often accompanied and followed by the rapid decline of other transportation resources. There was indeed a considerable popular opposition in the Balkan countries to the building of railroads, notably because they were to be chiefly financed, indirectly if not directly, by rural folk, or the sector of society most deprived economically. In Serbia and Bulgaria, in particular, many persons held that the countries ought first to acquire the kind of vehicles and build the kind of roads that would enable their peasantries to bring rural goods to market during all seasons of the year. Second, they contended that industrially backward nations should concentrate on the improvement of industrial production for domestic consumption rather than on transportation, which was advantageous primarily to those countries of Europe that were the most highly developed economically. In effect, Balkan railroads remained financially passive for the first two decades of their existence, since the main articles transported thereby—agricultural goods destined for foreign markets—were available only during three months of the year. During the rest of the year, railroad traffic was largely confined to passengers and mail.

Moreover, the new Balkan states were not free to determine the direction of the railways but had to agree to compromise solutions amenable to the politically or industrially great powers. Austria-Hungary thus thwarted Serbian preferences for a railway from Belgrade to an Adriatic port that was not under Austro-Hungarian rule, notably to Bar (Antivari), Ulcinj (Dulcigno), Durrës (Durazzo) or Shën Gjin (St. John of Medua). Even the formerly powerful Ottoman Empire was reduced to a position of humiliating inferiority vis-à-vis the steampower states. Henry Noel Brailsford vividly describes the kind of railroads that the great powers and European financial interests imposed upon Balkan territories that remained politically Ottoman until 1912:

> It seemed as though the line had laid itself across the countryside in the track of some writhing serpent. It curled in sinuous folds, it described enormous arcs, it bent and doubled so that a passing train resembled nothing so much as a kitten in pursuit of its own tail. Yet the country was a vast level plain. . . . And oddly enough this railway did not seem to serve any visible town. Indeed, a plausible theory of its gyrations and its undulations might have been that it was desperately trying to dodge the towns. Stations, indeed, there were, but they were at every conceivable distance from the centres of population—one, two, or even five miles away. The explanation was [that the private company which had built and owned the line had insisted upon and obtained] a kilometric guarantee. In order to induce the European financiers—who all the while were bribing and competing to obtain the favour—to perform the onerous work of "opening up Turkey," the Government agreed to guarantee the fortunate company an assured profit, reckoned at so much on every mile or kilometre of rails. . . . In order to make certain that the Turkish Government will pay this annual tribute, the tithes of the luckless provinces through which it passes are mortgaged. Be the season good or bad, whether famine rages or massacre decimates, and whatever the deficit in Constantinople itself may be, so much of the tithes of grain are annually set aside, a first charge on the whole amount, to assure the punctual payment of this debt. And, further, since the financiers know only too well how corrupt Turkish officials are, the collection of this mortgaged revenue is placed in the hands of some European official responsible ultimately to the great Powers.[7]

The building of railways in Slovenia was initiated between 1846 and 1857. In the Balkans proper, the first railroad was the Cernavoda-Constanţa line in the Ottoman (now Rumanian) province of Dobruja, built by an English company shortly

[7] Henry Noel Brailsford, *The War of Steel and Gold: A Study of the Armed Peace* (London: G. Bell and Sons Ltd., 1914), pp. 83–85.

after the Crimean War. In Croatia, the first railways date back
to the early 1860's; in the major European provinces of the
Ottoman Empire and in Greece and Rumania, to the late
1860's; in Serbia, to the 1880's; in Albania proper, there was no
railroad until 1947.

Railroad building was accompanied by numerous financial
irregularities and scandals, the most notorious of which may
have been the bribery of high personages in the Serbian government and of members of the Serbian National Assembly by various financial groups desirous of winning the contract for the
construction of the Belgrade-to-Niš railway, which was initially
given to the publicly French but covertly Austrian Union
Générale, the bankruptcy of which was announced in February
1882. The irregularities and scandals, however, were essentially a characteristic of European rather than specifically Balkan society and should be set in the framework of the Panama
and other scandals that characterized the 1880's and 1890's as
an era of *trasformismo,* a time particularly attuned to political expediency and commercial and financial opportun-
ism.

By 1913, at great cost to the Balkan peoples, there were in
the peninsula over 8,200 kilometers of rail. In the early 1920's,
the railway density per 1,000 square kilometers of territory
varied as follows in the different Balkan and adjacent provinces: Albania, 0; Greece, 21.9 kilometers; Bosnia-Hercegovina, 24.5; Bulgaria, 27.7; Serbia and Serbian Macedonia, 28.5;
Wallachia and Moldavia, 31.5; Croatia, 52.8; Transylvania,
54.8; Slovenia, 69; Bukovina, 70.5; Bačka, 101.8. We may com-
pare these figures to a density of 13 kilometers of rail in the
former territories of the Russian Empire, 67 in Italy, 97 in
France and the Netherlands, 123 in Germany, and 370 in Bel-
gium. In Greece and Bosnia-Hercegovina, however, the density
should be reduced considerably in view of the fact that so
much of the track was narrow-gauge. Moreover, the rolling
stock available to the Balkan countries was very much less than

the stock at the disposal of the countries of Western and Central Europe.

THE REVOLUTION

After 1880, the governments of Rumania, Serbia, Bulgaria, and Greece, and the Austro-Hungarian administration of Bosnia-Hercegovina, all pursued a policy of industrialization, closely linked to but inadequately coordinated with the program of railway construction. All efforts at industrialization met with some degree of success, but in no case was there an industrial "take-off"—the establishment of a self-sustaining industrial economy.

Industrialization was not easy to achieve for several important reasons. First of all, the Balkan countries were the last in Europe, slower even than Russia, to attempt industrialization. In spite of this fact, they pursued a development pattern set by the countries that were among the first to industrialize: England, France, and Germany. But this pattern was essentially a model for countries with the advantage of being first, second, or third, not for those that were the last. In other words, the Balkan countries followed the wrong models.

Moreover, when they tried to imitate the post-1880 European pattern of industrialization by setting up protective tariffs, the highly industrialized countries set impediments in their way by trying to preserve intact the provisions of the Congress of Berlin (1878), which denied Serbia, Bulgaria, and Rumania the right to establish protective tariffs. The aim of the great powers was to retain their extraterritorial rights. In the centuries of its greatness, the Ottoman Empire had freely extended such rights, known as capitulations, to one European country after another. In the eighteenth century, the great powers took advantage of these rights to prevent the improvement of Ottoman manufactures. In the nineteenth, they obliged the new Balkan states to submit to similar terms. The economic provisions of the Congress of Berlin thus represent a continuation of a policy designed to maintain the Balkans as a reservoir of raw materials for the industrial states.

By capturing the world market for industrial goods, especially cotton textiles, Britain had become the primary industrial state in the world. Thus in 1814, British manufacturers exported 32 yards of cotton cloth for every 24 consumed at home; by 1850, the ratio was 39 to 24. The countries of Western and Central Europe copied the British example. On the other hand, the Balkan states, the last in Europe to industrialize or institute a modern technology, could not compete in the world market with the steampower and multipower states. At the same time, being thwarted until the very last years of the century—and in the case of Greece as late as 1910—in their aspirations to protect domestic industry, they could not rapidly create a home market for their new industrial products. In Rumania, industrialization was somewhat easier than in the other Balkan countries, partly because, as the chief exporters of Balkan grains, Rumanian landowners had been able to accumulate greater amounts of capital than their counterparts in the other Balkan states. Second, Rumanian petroleum production, rising from 8,000 barrels in 1860 to 383,000 in 1890 and 13,-500,000 in 1913, drew foreign capital into the country. In spite of a perceptibly greater attractiveness to foreign investors, however, Rumania too failed to achieve an industrial "take-off."

Prerequisite to an industrial "take-off" is economic growth, which we may define as an increase in the real per capita labor product. Such growth can be achieved by improving the average quality of labor, by using labor resources more efficiently, and by investing in machinery and other capital goods. These three changes can be brought about either by private enterprise or by the government, but in either case the agent must be free from outside control and able to act independently in dealing with others. Thus if the government is in charge of the economic growth program, it must be able to negotiate on an equal footing with other governments; similarly, if private enterprise undertakes the task, it must be able to deal on a reciprocal basis with private businesses in other countries. If the program is to be handled by private enterprise rather than by the government, however, one further requirement is necessary: The culture must be a relatively stable one in which goals have been well defined and have to some extent already been realized and in which change can be accepted as part of the normal routine because this change is not drastic but involves only a slight modification of the society's value system and institutions.

Since effective change in the Balkans would have required a metamorphosis of prevailing values and structures, it was well beyond the capabilities of private enterprise. At the same time, changes made by the governments failed to culminate in an increase in the per capita labor product. This failure may be ascribed to the fact that the Balkan economies and technologies were dominated from without and that the initial agents of industrialization—the Balkan bourgeoisies—failed to achieve a reciprocal relationship with the bourgeoisies of the technologically superior and politically dominant states. There was, in effect, no world bourgeoisie, but a multiplicity of national and provincial bourgeoisies, some of which tended to be dominant, while others were dominated. The Balkan bourgeoisies fell, in general, in the latter category.

In recent centuries, however, various human groups have sought to reduce the degree to which they were dominated by embracing some ideology and attempting to endow it with objective force. Thus, the goal of laissez faire was to free the bourgeoisie from the control of the nobility, unenlightened monarchs, and other dominant figures and status groups; the aim of socialism was to free the working class from the control of the bourgeoisie; the theory of nationality was intended to free the dominated nations from the controls of the dominant ones, or from domination by "universal," multinational, or antinational states.

Long aware of the diverse ways in which they were dominated, the most intelligent and most sensitive members of the middle elements of Balkan society systematically denounced their condition of inferiority, especially during the 1870's and 1880's. In Rumania, the unsatisfactory nature of the relationship between the dominating European powers and the dominated Balkan states was defined with particular cogency by the historian Alexander D. Xenopol, who, a year after the Congress of Berlin, bitterly censured Western Europe for monopolizing the work of industry, which he described as ennobling, better recompensed, and energy-saving, and for relegating the rude, heavy, fatiguing, demeaning work of unmechanized agriculture to the peoples of the rest of the world, among them the Rumanians and other Eastern Europeans.[8]

Although some Balkan merchants, such as those of Varna, were hostile to industrialization, a large segment of the Rumanian, Greek, Serbian, and Bulgarian bourgeoisies welcomed such a program. Industrialization policies were undertaken during the two or three decades preceding World War I, and were resumed during the 1920's and after the economic crisis of the early 1930's. In the interwar era, however, and especially during the 1930's, the Balkan bourgeoisies were less confident, less exuberant, less self-reliant than they had been on the eve of World War I.

One reason for this was that they had become fearful of the possible consequences of rapid industrialization—notably, of proletarian revolution. An idea consequently advanced by some bourgeois leaders, especially in Yugoslavia, successor state to the former Serbia, was that, before a large industrial

[8] For Xenopol's views, see Henry L. Roberts, *Rumania: Political Problems of an Agrarian State* (New Haven: Yale University Press; London: Oxford University Press, 1951), p. 335.

proletariat developed, a powerful, homogeneous bourgeoisie should be created, one that was untroubled by differences of religion, dialect, or provincial origin. In other words, they sought to bring about immediately what had actually occurred in Western and Central Europe only after the rise of an industrial working class.

A second bourgeois group, most vociferous in the territories that had remained under Austro-Hungarian rule until 1918, regretted the breakup of the Austro-Hungarian Empire and the subdivision of large estates and, following the example of the Croatian economist Otto Frangeš, yearned to integrate or reintegrate Southeastern Europe into a Middle European "great-space" economy (*Grossraumwirtschaft*). But this was almost tantamount to a social and cultural death-wish, for the only Middle European great-space economy then in the offing was the "prosperity sphere" of expanding fascist Germany, in which the Balkan states could expect to be welcomed only as subservient satellites.

Under the intellectual leadership of the Rumanian economist Mihail Manoilescu, a third bourgeois group developed a theory that divided the world into economically advanced and economically retarded countries. According to this group, countries technologically backward could improve their low labor productivity only if they embraced protectionism. Manifesting another aspect of the fear and despondency of the Balkan bourgeoisies, however, Manoilescu and his adherents further contended that protectionism would allow a technologically backward state to industrialize effectively only if the state dealt with the threats of class struggle and proletarian revolution. The only way to do this would be to organize the society on a vertical basis into status groups or corporate bodies, each subject to a different set of laws, with conflicts between vertical units held in check by an authoritarian state.

The alternating bourgeois sentiments of overconfidence or indifference to public opinion and of deep anxiety, which culminated in bourgeois subservience to the most technologically advanced and most neurotic state in Europe, Nazi Germany, or in flight to Western Europe, North Africa, and America, alienated the common folk more and more from the bourgeoisies. Left leaderless or with leaders in whom they could not confide, a significant minority, or perhaps even a majority, of the people in Yugoslavia and Greece transferred their allegiance during World War II to a set of leaders who espoused a Communist ideology and directed movements of national liberation. In the other Balkan countries, where the bourgeoisies and official and landowning elements had identified their interests more thoroughly with German, Italian, or native fascism, or with the principle of a German or Italian great-space economy, a new Communist leadership came to power partly as the result of a Churchill-Stalin agreement that provided for the establishment—at the close of the war against Nazi Germany—of a preponderance of Soviet influence in Rumania and Bulgaria, of a balance between Soviet and Western influence in Yugoslavia, and of a preponderance of Western influence in Greece.

The terms of the Churchill-Stalin agreement were in keeping with traditional Russian policies. Ever since the time of Catherine II, Russian governments had thought primarily in terms of the division of the Balkans into three spheres of influence: a Russian zone in the east, a zone of the maritime powers in the south and extreme west, and a Central European or a joint sphere of influence in the central and nonmaritime western portions of the Balkans. Since at the time of the Churchill-Stalin agreement Britain and the Soviet Union were jointly engaged in a life-and-death struggle against Germany, the customary provisions for a zone of Central European (German) influence had to yield to the equally old idea of a joint sphere of influence.

As a consequence of the Soviet-British agreement, Britain and the United States were able to pursue in Greece, where a substantial segment of the population sympathized with communism, policies that would lead to the defeat of the Communists in the Greek Civil War of 1946–1949. In Rumania and Bulgaria, on the other hand, native Communists dependent on the USSR succeeded in extending their authority. In Yugoslavia, victory went to the native communism of the war leader Josip Broz Tito and to the ideology of "different roads to socialism."

Albania presents a special problem. There, Communist leaders rose to ascendancy with the aid of Yugoslav communism, but after an open ideological and political conflict developed between Yugoslav and Soviet Communists in 1948, they oriented their domestic and foreign policies around the Soviet example. In the current ideological and political dispute between Soviet and Chinese communism, Albania is in the Chinese camp, the camp of the third set of countries to industrialize under Communist leadership.

By 1960, after pursuing policies with different psychological foundations and economic principles but purportedly with common social goals, Rumania and Yugoslavia succeeded in achieving an industrial "take-off." Bulgaria is in close pursuit, while backward Albania has achieved in two decades what, under bourgeois leadership, might have taken half a century. Greece, however, has also made noteworthy progress toward effective industrialization, and has done this under bourgeois leadership (see Figure 2).

Before trying to explain the Balkan industrial "take-off," let us cite some facts which tellingly demonstrate the technological progress that has been made. Bulgaria increased its production of lignite by the early 1960's to 20 million tons or more as against 1 or 2 million before World War II, embarked upon important irrigation projects that have brought one-sixth of the cultivated surface under irrigation, greatly expanded its hydroelectric production, and increased its steel production from 6,000 tons in 1938 to 211,000 in 1958. During the same

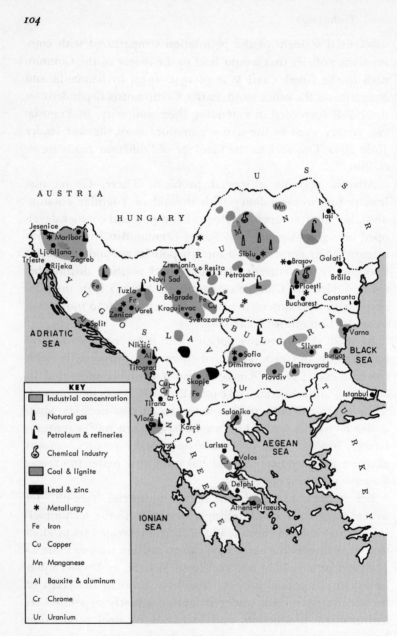

Figure 2. Balkan Industry: The 1960's

period, Rumania increased its steel production from 284,000 to 934,000 tons. Furthermore, between 1938 and 1962, Rumanian petroleum and lignite production was doubled, Rumanian production of natural gas was increased tenfold, and the production of coal rose to 5 million tons, twelve times the prewar figure. In Yugoslavia, steel production rose from 230,000 tons in 1938 to 1.1 million tons in 1958 and 1.5 million tons in the mid-1960's. Moreover, by the mid-1960's, Yugoslavia was producing 25 million tons of lignite, 1.5 million tons of petroleum, 1.2 million tons of bauxite, and had raised its hydroelectric production to 10 billion kilowatt hours. It may be even more to the point to note that in the period 1950–1965 the average yearly increase in the national product has been on the order of 13 per cent, as against an annual demographic increase of 1.3 per cent. The average annual increase in the per capita national product has thus been on the order of 10 per cent. Similar growth rates have been attained in Rumania and Bulgaria.

Without aiming to please or denounce any particular group in any general philosophical sense, we are left with the feeling that the Communists were the only group in the Balkans ready to assume the kind of risks that the "conquering bourgeoisies" had taken in the countries of Europe which were among the first to industrialize. But the success of communism in the Soviet Union, in Central Europe, in the Balkans, and in China is not a victory of communism alone—often waged and won with an obdurate nonchalance to human suffering—but of the dialogue between capitalism and communism. Without that dialogue or competition, the technological achievements of communism would surely have been less great. The expansion of communism pushed the United States and the countries of Western Europe into espousing the enlightened principle of massive economic aid to underdeveloped countries. The basic aim of such assistance was to stop the spread of communism or to divide the Communist states, but United States and Western European aid in money, raw materials, food, arms, and credits to Yugoslavia in the decade after that country's break with Stalin enabled the Yugoslavs both to preserve their political independence of the Soviet Union and to lay a new groundwork for an industrial "take-off." The United States poured into Greece more than $3 billion in aid from the close of World War II to the end of 1963, or more aid per capita than to any other country in the world. Despite this assistance, however, the annual growth rate in Greece was only 6.5 per cent between 1950 and 1956 and 5.5 per cent between 1956 and 1962, or about half the growth rate in the Communist states. The chief reason for the difference may be that Greece has concentrated upon improving consumption, with the consequent result that funds available for investment in capital goods were reduced. Partly as a means of driving her closer to an industrial "take-off," the countries of Western Europe admitted Greece to associate membership in the customs union of the Common Market in November, 1962, allowing her to dismantle her protective tariffs slowly while pursuing a policy of encouraging business consolidations, welcoming foreign capital, and eliminating marginal enterprise—a program bound, in the short run, to arouse popular discontent.

To the advantage of both East and West, however, the dialogue between communism and capitalism, made more imperative than ever by the threat of nuclear war, continues to grow.

IV

SOCIETY

◇━◎◎━◇

A society is a group of communities with a common network of interdependent systems for the management of social strains and solidarities. Every society has its own way of organizing interpersonal and intergroup relationships so that the members of the society are in frequent or regular, if generally indirect, communication with each other at all or nearly all levels of life—religion, art, play, production, consumption, education, exchange and so forth. In addition, every society has its own set of social structures.

Social structure refers not to the particular parts of a society, or to the role-players, but to the wholes that remain much the same generation after generation, in spite of the fact that the players constantly change. Class structure, patterns of consumption, patterns of exchange, and other structural complexes identify functional rather than organizational aspects of society. Moreover, behind the functions or social structures, and woven into them, are the fundamental values of a society. Functional or structural change is therefore ordinarily taboo.

Societies, however, remain always in a precarious equilibrium. They are not only fields of structural solidarity, but also

of structural strain and stress. In other words, they allow the
existence of variant social structures—at a potential level if
not at the level of reality. Under certain conditions, an open
struggle ensues between the defenders of the dominant structures and the role-players who identify themselves with the
variant patterns. When several structures change simultaneously, the change is said to be a revolution.

Structural change and ethnic change are the themes of the
present chapter. After dealing with the problem of ethnic
change, that is, with the almost total transformation of roles
and the partial transformation of structures, especially linguistic, we shall proceed to study the Balkans as a general field of
structural solidarities and tensions.

RACES, PEOPLES, AND NATIONS

The ethnic affiliation of the inhabitants of the Balkans can be
identified with any degree of assurance only since 2000 B.C. At
that time, three main ethnic groups occupied the peninsula:
Illyrians in the west; Daco-Mysians, Thracians, and Armeno-
Phrygians in the east; and Pelasgians in the southern maritime
fringes. The last group was apparently related to the Lydians,
Carians, and Lycians of western Anatolia, and it may possibly
have been the creator of the so-called Dimini culture of
Thessaly.

According to a general scholarly view, Indo-European linguistic groups—Illyrians, Achaeans, Dorians, and Thracians—continued to penetrate southward into the Balkans during the
second millennium. The Achaeans and Dorians ultimately settled in the southernmost areas, where they mingled with or
destroyed the former Pelasgians. Disagreeing with the view
that the Illyrians were a group of new immigrants, Albanian
scholars maintain that they were an old Balkan ethnic element, like the Pelasgians. They base their interpretation on
certain archeological findings which appear to show a continu-

ity of cultures in Slovenia, Bosnia, and Hercegovina between the prebronze and bronze ages.

Shortly after 400 B.C. began an era of new ethnic formations, heralded by the southward penetration of the Celts to the Drava, Sava, and middle Danube, and the northward dispersal of the Illyrian Neuri, identified by some Soviet scholars as ancestors of the Slavs. Between 380 and 360 B.C., the Celts moved into the Morava valley, where they mingled with the Daco-Mysians and drove a wedge between the Illyrians and Thracians. In addition, they forced the Illyrians of the northern Adriatic to withdraw to the mouth of the Neretva in Hercegovina. At the same time, a population of diverse linguistic affiliation and ethnic origin known as the Scythians invaded what we now designate as Hungary by way of the Ukrainian steppes and then spread into Dacia (modern Rumania). In the next century, Celtic groups pushed southward from the Danube and Sava into Thrace and Macedonia. As a result of cultural and biological intermingling, Illyrians and Thracians were thus often transformed into Celto-Illyrians and Celto-Thracians.

The Roman conquest of the Balkans, carried out between the latter part of the third century B.C. and the opening of the second century A.D., added still more to the ethnic and linguistic complexities. Among the last areas to come under Roman rule (101–107 A.D.) and among the first to be abandoned (270–275) was Dacia. Today, however, Dacia, or modern Rumania, is linguistically the most Romanized of all the Balkan provinces and consequently confronts scholars with the interesting and important question of how its Romanization occurred.

At the close of the fifth century the Balkans formed two urban linguistic zones, a Roman in the north and west and a Greek zone in the south and east, with the line of division running from Alessio (Lesh, now in Albania) on the Adriatic to Skoplje (Skopje), Niš, Pirot, and Nikopol, with the area from the Balkan foothills to the Danube falling under Roman linguistic influence. This was somewhat east of the line along which the Roman Empire had been separated in 395 A.D. into a western and eastern complex of territories. The zone of Romanization comprised, however, two noncontiguous blocs: an Adriatic zone, in which the population spoke a southern Italic language known as "Roman" or "Dalmatian," and a Danubian zone, in which the inhabitants spoke an idiom replete with what we now call "Balkanisms." In the mountainous interior between the two lay a zone of lightly Romanized Illyrians and, intervening between the Romanized lower Danube and the Hellenized south, a highly mixed zone, including Thracian Besses in the district of Tatar Pazardžik, Thracian Sapes in the region between Kratovo and Sofia, Celto-Illyrian Scordisci and remnants of Daco-Mysians between the province of Srem in the northwest and the district of Serdica (modern Sofia) in the southeast, Thracian Paeonians to the east of the middle Vardar, and Celto-Thracians or Celto-Mysians in the district of Philippopolis. We infer the presence in the last region of Thracians, Celts, or Daco-Mysians, or of all three, from the fact that the Slavs who later settled there derived their own name for the city of Philippopolis—Plovdiv and Plovdin—directly from the Thracian or Daco-Mysian Pulpudeva or from the Thraco-Mysian with the Celtic ending *-dun*. Some of the populations inhabiting the rural areas of the southeastern interior were probably Hellenized, but the soldiery was everywhere at least superficially Romanized. Moreover, Goths occupied certain parts of Croatia, an area in northeastern Albania and adjacent districts to the north, the Dobruja, the region between the Balkan foothills and Danubian Nikopol, and large parts of Dacia.

Goths had settled in Dacia following the withdrawal of the Roman legions. The departure of Roman officials and soldiers also resulted in a new influx of Sarmatians, a people speaking a language similar to Iranian, some elements of whom had been present in the country for several centuries. The inhabitants of Dacia then also included the Carps, a Carpathian people that had successfully resisted Romanization, and the Germanic Gepids. There were doubtless other ethnic and linguistic groups at the end of the fifth century, including even some Slavs. But were there any people left who spoke a Romance dialect?

Rumanian and Hungarian scholars have long been divided in their answers to this question, the Hungarian view being that there were none or very few, since the Magyars do not appear to have encountered any when traversing the former Dacia in the ninth century. The general Rumanian version is that Romance-speaking populations—Daco-Romans—never ceased to exist in some districts of the country, and Rumanian scholars have conclusively demonstrated in recent decades that some Romanized groups continued to be found in Dacia well into the fifth and sixth centuries. But the question then arises as to the fate of these groups following the Slavic and Avar invasions of the sixth and seventh centuries.

The movement of Slavs from north of the Carpathians to the middle Danube and the left bank of the Sava appears to have been a long process, beginning in the first and second and continuing into the fifth and sixth centuries. In the early part of the sixth century, Slavic bands began to make incursions deep into Thessaly, Epirus, Illyricum, and Thrace, and in the latter part of the sixth and first quarter of the seventh century, Slavs and Mongol or Turkic Avars jointly organized numerous invasions directed against the maritime cities of the Adriatic, Aegean, and Pontus Euxinus.

Arnold J. Toynbee cites a passage from the annals of Theophylactus Simocatta concerning one of the earliest recorded contacts, notably in 591 A.D., between Slavs and the East Roman Empire:

> Three men of Slav race without weapons or military equipment were captured by the Imperial Body-Guard. Their only baggage consisted of harps, and they carried nothing else with

them. . . . They carried harps because they were not trained
to bear arms. Their country [on the boundary of "the Western
Ocean" or Baltic] was ignorant of iron, and this accounted for
their peaceful and harmonious life. . . . They were a people
among whom war was unheard-of; and it was only natural there
should be a bucolic note in their musical technique.[1]

Toynbee then goes on to conclude that Slavic history begins
only after the Avars compelled the Slavs to fight for and beside
them. In 584 A.D., however, John of Ephesus reported that the
Slavs were capable of waging war more effectively than the Romans, and the "Miracles of St. Demetrius," or accounts of the
first and second sieges of Salonika by the Slavs at the end of the
sixth and opening of the seventh century, relate that the Slavs
possessed arms of a kind that "no man of our era has ever seen,
or has ever known their names." [2] Several centuries earlier the
Slavs may have been poorly armed. But by the latter half of
the sixth century, having come into contact with Gothic,
Roman, and Hunnic, as well as Avar, arms, they were no
longer the "unarmed folk" (ἔθνη ἄοπλα) of Constantine
Porphyrogenitus or the "weaponless" folk (*armis despecti*) of
Jordanes.

Upon the advent of the Slavs into the heart and deep into
the southernmost parts of the Balkan peninsula, the Romanized populations of the Danube took flight into the Transylva-
nian, Balkan, Rhodope, and Pindus mountains; some Illyrians
and Daco-Mysians fled into the wild highlands of Albania; the
Dalmatian Latini locked themselves in their Adriatic island
and coastal fortresses; and the Greeks found refuge in the Aegean and Pontic cities. Whereas Danubian Romans and Adriatic Latini had formerly lived at great distances from each

[1] Arnold J. Toynbee, *A Study of History*, Vol. II (Published under the
auspices of the Royal Institute for International Affairs by Oxford University Press, London, 1934), p. 318.

[2] Gavro A. Škrivanić, *Oružje u srednjovekovnoj Srbiji, Bosni i Dubrov-
niku* (Belgrade: Srpska Akademija Nauka, 1957), p. 204. [Summary in English, "Armour and Weapons in Medieval Serbia, Bosnia, and Dubrovnik,"
pp. 201–05.]

other, they now became neighbors. In language and way of life, however, distinctions were perpetuated, and for the La- tini, the Danubian Romans in their new Dinaric mountain homes were *Nigri Latini, Maurovalachi,* or Morlaks: Black Vlachs.

Along the Dinaric chain the Morlaks ultimately occupied a series of mountain heights from Kotor (Cattaro) in the south to Senj (Segna) in the north. But in addition to the complex of Dinaric Valachiae (Vlach settlements or Vlach countries), there emerged a series of other Valachiae: an Old Valachia (Stari Vlah) in the mountain corridor dividing Bosnia-Herce- govina and Montenegro from Serbia, an Upper Valachia in Epirus, a Valachia Major in Thessaly, a Valachia Minor in Aetolia and Acarnania, a Valachia (Vlachorynchinoi) in south- ern Macedonia, a series of Balkan and Rhodope Valachiae, another group of Valachiae stretching from the Dobruja southward to Anchialos on the Black Sea, a White Valachia (Wallachia) on the lower Danube, a Black Valachia (Molda- via) from the Carpathians to the Prut River, a Valachia Minor (often known as Oltenia) to the west of Black Valachia, Va- lachiae projecting from the Carpathians into Transylvania, a Romanija in Bosnia, and yet other Valachiae.

Large as may have been the Valachiae, still larger were the Sclaviniae or settlements of Slavs. Indeed, the Vlachs occupied the high country, land of refugees fleeing from foreign in- vaders or from the authority of empires, while the Slavs settled in the plains and along the middle and lower courses of rivers. The relationship between Vlachs and Slavs exposes a principle of human development, a kind of law of history: the conquer- ors occupy the most easily exploitable resources, the rebels withdraw to less hospitable lands, which offer them at least the advantage of preserving their freedom. The un-Romanized Carps were thus mountaineers, the Romanized Dacians were plainsmen. Following the Slavic invasions, the Romanized plainsmen were forced into the mountains and the Slavs occupied the plains. As a result of the Ottoman conquest, many Slav peasants abandoned the plains to join the Vlach folk of the mountains, and the plains came into the possession of Turks and Muslim Albanians.

Between the ninth and fifteenth centuries, the southernmost Sclaviniae, notably those of the Peloponnesus, were largely eliminated as a result of the Byzantine policy of recolonizing these territories with Greeks from southern Italy and of the population transfer policies of the Ottoman Empire. To prevent the emergence of a possibly dominant nationality or triumph of the principle of nationality, Byzantium settled Armenians, Turks, and Monophysite Syrians in Macedonia and Thrace. Ottomans and Habsburgs pursued similar strategies, for it is a condition of empire to maintain or create enclaves of peoples to obstruct the formation of nationality.

Partly as a result of the policies of empires and even more as a consequence of the unequal rate of cultural evolution and of the long succession of migrations and invasions, peoples without a precise consciousness of cultural or national identity came to inhabit extensive Balkan areas. Discovering such peoples in Epirus, Acarnania, and Aetolia, Euripides called them *Mixobarbaroi,* a term long used in one or both of two senses. Mixobarbaroi were semibarbarians or rural folk without an important city culture of their own or without an imperial, ecumenical, or missionary religion, but who were acculturated through their contacts with peoples, such as the Greeks or Romans, who did possess a city culture and an ecumenical religion. Second, Mixobarbaroi were rural folk with a fluctuating or floating sense of ethnic consciousness, identifying themselves, or identified by others, first with one and then with another and sometimes with several nationalities. A Greek chronicle from the monastery of Panteleimon on Lake Janina thus describes a certain Vonko, who conquered Arta in 1400, as a *Servalvanitovoulgarovlachos,* a Serbo-Albanian-Bulgarian-Vlach. *Mixobarbara,* or lands of Mixobarbaroi, continued to exist in the Balkans until the beginning of the twentieth century. Macedonia and the Dobruja are notable examples of such provinces.

To the ethnic changes we have already indicated, we should add the entry into the peninsula of large numbers of Turkic peoples. For example, during the second half of the fifth century, Turkic Bulgars from the Don and Volga settled along the left bank of the lower Danube, arriving at the invitation of Byzantium, which needed their aid against the Goths. After accepting Avar rule for almost a century and then coming under pressure from the steppic Turkic state of Khazaria, some 10,000 to 25,000 Bulgars crossed the Danube in 679 A.D. to settle in the "crazy thicket" (Deli Orman) district of the Dobruja, then occupied by Severian Slavs. Seizing Serdica in 809 A.D., the Bulgars proceeded to create a Bulgarian Empire, the language of which became increasingly Slavic, particularly after the translation of the scriptures into the Slavic dialect of southern Macedonia and the conversion of the Bulgarian *khakan* and his subjects to Christianity during the second half of the ninth century.

Numerically more important than the Turkic Bulgars, however, were other Turkic groups that surged forward from the steppes of Southeastern Europe and from Anatolia: Pečenegs, Cumanians, Tartars, and Ottoman Turks. Under pressure from the Cumanians, Pečenegs moved into the Dobruja. To prevent a resurgence of the Slavs of Bulgaria, who had reverted to Byzantine control at the beginning of the eleventh century, Byzantium allowed other Pečenegs to settle along the northern limits of Hellenism, especially around Adrianople and Philippopolis. To separate the Slavs of the western from those of the eastern areas, a Pečeneg tribe was allowed to move into the region that now forms eastern Serbia and western Bulgaria.

The Cumanians, however, overran a still larger territory and were probably numerically the most significant of the Turkic groups, settling in the lightly wooded sandy area between the

Danube and the Tisza and in the region between the Dnieper and lower Danube, including southeastern Moldavia, Wallachia, and Oltenia, where they created their own political state. Cumanians also settled south of the Danube, notably in the Byzantine province of Paristrion around and north of Varna, and appear to have extended into northern Macedonia (Kumanovo). In Transylvania, they were Magyarized through their contacts with the Finno-Ugrian Magyars of Hungary and their conversion to Roman Catholicism; in Wallachia and Moldavia, they were Romanized; in Bulgaria, they were Slavicized or Romanized. Moreover, Cumanians played a key role in the forging of Rumanian and Vlacho-Bulgarian states.

The great Mongol invasion of 1241 and repeated subsequent Tartar incursions, first under Mongol and later under Ottoman sponsorship or on their own initiative, brought yet other Turkic elements to the eastern Balkans, especially to Moldavia, the Dobruja, and eastern Bulgaria. Politically and religiously most important was the last Turkic group to penetrate the Balkans, the Muslim Ottoman Turks. From a linguistic and biological point of view, however, the Ottoman Turks —if we exclude the Yürük shepherd folk of Anatolia, Thrace, and Macedonia—were the least Turkic of all the Turks to enter the Balkan peninsula.

The impact of Ottoman rule on the Balkan ethnic structure was nevertheless of inestimable significance. Ottoman Turks settled in the plains and river basins of the eastern and central Balkans and in the towns of the entire peninsula. Many Slavs abandoned the lowlands to settle in the uplands, where they Slavicized the Vlachs but adopted their pastoral habits. Furthermore, Slavs and Slavicized Vlachs migrated in increasingly large numbers to Dalmatia, with a resultant rapid recession of the Romanic Dalmatian dialect before various Serbo-Croatian idioms. In the sixteenth century, Italian was the language of commerce in Venetian Dalmatia and in Ragusa, but the language of the hearth was predominantly Slavic and the language of literature was both Slavic and Italian. By the seventeenth century, the number of speakers of Romanic Dalmatian was negligible, and in 1898 the last speaker of this idiom died on the island of Krk (Veglia). The *Latini* and Morlaks were thus more or less completely Slavicized.

North of the lower Danube, the process occurred in reverse. Following the Mongol conquest of Kievan Rus and the Mongol ravages of Hungary, the Vlachs of the Carpathian uplands descended to the plains, where they mingled with and Romanized Slavs, Cumanians, and other ethnic groups. Moreover, the Ottoman conquest aided Romanization in Wallachia and Moldavia in two fundamental ways. First, the weakening of the Slavic states gave the Rumanians an opportunity to create, albeit temporarily, more effective political entities of their own. Second, they were assisted in that enterprise by their ability to draw on Serbian and Bulgarian scholars and administrators fleeing Ottoman rule after the fall of Bulgaria and Serbia. Among elite groups, some Slavicization was manifest in the Wallachian and Moldavian principalities both before and after they became Ottoman tributaries, and much Hellenization occurred in the two provinces during the seventeenth and eighteenth centuries, particularly after the office of *hospodar* or Ottoman governor fell into the hands of men of wealth in Constantinople who were known as Phanariots. At the folk level, however, the process of Romanization continued unbroken.

As a consequence of Ottoman rule, by the end of the seventeenth century almost certainly a fifth and perhaps nearly a third of the population of the eastern areas was ethnically or linguistically Turkic, whereas in the western areas the number was less than 10 per cent. Thus, while the Slavic character of the western and the Romanic character of the trans-Danubian eastern territories was affirmed and the linguistic Hellenism of the southern maritime zone was not seriously challenged until the great Albanian incursions of the eighteenth century, the ethnic future of the eastern and southern continental regions was a big question mark: Would they ultimately become singularly Hellenic, Turkic, Albanian, Slavic, or Romanic, or would they retain their conglomerate character?

In the northwestern and north central areas, the Germanic ethnic element grew rapidly after the Austro-Turkish war of 1683–1699. Throughout this period the Protestant Saxons of Transylvania retained their identity as a separate nation. Then, in the eighteenth century, the Habsburg monarchy welcomed the settlement of Roman Catholic colonists from the Rhineland and other sections of Germany and from Lorraine and Italy in the provinces taken from the Turks (Hungary, Transylvania, Banat, Syrmia, and Slavonia). The monarchy had two reasons for encouraging this colonization: to use the new inhabitants as a lever and bulwark against the rebellious Magyars and Protestant Saxons and to repopulate the devastated plains. In the nineteenth century, Germanization proceeded apace even in Dalmatia and, after 1878, in Bosnia-Hercegovina, which the Turks had been forced to place under an Austro-Hungarian administration. In Hungary, on the other hand, the Magyar minority succeeded in becoming a majority through the assimilation of many Germans, Slavs, Jews, and other ethnic groups.

During and after the Napoleonic wars, a series of autonomous or nominally independent Balkan states arose along the Danube (Serbia, Wallachia and Moldavia united as Rumania, and Bulgaria) or on the sea (Greece); Montenegro already had a considerable degree of autonomy. This increase in the number of self-governing states immediately raised the question of which would be victor, the revolutionary principle of nationality as represented by the new states or the principle of empire as embodied in the Habsburg, Ottoman, and Russian monarchies. In the long run (1804–1918), the empires collapsed and, with the creation between 1912 and 1918 of a Serb-Croat-Slovene State (Yugoslavia), an enlarged Rumania, an enlarged

Bulgaria, and a nominally independent Albania, the theory of nationality triumphed.

The period since 1918 has been typically an era of striving to mold a homogeneous nationality or a cluster of mutually compatible subnationalities. Threatened by and accommodating themselves to German and Italian fascism and developing authoritarianisms of their own during the interwar and World War II periods, the Balkan states almost foundered in the sea of nationality conflict. After surviving World War II, however, they have at last almost realized their goal of national homogeneity even without major boundary revisions, largely by carrying out the following during one or both of the postwar periods:

1. Subdivision of large estates, resulting in the expropriation of Germans and Magyars in Rumania and Yugoslavia and of Turks in Bulgaria, Greece, and Yugoslavia.
2. Nationalization of enterprises known to have collaborated with the enemy during World War II.
3. Exchange of populations, involving more than two million persons during the first postwar period, with Greeks going from Turkey and Bulgaria to Greece, Macedonian Slavs from Greece to Bulgaria, and Turks from Bulgaria and Greece to Turkey.
4. "Voluntary" expatriation of minority ethnic and religious groups to the countries of their choice.
5. Expulsion after World War II of a large portion of the German minority from Yugoslavia and Rumania and the virtual expulsion of the Turkish minority from Bulgaria.
6. Establishment of limitations upon the movements of populations engaging in transhumance or seasonal migrations, thus facilitating their assimilation into the settled folk.
7. Pursuit of other assimilationist policies, including the non-enforcement of minority "rights" and the maintenance of

educational facilities and employment opportunities for minority nationalities at a lower level.

In all of the Balkan countries today, 80 to 90 per cent of the population is composed of a dominant nationality or of several subnational groups. In Yugoslavia, where the principle of subnationality is operative, the subnationalities comprise Serbians, Croatians, Slovenians, and Macedonian Slavs. In Rumanian Transylvania and in Yugoslav Macedonia and Vojvodina, the minority nationalities are still very large, and in Yugoslavia's Kosmet (Kosovo-Metohija), the Albanians continue to constitute a majority. By and large, however, there is now almost an end to the maze of ethnic enclaves existent already in antiquity but much complicated by the migrations of peoples.

Nationality and subnationality, however, do not constitute race. On the basis of the fragmentary information available, every ethnic group comprised several different physical types even before its entry into the Balkan peninsula. Even territorially small Montenegro, traditionally (since the end of the nineteenth century) noted for its Dinaric race, the very existence of which modern physical anthropology now questions, manifests considerable racial diversity. In fact, at the close of the nineteenth century one could discern three Montenegrin physical types: a relatively short, brown-haired, dark-skinned, and either blue- or tawny-eyed inhabitant of Old Montenegro; a taller, more thick-set, auburn-haired, blue- or gray-eyed inhabitant of the Brda or northeastern mountain districts; and a very tall solidly built type with long legs and a relatively short body and blond hair (but sometimes with very dark hair and skin) found in the North Border area. Moreover, there was a great difference in Montenegro between the height of men and that of women, the average height of women tending to be under 5 ft. 3 in. and the average height of men 5 ft. 10 in., largely because women were overworked, underfed, and often not given an opportunity to reach their full stature, for it was common practice to marry girls when they were 10 to 15 years of age and thus oblige them to become mothers of two, three or four infants before they were twenty. Finally, variations from the median types were evident in all geographic areas.

Prehistoric, early historic, and medieval human skulls discovered in Balkan tombs and cemeteries tend to indicate a greater dolichocephaly or narrow-headedness and a less marked condition of brachycephaly or broad-headedness than in modern times. The conclusion is inescapable nonetheless that subracial diversity has prevailed in the Balkans for many millennia. The necropolis (cemetery) of prehistoric Glasinac, northeast of Sarajevo, thus shows that 24 per cent of the prehistoric population of that region was brachycephalic and 76 per cent dolichocephalic and mesocephalic (medium-sized). The cephalic-index distribution in modern Bosnia is almost a reversal of the prehistoric Glasinac situation, but the latter finds an apparent parallel in modern Bulgaria, where 23 per cent of the population is brachycephalic and 77 per cent dolichocephalic and mesocephalic, and in modern Serbia, where 30 per cent is brachycephalic and 70 per cent dolichocephalic and mesocephalic. In fact, however, western Serbia, western Macedonia, and western Greece are brachycephalic, whereas eastern Serbia, eastern Macedonia, and eastern Greece are predominantly dolichocephalic (index of 75 and less) and mesocephalic (index of 75.1–80). Every Balkan nationality is a complex mixture of Caucasian physical types, and even on the basis of the average cephalic index, no Balkan country may claim racial purity.

MACROSOCIETY: ESTATES STATES

Indo-European societies, as we have already noted, tended in their early history toward a tripartite mode of thought and social organization. In the macrosocial sphere, this orientation embodied a division of the members of various political or

KEY

SOUTH SLAVIC DIALECT GROUPS

Slovenian. From Maribor in NE to Klagenfurt (in Austria) in N and Gorizia in W.

Kajkavian or Croatian of Zagreb area. Since 1848 literary language of area is Štokavian.

Čakavian or SW Croatian. Partly submerged since 16th century by Štokavian.

Serbo-Croatian or Štokavian. Literary languages of Serbia, Croatia, Montenegro, and Bosnia-Hercegovina are based on these dialects.

East Serbian Štokavian. Linguistically close to Bulgarian and Macedonian as well as to Serbo-Croatian.

Macedonian-Slavic. Intermediate between East Serbian and Bulgarian.

Bulgarian. Affinities with East Slavic languages as well as with Serbian and Macedonian. Various dialects.

OTHER LINGUISTIC GROUPS

G Greek.

GA Gheg. Northern and central Albanian dialects.

TA Tosk. Southern Albanian dialects.

R Rumanian of NE areas.

V Vlach or Macedo-Rumanian. Rumanian of Thessaly, Macedonia, and the Pindus.

T Turkic dialects.

H Hungarian.

S Saxon. Spoken by descendants of medieval German colonists.

A Austro-German.

I Italian.

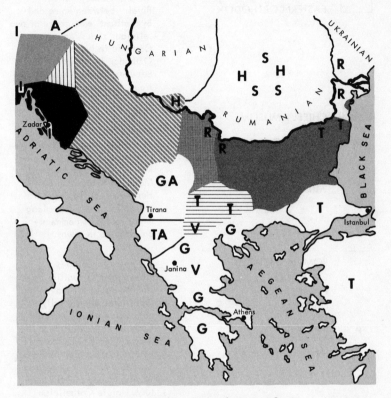

Figure 3a. Language Areas, 1960

NOTE: For similar but more detailed versions of linguistic distribution in part of the Balkans (excluding Rumania), see P. Vidal de La Blache and L. Gallois (eds.), *Géographie universelle*, VII, *Méditerranée*, Part 2 (actually the second volume of tome VII), section on "Pays balkaniques," by Y. Chataigneau and Jules Sion (Paris: Armand Colin, 1934), p. 405; Werner Markert (ed.), *Osteuropa-Handbuch: Jugoslawien* (Köln/Graz: Böhlau-Verlag, 1954), map II (between pp. 32 and 33). Our map of language areas is also partly based on Pavle Ivić, *Die serbokroatischen Dialekte. Ihre Struktur und Entwicklung, I. Allgemeines und die štokavische Dialekt-gruppe* (Slavistic Printings and Reprintings, XVIII, C. H. van Schooneveld (ed.) 's-Gravenhage: Mouton & Co., 1958).

KEY

ROMAN CATHOLIC

EASTERN ORTHODOX

Christianity spreads between
1st and 12th centuries.
Rivalry between Rome and
Byzantium: emergence of two
religious zones, Roman
Catholic in N and W and
Orthodox in S and E.
Between the two, a zone of
transitional religion.

CHIEFLY MUSLIM

M   ORTHODOX OR
ROMAN CATHOLIC
WITH MUSLIM
MINORITIES

Islamic communities arise
between 14th and 17th
centuries in zone of heresies
(Mithraic Danube, Paulician
Rhodope Bulgaria, Bogomil
Macedonia and Bosnia-
Hercegovina), in pastoral
mountainous regions, along
major routes of communi-
cation, and in towns.

ROMAN CATHOLIC,
ORTHODOX,
PROTESTANT,
UNIATE

P   PROTESTANT

L   LUTHERAN

As in rest of Europe,
Protestant communities arise
in 16th century. Slovenian
Protestants aim initially at
conversion of all Orthodox,
Catholic, and Muslim South
Slavs. Nobility of Transyl-
vania espouses Calvinism,
Saxons embrace Lutheranism.
Arising at end of 16th cen-
tury, Uniate Catholicism
aims at recovery of losses to
Protestantism and Orthodoxy.

J   JUDAIC

Judaic communities in Hellenistic Greece. Hungarian,
Iberian, and Italian Jews
emigrate to Ottoman areas in
15th and 16th centuries,
Ukrainian (or Polish) Jews
to Moldavia and Wallachia
since mid-17th century. Nazi
Germany exterminates
thousands of Balkan Jews.
Rumanian Jews go to Israel
after World War II.

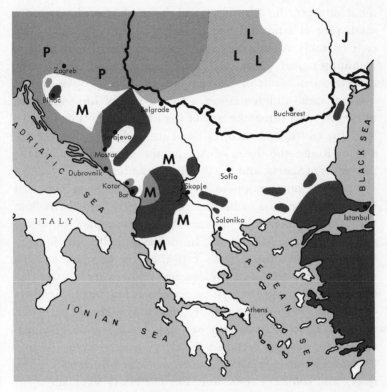

Figure 3b. Religious Distribution, 1960

NOTE: For similar but more detailed versions of religious distribution in part of the Balkans (excluding Rumania), see P. Vidal de La Blache and L. Gallois (eds.), *Géographie universelle*, VII, *Méditerranée*, Part 2 (actually the second volume of tome VII), section on "Pays balkaniques," by Y. Chataigneau and Jules Sion (Paris: Armand Colin, 1934), p. 404: Werner Markert (ed.), *Osteuropa-Handbuch: Jugoslawien* (Köln/Graz: Böhlau-Verlag, 1954), map VIII (between pp. 177 and 178).

tribal entities into three orders, estates, or *bioi:* makers of sacrifices, protectors, and producers. In Aryan India, the three orders were. respectively, the *brâhmana, kshatriya,* and *vaiçya.* In Rome, they were the *flamines, milites,* and *quirites,* or the three tribes of the Ramnes (cult experts), Luceres (warriors), and Titienses (herdsmen). In ancient Greece, they comprised the demiurges, the aristocrats, and the producers who owned a small plot of land and had the right to be represented in a civic assembly. Among the pagan Scandinavians, they were *Godi* (demiurge), *Jarl* (earl), and *Karl* (free farmer). Very early, however, as a result of the conquest of other peoples and of internal social differentiation, a fourth way of life was added to the previous three, the way of life of dependents or inferior folk: the *çûdra,* or human cattle of the Indian system, the clients of Rome, the thetes of Athens, the *penestai* of Thessaly, the helots of Sparta, and the thralls of Scandinavia.

There is some reason to suppose that the Slavs possessed three orders or ways of life before their entry into the Balkan peninsula. In their new homelands, however, they too developed a system of four estates. In medieval Serbia, the four estates comprised the priest's cap (*popova kapa*), the great protectors (*vlastela*) and professional soldiery (*voin*), the free farmers (*sebri*), and the serfs or persons of low birth. Members of the last group were variously known as *meropsi,* pareques, villeins (*villani* or *posadnici*), or *kmeti.* In neighboring Dalmatia, the four estates included the clergy (successors to the pre-Christian Roman *flamines*), patricians (*sjor* or *vlastela*), plebs (*puk*), and *coloni* or *contadini.* The last estate was made up of fisherfolk and peasants who were contractually bound to render a fixed portion of their produce to their lords in return for military and other forms of protection.

In the other Slavic and in the Greek portions of the peninsula, there were four similar basic estates or ways of life during the Middle Ages. The medieval history of Wallachia and Moldavia is more obscure, but it is virtually certain that they had

three estates: clergy, boyars, and free hereditary small land-
holders known as *moşneni* or *răzăşi*. A fourth estate of Walla-
cho-Moldavian client peasants known as villeins (*vecini*) or
rumâni has been documented only since the fifteenth century.
It may, however, have come into being in an earlier period.

Although basically divided into four estates, Balkan society
was very much more complex. In the multinational fourteenth-
century state of Emperor Stephen Dušan of Serbia, for example, there existed, beside the four functional estates we have
already identified, four specially recognized ethnic estates:
Vlachs, Albanians, Saxons, and Latins. A fifth ethnic estate of
Greeks or Romans (the designation generally applied to the
subjects of the Byzantine Empire) might have been ultimately
established if Serbian imperial enterprise had been less ephem-
eral. There thus prevailed a tendency in medieval Serbia toward setting up the kind of estates system that evolved in
Transylvania, where society continued to be divided into three
privileged ethnic estates—Magyars, Saxons, and Szeklers—
until 1863.

Contrary to common belief, the estates society was not an
immobile social system. Indeed, efforts were exerted in Serbia,
especially after 1300, to prevent intermarriage between Vlachs
and *sebri* (freemen of the third estate), but these efforts had to
be made because an intermingling of Serbian farmers and
Vlach herdsmen had doubtless already occurred on an inten-
sive scale. The legal obstacle may have slowed down the process, but there is no reason to suppose that it stopped intermingling altogether. The principle of kinship, it is true, was a
deterrent to social mobility, but another principle of the
estates society—adoption or initiation—facilitated some degree of movement from one estate into another.

There even emerged certain groups that were not directly
affiliated with any of the functional or ethnic estates. Among
these was the *svobodnik,* a former serf or slave who was granted
personal freedom but failed to obtain admission into the estate

of *sebri* because he lacked a hereditary right to the ownership of a plot of land. Another was the *sokalnik,* a very numerous social category, the exact duties of which modern scholars still dispute. *Sokalniks* may have been temple or state butchers, cooks, bakers, or masons; judicial officers like the medieval English sokemen; or lower officials charged with the collection of the tithe in grains and enjoying judicial powers in matters relating to their function. In any case, such "public workers" were recruited in part from among the younger sons of Orthodox priests. There was in addition a group of underground demiurges, public workers expelled from the estate of official propitiators in the centuries following the conversion of the South Slavs to Orthodox Christianity: magicians, poisoners, heretics, and shamans or practitioners of *vlăhovstvo.*

The first three estates—propitiation, protection, and production—initially enjoyed almost equal esteem. During the thirteenth, fourteenth, and fifteenth centuries, however, the third estate of free smallholders experienced considerable social differentiation in all the Balkan provinces: Although some members improved their condition, others lost their land or freedom, and the order itself was pushed into a position of inferiority.

In declining Byzantium, the transfer of commercial franchises to Venice and Genoa deprived the state of revenues with which to remunerate its bureaucracy, and the government had to resort to the levy of higher taxes to pay its officials. This new tax structure, however, caused the impoverishment of many members of the free peasantry. In dire need of loans and protection against extortionist tax collectors and pitiless mercenaries, many free farmers recognized the authority of powerful lords who promised to satisfy their needs. Formerly free peasants thus bound themselves and their descendants to provide their superiors each year with a designated quantity of labor, as well as a portion of their crop. In turn, many lords succeeded in transforming their *pronoia* or conditional properties into hereditary lands.

In the Slavic areas, there was a similar evolution toward the formation of great holdings and the transformation of benefices or conditional properties into hereditary properties. Here, however, one other reason accounted for the new trend, notably population growth. As the rural population increased, the size of the plots of land available to the peasantry diminished correspondingly. Moreover, as in Byzantium, powerful lords then took advantage of their power to hasten the process of reducing hereditary small landholdings.

On the other hand, the expansion of mining and the growth of towns in the Slavic areas led to the rise of native artisans and merchants, side by side with the artisans and great merchants of foreign extraction—Saxons, *Latini* (mostly Ragusans), and Greeks. In the Serbian towns of the interior, these new "middle elements" were still weak, however, and were further quickly deprived of the one institution that might have become an instrument of their eventual ascendancy: an assembly of the third estate. In effect, the Law Code of Stephen Dušan and of the Serbian ecclesiastic and noble estates encouraged the growth of a market economy, made corvée obligations uniform throughout the realm, subjected the Emperor himself to the provisions of the law, and authorized assemblies of the priest's cap and of the *vlastela*. But it forbade an assembly of *sebri* (freemen), and particularly their assembly as an estate, under threat to organizers and participants of the loss of both ears (hence of all reason) and of the branding of the cheeks (thus the permanent tarnishing of the face).

Instituted in 1349 by an assembly of the first two estates, the provisions of the Law Code in regard to the *sebri* are a regional reflection of a general seigniorial reaction, European in character, that culminated in the Hundred Years' War. The war to which we allude, of course, was not simply the war between France and England but the complex strife of Catholic against Catholic, Christian against Muslim, Orthodox against Catholic, Hussite against Imperial and Catholic, Taborite against Utraquist, Poland and Lithuania against the Teutonic Order, Ottoman against the kingdom of Hungary and the fragments of the empires of Byzantium and of Dušan, Muscovite against Tartar and Novgorodian, Venice and Milan against Genoa, Tamerlane against Bayezid, Denmark against the Hanse, one feudal lord against another, mercenary against peasant, peasant against lord.

In the Balkans, a crucial aspect of this conflict was the attempt on the part of lords, patricians, or aristocrats to transform themselves into a largely closed estate, ally themselves with powerful foreign merchants, seize the land and revenues of the peasantry, and curb the aspirations of native "middle elements," regardless of whether these were a potentially rising group, as in the Slavic portions of the Balkans, or a seemingly declining group, as in the Greek areas. In 1341 and 1342, the middle elements of Adrianople and Salonika and the peasantry of Didymotichon took up arms against the aristocrats and absentee landlords. In Salonika, a group known as the Zealots seized power between 1342 and 1349 and proceeded to confiscate the properties of magnates and of churches and monasteries and to transfer a part of them to the poor. It also made use of the newly available funds and materials to repair the walls of the city and create a people's army. Finally, it opened careers to talent and wealth. Partly as a result of a split between the middle elements and the poor and of divergences within the middle elements themselves, however, the aristocrats soon prevailed again. Similar conflicts in the Adriatic towns of Cattaro (Kotor) and Antivari (Bar) similarly culminated in a victory for the patricians or nobility that was sealed by the transformation of the Antivari general assembly of elders into a Grand Council and of the general assembly of Cattaro into a Senate.

There are many explanations for the relative ease with which the Ottoman Turks spread across the Balkans during the second half of the fourteenth century, but this transformation of Balkan society into a field of strain, stress, and strife was one important factor in their initial expansion (as well as in their later conquest of Hungary). But however welcome Ottoman rule may have been at first to an unknown number of peasants and middle elements, it did not lead to an abolition of estates. Instead, the already modified system of estates was altered again to suit Ottoman requirements.

On the basis of Ottoman social theory, derived in part from the Arabs, Ottoman society was a vertically structured social order of four pillars or estates: men of the faith and law (*'ulemâ*), men of the sword (*'asker*), merchants and craftsmen (*tüccar*), and *raya* or husbandmen. One may also conceive it, however, as a society of six estates (excluding slaves, who were not legally persons): the *'ulemâ* or Muslim institution; the *'asker* or ruling institution, many of whose members engaged in trade and were thus closely associated with the new "third estate" of non-Muslim businessmen; the fourth estate of the privileged *raya* or auxiliary *'asker* of Orthodox Christians; the pseudoestate of the oppressed *raya;* and the collection of estates of self-governing foreign communities (and their Ottoman protégés) protected by international agreements.

In fact, however, the Ottoman social order was even more complex, since it assumed two forms, religious and functional. In terms of the religious form, it was ostensibly divided into four officially autonomous communities called *millets:* Muslims, Orthodox Christians, Jews, and Gregorian (Monophysite) Armenians. But the Muslims were further subdivided into two broad religious groups, the heretical *Şi'a* and the "orthodox" Sunni, the latter subdivided into a multitude of brotherhoods of varying orthodoxy. Although the Orthodox Christians were all theoretically subject to the Patriarch of Constantinople, they were separated in some periods into at least two self-governing churches (Greek and Serbian), each enjoying jurisdiction over different combinations of ethnic groups and subcultures. As for the Jews, they constituted four main religious and cultural groups until the second half of the seventeenth century, when some of the adherents of the sect of Shabbethai Zebi (Zevi), following the example of their leader, espoused Islam while retaining a portion of their Judaic heritage. The Armenian *millet* embraced not only Monophysites but Roman Catholics, Nestorians, and Jacobites. The latter churches, however, were sometimes able to acquire special charters setting them apart, to some extent, from the Armenian group. In actuality, therefore, the total number of Ottoman religious groups was closer to three or four times the official number.

In terms of the functional classifications, Ottoman society was organized into a pseudo-order of men of the faith and law, separated into as many tangible orders as there were *millets;* an order of the sword, separated into a military and ruling estate of dominant Muslims and an auxiliary order of dependent but privileged Orthodox Christians; a business order of Jews, Orthodox Christians, Gregorian Armenians, and converts or descendants of converts to Islam, whose members derived a sense of communion through the frequent exercise of a common craft in a common guild with a common patron saint or prophet. To these one must add the pariah *raya* of Orthodox Christian peasants and the privileged foreign communities.[3]

The system of estates or social "conditions" was grossly imperfect. Both in practice and theory, "ritually correct rebellion" was permissible, although punishable if unsuccessful. We

---

[3] The paragraphs on Ottoman estates follow very closely a section in Traian Stoianovich, "Factors in the Decline of Ottoman Society in the Balkans," *Slavic Review*, XXI (December 1962), 623–25; see also Stoianovich, "The Social Foundations of Balkan Politics, 1750–1941," in Charles and Barbara Jelavich (eds.), *The Balkans in Transition* (Berkeley and Los Angeles: University of California Press, 1963), pp. 298–303.

may define ritually correct rebellion as rebellion in which the essential object was the transfer of power from one group of individuals to another for the purpose of correcting flaws in the management of the existing estates structures or of government and the economy. Rebellion ceased to be ritually correct if the aim of the rebels widened to include revolution; that is, if their goal became the abolition of the existing system as distinct from the correction of imperfections in the system.

Ritually correct rebellions against the sultan or very arbiter of the system, the gazi (warrior of the Faith) of gazis and padishah, thus occurred repeatedly. Quarrels or disagreements between the estates were indeed normal, and the state was often absorbed with the problem of resolving such conflicts. These rebellions and rivalries did not constitute a threat to the basic purposes of the existing social structure; often, in fact, their aim was to reaffirm those purposes. Nevertheless, by the close of the eighteenth century, there had come into being a real threat to the Ottoman system of maintaining stability and even to the very principle of estates society. How this happened and the ultimate consequences thereof will be the subjects of the remainder of this chapter.

KINSHIP, CLANSHIP, AND MEN'S SOCIETIES

One of the results of medieval social differentiation and of the development of state officialdoms in the Slavic areas was a decline in the importance of distant kinship relations and a virtual disappearance of clans as effective political, economic, and religious units. In other words, the decline of family solidarity, which had been initiated in Mycenaean Greece (second millennium) and had spread ever more widely through the Balkan peninsula during the Roman era, now gained a new momentum. Ottoman rule accelerated this process in regard to Muslim families but slowed it down, halted, or reversed it in the case of Christians.

The sense of family solidarity was weakened among Balkan Muslims by the very fact of their recent apostasy, or abandonment of one faith and civilization for another. Often motivated by the desire to preserve old or acquire new wealth and privilege or by the need for a new identity on the part of some of the conquered populations, especially those that had been resettled in regions distant from their old homes and families, the conversions generally constituted a significant break with the most recent old tradition, that is, with Christianity and some of the political and social institutions of medieval civilization. In addition, their sense of kinship suffered as a result of the very nature of Ottoman military life, which was divided into a campaigning season (from St. George's Day to St. Demetrius' Day) and a billeting season, with different wives and concubines in different camps and billets. Count Ferrières-Sauveboeuf describes the events that occurred after the Grand Vizier in 1788 encamped his army near the gates of Sofia in order to prepare an offensive against Austria:

> Nothing created a greater stir in this city than the betrothals of the Janissaries to the young local [supposedly Muslim] beauties, who apparently thought that the army would never again quit their territory. Nearly all the young ladies got married and spent their honeymoon quite pleasantly. The latter was succeeded, however, by a general abandonment and the most complete widowhood. As the Vizier left Sofia to pitch camp near Niš, it was not without difficulty that the belles were turned away, for they missed the Janissaries too exceedingly not to want to follow them. I saw a group of them being brought back in carts, but since they had disobeyed orders they were now threatened, in the event of a repetition of the offense, with a not very delicate ceremony commonly practiced in Turkey: the authorities would slip a cat into their ordinarily ample bloomers; and this poor beast, flogged without mercy, would hardly show claws of velvet.[4]

[4] [Louis-François] de Ferrières-Sauveboeuf, *Mémoires historiques, politiques et géographiques des voyages faits en Turquie, en Perse et en Arabie, depuis 1782, jusqu'en 1789,* 2 vols. (Paris: Buisson, 1790), Vol. II, p. 253.

A sentiment of some degree of family solidarity was doubtless not altogether wanting among Muslims, especially among men of wealth and influence. A German-Imperial (Austrian) ambassadorial report of 1779 thus observes that Ottoman luminaries were "very careful in their marriage alliances," while consulting "only their taste in choosing concubines." [5] Another indication that Muslim families were not invariably seasonal and occasional affairs is the popularity of the practice of transforming properties into special pious (*vakf*) holdings. The transfer entailed the donation of a property to a mosque or some other religious establishment, but very commonly the donation was made with the proviso that the descendants of the author of the testament should continue to receive a portion of the revenues derived from the property until the family was extinct. In this way, much private property was rescued from state confiscation. If Muslims had failed altogether to perceive a sense of family responsibility, it is unlikely they would have felt a need to resort to such practices.

By and large, however, we are forced to conclude that the institutions of polygamy and concubinage were unsuitable as instruments of family solidarity. Since they were frequently abandoned when they were no longer wanted, wives and concubines of Muslim men often had recourse to abortion and other birth control measures. A typical Muslim family thus might be said to have consisted of one man, several or many women, but relatively few children in proportion to the total number of adults. The comments of a French consul on Muslim sexual habits in general, and particularly on the practices of Moreot women of Muslim faith during the latter part of the eighteenth century, provide both a description and an analysis:

> Although they are often Greeks themselves, unlike the latter they rarely have a large number of children. This may be ex-

5 Stoianovich, "The Social Foundations of Balkan Politics," in Jelavich, *op. cit.,* p. 301.

plained, on the one hand, by the institution of polygamy and, on the other, by the frightful art of abortion, which is familiar to them. Nowhere have the effects of abortion been so harmful [as among the Turks], nor so solemnly consecrated. Avowed publicly in the family of the Sultan, who condemns his sisters and nieces to sterility, these horrible means of depopulation pass on to the different strata of society. When suspected of infidelity, the wives of a Turk do not hesitate to commit the crime. They even resort to it, and without remorse, with the sole object of conserving their attractiveness and protecting the beauty that gives them an empire over their rivals, with whom they never cease to be at war.[6]

Added to abortion and infanticide were the ravages of venereal disease, all of which resulted by the eighteenth century in a low rate of fertility for Muslims in many Balkan areas. The population balance thus shifted in favor of the Christians in certain predominantly Muslim provinces such as Bosnia-Hercegovina, where the ratio of Muslims to the total population fell from two-thirds in the seventeenth century to two-fifths at the end of the eighteenth.

The trend among Christians, on the other hand, was toward the extension of kinship and quasi-kinship relations and the revival of the extended family. Very broadly speaking, Christian rural-familial relationships developed along two lines, one confined to the western mountain areas of Hercegovina, Montenegro, nothern Albania, Epirus, and Mani (in the Morea), while the other prevailed in the rest of the Balkans. In both types, the extended family was dominant. In other words, a family or household generally comprised more than a husband, wife, and children; often it would include several brothers, their respective wives and children, and, if still alive, the fa-

---

[6] François Charles Hugues Laurent Pouqueville, *Voyage en Morée, à Constantinople, en Albanie, et dans plusieurs autres parties de l'Empire othoman, pendant les années 1798, 1799, 1800 et 1801* (Paris: Gabon, 1805), Vol. I, p. 265. Translated in Stoianovich, "Factors in the Decline of Ottoman Society," *Slavic Review*, XXI (December 1962), 630.

ther and mother of the brothers. The size of households varied greatly; some South Slavic units numbered more than a hundred persons, but others were very small. During most of the last two or three centuries of Ottoman rule, however, the average number of persons in a South Slavic rural household seems to have been close to ten. In any case, the Balkan Christian rural family was probably larger and stronger by the end of the eighteenth century than ever before, or at least as large as in any past period. Thereafter, the process was reversed, and we note that the family declined in the Serbian district of Gruža from 9 members in 1844 to 6.2 in 1905, 5.9 in 1910, and 5.5 in 1931; in Croatia it declined from 8.4 members in 1857 to 4.9 in 1910 and 4.4 in 1953.

Generally known in Serbian areas as a *kuća,* a household was a group of persons closely related by birth or admitted by adoption. All members were destined to engage eventually in production for the entire group, and they regarded land and cattle as the common property of the group. The household was thus a corporate organization, aiming to perpetuate itself and its properties beyond the lifetime of any existing set of members, although it was sometimes dissolved by war, famine, epidemics, or quarrels. Noting the economic aspects of the *kuća* or Serbian household, eighteenth-century Austrian observers defined it as a *Wirth*—a household enterprise.

Above and beyond the household were the autonomous villages and federations of rural communes, similarly organized on a corporate basis. Many of the members of such units were related by kinship, but the territorial units themselves were not kinship organizations except vestigially. Kinship, however, was very important to the Christian peasantry, for it assured the peasant of an abundance of labor power—through the institution of mutual aid among kin and "friends" to assure the completion of certain tasks that might otherwise remain undone—and of protection against hostile families and aggres-

Family affiliation was asymmetrically bilateral, with relationships in the masculine line—"kin through blood"—being counted to the sixth, seventh, or eighth degree, and sometimes beyond, and kinship through the female line—"kin through milk"—only to the second or third degree. Consequently, in the greater part of the Balkans, kinship—as distinct from the household—was a personal rather than corporate institution, for the kin of one generation was not exactly the same as the kin of another. Moreover, in highly urbanized districts, and notably in the plains and maritime regions of the south and southeast, kinship relations were not as extensive as among most of the Slavs or among the Greeks of the highlands. Regions along routes of trade and imperial communication, such as the Vardar-Moravia axis, often valued kinship quite as much as the inhabitants of the high mountains, but in their songs they own that conformity to the kinship code is sometimes unduly onerous:

> An innocent lamb hath no sin,
> A pretty maiden hath no kin.[7]

Exogamy—taboo upon marriage between members of a given group—was the rule between kin, but in most of the Balkans there was no specifically exogamous corporate entity apart from the household into which one was born or initiated. In the southwestern mountain provinces, on the other hand, from Mani in the south to Hercegovina in the north, clanship and phratries prevailed. The number of corporate kinship units here rose to two if exogamy was confined to the phratry, or subclan, and to three if it extended to the clan. In those

---

[7] M.[ilan] Dj.[uro] Milićević, *Kraljevina Srbija: Novi krajevi* (Belgrade: Državna Štamparija, 1884), pp. 262–63; Jovan Cvijić, *La Péninsule balkanique: Géographie humaine* (Paris: Armand Colin, 1918), p. 391. [Author's translation]

cases where the clan was endogamous, or favorable to clan-inbreeding, it served to regulate the flow of marriageable girls from one phratry into another and thus tended to inspire among member phratries a sense of solidarity against intruders.

This kind of biosocial arrangement was not new to the area, although it had twice experienced a decline—once in Roman and then in late medieval (pre-Ottoman) times—before its ultimate ruin during the last hundred years. Even in the Roman era, when the clan structure was being undermined, the Celto-Illyrians of Pannonia were separated into *civitates* or tribal territories, and each *civitas* was subdivided into several *pagi*. Although generally described as a territorial unit, the *pagus* was essentially a group of families who practiced exogamy and a common agrarian cult and traced their origins to a common ancestor, mythical or real. Indeed, the *pagus* closely resembled the Sanskrit *sapa,* Germanic *Zippe,* and early South Slavic *župa,* a cluster of families with a common house or place of assembly. It was also an older version of the South Slavic *bratstvo* (literally, phratry), or group of families with a common *slava* or saint's day.

In Ottoman times, the kinship organization of the southwestern Balkans comprised three fundamental units: households, which were hereditary members of a given phratry, and two or more phratries, which together constituted either an exogamous or endogamous clan. Diagrammatically, it asssumed the shape shown in Figure 4 (p. 140).

In a modified form, this organization penetrated northeastward into Serbia, where, side by side with the institution of household and personal kinship appeared phratries practicing exogamy but lacking a clan structure.

The strengthening of the rural Christian family during the Ottoman era was accompanied by the strengthening and extension of various forms of initiatory and contractual kinship associations:

1. Godfatherhood relationships sanctioned by a church ceremony.
2. The institution of the haircutting godfather (*šišani kum* or *striženi kum*), or the father-son relationship established

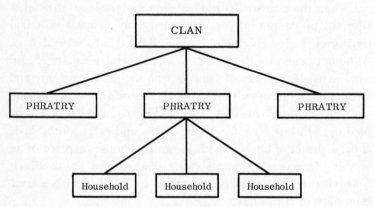

Figure 4. Family and Clan Structure

through the pagan ceremony of the first haircut, known in Byzantium as *trichokouria*.
3. Foster brother or foster sister (*pobratimstvo, posestrimstvo, adelfopoias, aderfopoitoi, bratimoi*) relationships, which were opposed by the Orthodox church during the Byzantine era but to which priests gave wide sanction during the Ottoman era.
4. Brother-of-the-cross affiliations (*stavroderfoi*), especially among the Greeks, whereby, upon the performance of a special initiatory ceremony by an Orthodox priest, two or more persons became brothers-of-the-cross and acquired rights of inheritance to each other's property.
5. Relationships of friendship (*prijateljstvo*) between families

not related by kinship (normally, whoever is not of one's kin, phratry, or clan, is an enemy or potential enemy unless designated as a friend).

6. *Tselingas* or *čelnik* associations of shepherds, often bound by kinship or quasi-kinship, as well as by economic ties, for a temporary period.

7. The expansion during the eighteenth century of Greek, Serbian, Vlach, Macedonian, and Bulgarian merchant *companiae* and of Greek and Greco-Albanian associations of seamen (*syntrofonaftai*).

One other form of association expanded during the latter centuries of Ottoman rule, the men's society or band. Men's societies in their original form reflect, in effect, a determination on the part of a portion of youth to reject agriculture and herding as a way of life in favor of hunting and the seizure of booty from enemies, ξένοι or merchant-adventurer *gosti*. Arising in or near agricultural societies, they represent either a rebellion against agriculture or against the submission of farming communities to the city.

In general, however, their members would return to the farming communities in the autumn, when the plowing, planting, and harvesting were over for the year. Thus, among the Celts, bands known as *fiana* lived with the clans from Samain (All Souls' Day, November 1) to Beltane (May Day), but after Beltane they would resume their life of hunting and banditry. So also, with a minor variation in the terminal dates of their activities, the Balkan *hajduks, hajduts,* or klephts. Often they would share their booty with farmers and herdsmen and dispose of their own portion through the aid of receivers. Their law, however, was the custom of the band, not the tradition of the ruling elders (gerontocracy) of the clan, household, or community.

The members of such men's societies were not ordinary thieves and cutthroats. In essence, they symbolized a variant value pattern which the gerontocracy frequently allowed as a means of diverting hostility from parents, household, kinfolk, community, and clan to other objects, and as a vicarious expression of their own hostility to the same objects. We may agree with the Serbian historian Slobodan Jovanović that men's societies (banditry)—*hajdučija*—are a manifestation of an "atavistic rebellion" if we define atavistic rebellion as rebellion in which the aim of the rebels is to bring down the newer (agricultural, urban, or imperial) and restore the older (pre-agricultural, preurban, or pre-imperial) culture. But it is altogether tendentious to view the existence of men's societies as evidence of "the anarchistic traits of the people." [8] On the contrary, the people lived in communities, clans, and many diverse kinds of associations, including bands, all of which had their own law.

Under Ottoman rule, however, there arose certain bands which displayed some of the characteristics of the men's societies described above but which differed from them in at least one essential respect. Aware of this difference, the Greeks carefully distinguished between the band of "tame klephts," which collaborated with the political authorities, and that of the "wild klephts," which opposed them. Still another category of band was that of the so-called *kirjalis,* who operated in the Rhodope Mountains and then spread to other areas during the latter part of the eighteenth and early part of the nineteenth century. While often opposed to existing political authority, the *kirjalis* committed acts of brigandage indiscriminately. In other words, they hardly intended to return to a community at St. Demetrius' Day except as predators.

The three types of men's societies are, of course, ideal constructs; in practice, the same band often behaved in various ways. The differences between the three categories, especially between the *hajduk* or wild klepht and the *kirjali,* were never-

8 Slobodan Jovanović, *Iz naše istorije i književnosti* (Belgrade: Srpska Književna Zadruga, 1931), pp. 16–17.

theless very important. Whereas the bands of wild klephts were generally made up of discontented rural youths, often coming from well-to-do and distinguished families, the *kirjalis* were recruited in large measure from urban and semiurban sources and from the riffraff and most deprived sectors of society: demobilized soldiers, "bachelors" and property-less menservants or farmhands (*momci*), and the "houseless," "barefoot," and "naked." Moreover, the wild klephts were almost wholly Christians, whereas the *kirjalis* constituted a highly mixed group: Christians, Muslims, Turks, Albanians, Bulgarians, Bosnians.

Floaters and vagabonds, *kirjalis* often obtained employment as security guards and were charged by their employers with carrying out raids against the domains of neighboring lords and with preventing or crushing retaliatory raids. When one employer did not suit them, they sought another, journeying from Albania to Bosnia, from Bosnia to Serbia and Bulgaria, from Bulgaria to Macedonia and Thessaly, into the Morea, and back to Albania. Numerous in quiet times they doubled and trebled in number during and after a war.

All three types of bands existed in the sixteenth century, and the growth of one generally stimulated the further development of the others. But while the tame klephts and the *kirjalis* were manifestations of a breakdown of social solidarities, the *hajduks* and wild klephts ultimately became an instrument of social cohesion. By 1573, Serbian and Bulgarian peasants were already in ·the habit of singing *hajduk* songs or *"Räyber Lieder"* while wending homeward from their fields. As the Ottoman government started to withdraw one privilege after another from the auxiliary *'asker* of Orthodox Christians, the latter shifted their support to Austria, Venice, and Russia, and readily furnished the *hajduk* bands with fresh contingents of fighters. The *hajduks* and wild klephts were particularly numerous along or near the Ottoman frontiers that bordered on independent Christian states, where, by the close of the eight-

eenth century, 10 per cent or more of the rural Christian population, or a third of the Christian male youth, were members of
wild outlaw bands.

The *hajduks* and wild klephts were not nationalists. In
spite of themselves, however, they were "nation"-oriented in
that their conception of the community—every forest and
every mountain, and every village and hamlet which sheltered
them in winter—was much broader than that of the leaders of
the clans, villages, and rural confederations. Although they did
not plan a national revolution, they were vulnerable to the
national ideology of the secular-oriented merchants and intel-
lectuals of their own faith and nationality who grew in number during the eighteenth century and entered into frequent
contact with Central Europe or with Russia and the Italian
states.

RE-VOLUTION AND REVOLUTION

In Serbia or Šumadija, where an intelligentsia was virtually
nonexistent at the end of the eighteenth century, Serbians
from Austrian Vojvodina filled the need for secretaries and
teachers during the Serbian war of independence (1804–1815).
A Serbian intelligentsia, however, was not the catalyst of the
national and social revolution, and even the "nation"-oriented
hajduks might have failed to take advantage of the opportunity to create an autonomous Serbian state during the Napoleonic era if the people had lacked a millenarian outlook. Millenarism, the belief in the coming of a messiah or liberating
ancestor or god, was not, of course, confined to Serbians; during various periods we discover millenarian manifestations
among Greeks, Vlachs, Bulgarians, Turks, and Balkan Jews.
The Serbian millenarian spirit, however, seems to have
reached a peak during the second half of the eighteenth century, almost concurrently with the French Revolution, although independently of it.

Many millenarian visions spread among the Serbs after the middle of the fifteenth century. During the last two decades of the sixteenth, when millenarism was rampant among almost every people of the Ottoman Empire, Serbians looked forward to the messianic return of St. Sava—historically, the thirteenth-century princely founder of a Serbian archbishopric, but mythically an ancestral hero or archetype. In the 1590's, along with other Balkan peoples, they rose in rebellion against Ottoman rule while the Turks were at war with the Germanic-Roman Empire (Austria) and the princes of Transylvania, Wallachia, and Moldavia, and with the Cossacks of the Ukrainian steppe. To put down the insurrection, the Turks ordered a *jihad*, or holy war: the cult of Mohammed against the cult of St. Sava. Removing what were supposedly the bones of St. Sava from the monastery of Mileševo, the Turks set fire to them in Belgrade. Even this, however, was insufficient to stifle forever popular belief in Sava's messianic return.

Furthermore, Serbian and Macedonian balladry envisioned the return of another culture hero, Kraljević Marko—historically, a fourteenth-century Serbian vassal of the Turks who was, from a poetic standpoint, a grand figure embracing the moral traits of Digenis Akritas and Dionysos. Legend held that Marko had temporarily withdrawn from earthly life to slumber and "bide his time" in some secret cavern—symbol of the Earth Mother—or in a cave near his Macedonian fortress of Prilep, or on a secret isle. But when "the time strikes" for Serbian renewal, he will rise and lead the Serbs and Slavs against the Turks and drive them "across the blue sea" whence they came.

To those beliefs were added many others during the eighteenth century, and certain natural occurrences—namely, the comets of 1781, 1797, and 1807; the eclipse of the moon on January 14, 1804, and the eclipse of the sun two weeks later on January 30; and the thunderstorm on January 14 (the Eve of St. Sava's), 1801—were interpreted as portents of liberation and renovation to be achieved by war, epidemic, and rebellion.

Finally, in the eighteenth century—or around the middle of the seventeenth, when Mediterranean and European Jews were being stirred by visions of Shabbethai Zevi—an "old man" of the Vasojević clan, a prophet by the name of Stanj, foretold the advent of a Serbian messiah, and for two centuries Serbians eagerly repeated his prophecy:

> From below the point where the Lim discharges into the [Drina, the Drina into the Sava, and the Sava into the] Danube [and presumably from the bowels of the earth and empire of the dead] will appear a dark man—*crni čovjek*—who will reveal himself as the king in moccasins. Until his coming there will be much evil, but he will liberate many Serbians. . . . The liberated will then live well, and the Mist Cap (*Crnokapa*) and Mist God (*Crnogaća*) will show up in our midst. The Turks will increasingly disappear from the face of the earth.[9]

Thus, on the eve of the Serbian social and national revolution—regardless of whether we accept the traditional date of 1804 or prefer to trace its beginning to the Austro-Turkish war of 1788–1791—there prevailed in Serbia what Vittorio Lanternari, in his analysis of dominated societies, calls a "premonitory religious movement of revival and transformation" [10] or a messianic cult of liberation, a fantasy of the sleeping god, hero,

[9] Veselin Čajkanović, *O srpskom vrhovnom bogu* (Belgrade: Srpska Kraljevska Akademija, 1941), p. 116. [Author's translation] For a fuller discussion of Stanj and other Serbian augurs, but at a lower analytical level, see M. Dj. Milićević, *Život Srba seljaka*, 2nd edition, revised and enlarged (Belgrade: Srpska Kraljevska Akademija, 1894), pp. 76–86. Our quotation comes from Čajkanović and differs slightly from the statements which Milićević's informants attribute to Stanj. Čajkanović situates Stanj in the eighteenth century, whereas Milićević leads us to believe he was a seventeenth-century figure. For a justification of my translation of *Crnokapa* and *Crnogaća*, see my forthcoming article on "Les structures millénaristes sud-slaves aux XVIIe et XVIIIe siècles," the subject of a paper for the First International Congress of Balkan Studies, Sofia, August 1966.

[10] Vittorio Lanternari, *The Religions of the Oppressed: A Study of Modern Messianic Cults*, Lisa Sergio, trans. (New York: Alfred A. Knopf,

or king who would awaken at the proper moment and, wearing perhaps a protective "mist cap" to make himself invisible to his enemies, a replica of the "dogskin" bonnet of the Greek god of death or of the *Tarnkappe* of the nebulous, nightmarish, underworld heroes and elves of Teutonic mythology, would free his people and allow them to revert to the mythical "golden age."

As we have said, this millenarian mental outlook reached its peak at the time of the Enlightenment, the French Revolution, and the Napoleonic Wars. At any other time, Serbian visions would probably have suffered the dismal fate of many past millenarian movements. If Serbia had not been looking forward to a messianic liberation, however, Enlightenment and Revolution would probably have been of no immediate ideological or social consequence in the Balkan interior. But as the Serbian goal of *re-volution,* a return to the "golden age," synchronized with the revolution in France and larger social and economic revolution that was taking place throughout the West, the impossible became a reality. From *re-volution* Serbia turned toward the enormously difficult task of creating a society based on the principles of liberty, nationality, and equality before the law.

In the Rumanian principalities and South Slavic provinces north and northwest of Serbia, and among the Greeks of Constantinople, Chios, Smyrna, Kydoniai, Janina, Ambelakia, Tyrnavos, Tripolissa, Corfu, Bucharest, and Iaşi, millenarian sentiments yielded at least superficially to the mental structure of the Enlightenment as the chief psychological and ideological agent of revolution. "People" in Michelet's sense were, of course, everywhere potentially of a millenarian outlook, but in the areas we have designated there were to be found certain social categories and institutions absent in Serbia or present only in protonuclear form: native urban and semiurban merchants, a native nobility and perhaps a native or Christian "nobility of the Robe," middle and higher schools, some private libraries, a considerable number of physicians trained in Italian or other European universities, a growing public of literate "middle elements," and, in the 1790's, a few private theaters and newspapers.

The most numerous intelligentsia, both ecclesiastical and secular, existed among the Greeks, the Balkan people with the longest heritage of literacy and bureaucracy. Around the middle of the eighteenth century, Greek ecclesiastical scholars were divided into two groups: "grammarians," who sought refuge in Aristotle and grammar; and "mathematicists," who found consolation in the science of Copernicus, Newton, Descartes, Locke, and Tycho Brahe. But beside these scholarly churchmen, there grew during the second half of the eighteenth century a secular intelligentsia of Phanariot "gentlemen scholars" and of heterogeneous "middle elements." The Phanariots were educated and wealthy Greeks, often of mercantile origin, who succeeded in winning appointment to high posts in the Ottoman government and in becoming lay administrators of the Greek Orthodox church and aspirants to the governorships of Wallachia and Moldavia. They constituted in fact a "nobility of the Robe." The middle elements comprised secretaries in the service of the Phanariot "nobility of the Robe"; merchants, who were often self-educated; and merchants' sons, who were educated in Western universities. Typical of these merchants' sons were the Drosos youths of Ambelakia who, after studying at Leipzig and Jena, returned to organize a little theater in their community, and Adamantios Korais, the son of a prominent Smyrniot merchant, who after trying his hand at merchantry and studying medicine at Montpellier, decided in favor of a literary and political-pamphleteering career in Paris, with the aim of converting fellow Greeks to the cause of the European Enlightenment and "liberal" aspects of the French Revolution. An example of an exceptional secretary in the temporary employ of Phanariots is the poet Rhigas Pheraios. After organizing a revolutionary club in Vienna with the object of transforming the Ottoman Empire into a pseudo-Jacobin republic, Rhigas was apprehended and turned over to the Turks in Belgrade, where he was duly executed in 1798.

As a group, merchants, secretaries, sons of merchants, and Phanariots preferred reform to revolution, and many were perfectly ready to continue to accept the *ancien régime,* particularly after 1789, when the official church took a strong stand against Westernism and modernism and threatened deviation with anathema. However, an important segment of the secular intelligentsia and merchants doing business with Russia and the West was favorably disposed toward organization in revolutionary clubs. Several such clubs, called *hetairies,* were formed during the French Revolutionary and Napoleonic era. Moreover, certain Greeks in the Macedonian community of Kozani took pride in being known as *Gallophrones* ("people who think in the French manner"), while some of the islanders of Samos rejoiced in the name of *Carmagnoles* (the name of a costume worn by French Revolutionists, of songs they sang, and of a dance they danced). Finally, in 1814, a secret revolutionary society known as the Philike Hetairia was founded in Odessa, a Russian port on the Black Sea opened only in 1794 but quickly transformed into a great grain emporium with a swarming population of Serbians, Greeks, Bulgarians, Italians, Jews, Russians, and Turks. Odessa was a nucleus of political intrigue and radical conspiracy that linked Russia to the Mediterranean spirit and élan of the Italian revolutionary group, the *Carbonari,* as St. Petersburg joined her to the philosophy, ideology, and industry of Western and Central Europe.

The ostensible purpose of the Philike Hetairia was the promotion of Greek culture, but its chief goal was the creation either of a Greek nation-state or of a neo-Byzantine empire. Of the 452 men officially enrolled in this club in 1819, 153 were merchants and shippers, 60 were notables, 36 were fighting men, 24 were priests, 23 were officials or secretaries, 22 were teachers and students, 10 were doctors, 4 were lawyers, 16 were members of miscellaneous professions; the professions of the remaining 104 persons are unknown. Thus, of the 348 persons whose professions we do know, 44 per cent were engaged in trade, 41 per cent were members of the bureaucracy and intelligentsia, and 10 per cent were fighting men joining a new kind of men's society.

The Philike Hetairia contacted other revolutionary or quasi-revolutionary groups, namely, the associates of the Serbian rebel leader Karageorge Petrović, the Kishinev branch of the revolutionary Russian Decembrists, the Phanariot Russian officer Alexander Ypsilanti, and the Rumanian *moşnean* (freeman) and ex-Russian officer Tudor Vladimirescu, and after 1819 it was ready to admit to membership, and even to positions of leadership, conservatives who embraced the objective of a national or Christian-Balkan state. The organization planned a general Balkan insurrection. In other words, it hoped to reproduce the kind of situation that had threatened in 1807 and 1808, when peasant disturbances broke out in the Banat and other Habsburg areas and the Ottoman Empire had to face simultaneously the blows of Russia in the northeast, Serbia in the north center, and Montenegro in the west. In those years, there had also been a peasant insurrection in Thessaly and Macedonia and klephtic attempts to join forces with the Serbian rebels.

Finally, this had been the turbulent era of what Bosnian Muslims called the *vampir,* the vampire-Empire and state of mind born of the improper death of the *ancien régime,* namely the French Revolution and Empire of Napoleon. Then master of the Ionian Islands and of Dalmatia, Ragusa, and the Bay of Kotor, Napoleon would unite the last three in 1809 to the Croatian Military Border and to Trieste, Istria, Carinthia, and Carniola, and call them the French Illyrian Provinces.

A general Balkan revolution failed to materialize in 1821, however, as it had failed in 1807. Miloš Obrenović of Serbia, leader of the Serbian insurrection of 1815 and organizer of a new Serbian state, refused to join the movement. The heterogeneous Balkan bands under the command of Ypsilanti found little support among the peasantry of Moldavia. The peasantry of Wallachia withdrew its support from Vladimirescu when he gave inadequate attention to their grievances against the seigniorial regime.

But revolution did come to the Morea or Peloponnesus and to neighboring Greek areas. The Greeks fought the Turks from 1821 to 1829, and engaged simultaneously in bitter internecine strife. Muslim Albanian troops in the employ of Mehmed Ali of Egypt intervened against them, but they received moral, financial, and volunteer-fighter aid from liberals in the Western European countries. They received additional aid in the form of joint French, British, and Russian naval action against the Ottoman fleet and of a Russian invasion of Moldavia, Wallachia, and Bulgaria. Of the European countries and provinces in which insurrection occurred during the 1820's—Wallachia, Moldavia, Greece, Italy, Spain, and Russia —Greece was the only one that could lay claim to a partly successful political and social revolution.

In one manner or another, however, all Balkan provinces felt the consequences of a half-century of revolution extending from 1788 to 1833. In the Ottoman Empire itself, the threat of revolution made imperative the reforms collectively known as the *Tanzimat* (1826–1876). To Wallachia and Moldavia it brought, under Russian sponsorship, a charter known as the Organic Statutes, and it deprived the Ottoman Empire of the right to preempt the raw materials of these provinces. To Serbia revolution brought autonomy, to Greece nominal independence. Finally, Bulgaria opened itself to the modern world, or to such outside influences as were acceptable to the various sectors of Bulgarian society.

A new generation of Bulgarians, nourished intellectually in the middle and higher schools and in the liberal and radical circles of Russia, Greece, Serbia, and Wallachia, espoused the cause of modern nationalism and social revolution. Even conservatives became nationalists, supporting the idea of a Turco-Bulgarian dual state (like the Austro-Hungarian dual state set up in 1867). Moreover, they led a movement that culminated, in 1870, in the emancipation of the Bulgarian Church from the Patriarchate of Constantinople. Actual political autonomy was won in 1878 through a combination of peasant rebellions (in Bosnia-Hercegovina and Macedonia, as well as Bulgaria), cooperation between *hajduts* and liberal and radical revolutionaries, and, most important of all, Russian aid.

The evaluation of the Serbian revolution by the nineteenth-century liberal folklorist, lexicographer, and man of letters Vuk Karadžić, and by the socialist Svetozar Marković, is almost equally applicable to the Greek and Bulgarian. In all three countries, the revolutions were national and social, involving, in the words of Marković, the "eradication of an entire unproductive class of people, who lived a completely different life, spoke a different language, worshipped another faith, and regarded the Serbian [and the Greek and Bulgarian] people as its property." [11] We may contest the view that the Turks and other Ottoman Muslims were an "unproductive class." On the other hand, we unreservedly agree that the revolutions overthrew the preexisting estates or vestiges of the estates structures. Although a new social order guaranteeing the security of property and based upon the principles of equality before the law, freedom of contract, and social mobility through free political and economic competition had to be fought for and won over and over again, many institutions resembling those that had been introduced only very recently in Western Europe itself—written constitutions, political parties with a variety of ideologies (liberalism, nationalism, progressivism, populism, utopian socialism, Marxism, and peasant-

---

[11] Woodford D. McClellan, *Svetozar Marković and the Origins of Balkan Socialism* (Princeton, N.J.: Princeton University Press, 1964), pp. 184–85.

ism), and educational facilities for an increasingly larger public—were rapidly brought into being.

In spite of all the changes, however, the Balkan revolutions remained an unfinished affair. From one point of view, this is not a very great indictment, for even the French Revolution was an "unfinished revolution" until the 1880's, perhaps even until the 1930's. By identifying the Balkan revolutions as "unfinished revolutions," we mean that they did not fully achieve the social structure that might have enabled them to perpetuate the new social system: a group of "middle elements" sufficiently large, homogeneous, and independent as to be able to manage the abnormal social strains created by two world wars, a world economic crisis, Communist revolution, fascist counterrevolution, economic change, technological backwardness, a "population explosion," and conflict between a multiplicity of cultural and political traditions.

Under a variety of circumstances to which we alluded briefly in our chapter on technology, the task of achieving "disalienation" or removing the condition of estrangement between the various sectors of society and generalizing, intensifying, socializing, or "completing" the revolution, giving it a new élan or taking it along new directions, ultimately fell to Communist leadership in Yugoslavia, Bulgaria, Rumania, and Albania, and reverted to bourgeois leadership in Greece. All five countries have realized this goal to a considerable degree. But the problem of managing a society is without a final solution, and so in Greece political and social discontent has been gathering since 1963, taking the form of criticism of "spendthrift" (now dowager) Queen Frederika, huge antigovernment manifestations, criticism of Britain and the United States for not allowing the union of Cyprus and Greece, and an end to stable government after the eight years of political stability (1955–1963) under Constantine Karamanlis of the "free enterprise" Radical Union. Strains are similarly manifest in the Communist states. In Yugoslavia, where they are most openly admitted, the national problem continues to pose difficulties. Among Communists themselves, at least three tendencies prevail: the conception of nationality, especially among Slovenians and Macedonians, as a supraclass and a virtually metaphysical category; the hope of some Serbians to rally all Yugoslavs around a Serbo-Croatian cultural nucleus; and the official program of promoting a voluntary integration of the subnationalities through the expansion of a socialist economy and the creation of an integrated national market. Balkan societies consequently continue to constitute a field of strain and stress, as well as a field of new and old solidarities.

V

ECONOMY

<>∞<>

It may appear that the primary economic difference between archaic and modern (or precapitalist and capitalist) societies is the lack of a market in the archaic society. In fact, however, archaic societies were not without a market of a kind. A more important distinction is that they lacked a clear concept of economic value.

ECONOMIC VALUE

We find the reason for the slow development of the concept of economic value in the very nature of the markets that did exist in prehistoric and premodern times—their purpose, the kinds of goods that were circulated there, and the characteristics of the market traders. As a system for the exchange of goods, the premodern market had indeed an economic basis. Moreover, its function was much broader than that of the modern market. It provided a setting not only for the exchange of goods, but for the holding of games, entertainment, feasts, and religious worship, and for the formation of political alliances. In the actual exchange of goods, however, the premodern market was at a disadvantage because "priced goods" did not exist —or if they did, were limited in number. Even among the Greeks, the concept of price arose only after coins were put into general use during the seventh and sixth centuries B.C. Long after that, however, many items continued to be regarded as "free goods," destined to circulate freely among members of the same family or clan, or as "ceremonial goods," reserved for exchange with other groups.

The Aegean portion of the Balkans was one of the first areas of the world into which the notion of price penetrated. Nevertheless, "priced goods" continued to be relatively few in number in the rural areas of the inland and more isolated portions of the Balkans until the middle of the nineteenth century. In western Serbia, for example, it was then still shameful and derogating—*sramota*—to sell locally produced food products ("free goods") or "ceremonial goods," such as towels, stockings, or shirts. In other words, although they were very important as items of exchange, such goods were not for sale. Among the few food products whose sale was permissible were cattle and salt, fundamentally because both could and did serve as a means of exchange or money and because cattle were not food so long as they were on the hoof. But when the moon was "empty," that is when there was a full moon, the sale of goods, particularly cattle, was ordinarily taboo.

Moreover, throughout the Balkans, sales and exchanges on a large scale were customarily confined to seasonal fairs. One of the most famous of such fairs during the Byzantine era, one that is still in existence today, was the autumnal fair of Salonika, organized for the feast of St. Demetrius. A Cappadocian traveler, Timarion, describes the international stamp of the visitors to the fair during the first half of the twelfth century:

> Not only do the natives of the country flock together to it in great numbers, but multitudes also come from all lands and of every race—Greeks, wherever they are found, the various tribes of Mysians [Moesians, or inhabitants of eastern Serbia and

northern Bulgaria] who dwell on our borders as far as the Ister [Danube] and Scythia, Campanians and other Italians, Iberians, Lusitanians, and Transalpine Celts.[1]

Fairs were places of exchange but they were also a time of ritual, festivity, and panegyric, and a place for the formation of alliances. Indeed, even as late as 1858, in their effort to bring down the authoritarian regime of Prince Alexander Karadjordjević, the first generation of Serbian Liberals sought allies mainly at monastic fairs. The partly political function of fairs was in fact an important vestigial characteristic of one of the basic purposes of gift exchange: to establish ties of friendship with another family or clan and placate its demons or ancestors through the exchange of objects, especially foods and ornaments, which were believed to be highly charged with what the ancient Greeks called *agalma* and which we might translate as "supernatural virtues."

But fairs differed from the earliest places of assembly at which gifts were ritually exchanged between neighboring groups in that they were open to professional traders as well. In other words, fairs were places of exchange honoring not only the principle of kinship and clanship, but also, and increasingly, that of the contract—the individual contract between two professional traders and the mixed contract between a professional trader and a clan or family as a whole.

The rise after the seventh century B.C. of professional traders, drawn from the urban societies of the southern or maritime regions, led to the development of the idea of price. As merchants became aware that different societies put a different value on the same object, they began to deal in those goods which allowed them to realize a high, or the highest, profit. But since clanship and kinship prevailed as strong principles of association in the central and northern areas at least until the second century A.D. and were revived in the sixth and sev-

---

[1] H. F. Tozer, "Byzantine Satire," *Journal of Hellenic Studies*, II (1881), 244–45.

enth and again in the fifteenth and sixteenth centuries, a full development of the concept of economic value was considerably delayed. Moreover, Greek law itself failed to distinguish between a community of persons brought together to practice a common cult or eat at a common table and an association of businessmen. A third obstacle to the full flowering of the concept of economic value was the fact that traders themselves were driven by the psychology of *prexis,* or the desire to take whatever can be taken. In practice, this resulted in piracy or banditry.

Precisely how, or to what degree, changes were made in the associations of traders during the first half of the Byzantine era remains uncertain. In the later medieval centuries, however, when Venetian, Genoese, and Ragusan merchants captured the international trade of Byzantium or of former Byzantine territories, there arose beside the traders' associations, which for centuries had been *de facto* partnerships, the institution of the *commenda* or *société en commandite.* This was a more formal business association, organized customarily for a period of three or four years. It generally had two or three members, one of them an active partner with full liability and the others with limited liability—that is, they were liable only to the extent of their capital investment.

During the second half of the fifteenth century, the practice of double-entry bookkeeping spread from Italy to Ragusa and eventually, by way of Ragusan and Italian merchants, to the great merchants of the Balkans. The practice was further reinforced through the migration to Balkan towns, during the sixteenth century, of almost a hundred thousand Spanish and Italian Jews.

Not until well into the nineteenth century, however, did the corporation, or limited liability company, start to take root in the Balkans. For example, the commercially and technologically backward principality of Serbia adopted a commercial code in 1860 that duplicated the provisions of Napoleon's

Code de commerce of 1807. The Serbian code recognized three basic types of business association: the simple partnership with unlimited liability; the mixed partnership, or *société en commandite*; and the *société anonyme,* or limited liability company, in which each owner is liable only to the extent of his share as an investor in the business.

Aided by improved business organization and practices, by the growth of cities and the creation of more rapid means of transportation and communication, and by changes in the social structure, the concept of economic value finally pushed into the background the older concepts of value.

FREEDOM AND SLAVERY

If we visualize a status scale for the societies of antiquity, with free status represented at one end and slave status at the other, we shall find that the vast majority of people were clustered at one end of the scale or the other—either free or slave. Thus, although there were certain social categories that combined some of the freeman's characteristics and some of the slave's, the likelihood was that one was either free and a person or unfree and an un-person. By the tenth or eleventh century A.D., however, a tendency that had started imperceptibly several centuries earlier became clearly evident: Slaves moved upward and freemen downward into serfdom.

The teachings of Christianity were partly responsible for the improvement in the slave's status, but the most important factor in the decline of slavery was that it became increasingly difficult and expensive to acquire slaves after political states were established in Eastern Europe. The slave trade did not, of course, cease altogether. Pagans, Muslims, Bogomils, and Orthodox Christians from many different areas of Eastern Europe and Western Asia continued to fill the need for slaves in Balkan and Mediterranean markets, but the movement of slaves from East to West was considerably less significant in 1400 than in 1200. Since their reproduction rate was low, the number of slaves declined very rapidly as the sources of supply dried up. As a result of this decline, the price of slaves in Crete and Ragusa increased more than five times between 1280 and 1400; by 1416, Ragusa forbade the slave trade.

As the supply of slaves diminished between the twelfth and fifteenth centuries, the status of many freemen deteriorated and the intermediate categories between the freeman and the slave—"the fourth estate"—grew in number. By tying the servile or dependent folk to the land, by augmenting compulsory labor services, by reducing freemen to a condition of dependency, the clerical estate and the estate of great protectors found a compensation for the inadequate supply of slaves. Moreover, the period between 1200 and 1450 was a time of growth of great properties, and the need for labor increased as the properties grew in size.

The Ottoman conquest of the Balkans tended to restore somewhat the former kind of freedom-slavery continuum, with most men either free or slave. In any event, slavery and the slave trade acquired a new importance during the second half of the fifteenth and the greater part of the sixteenth centuries. Slaves were normally taken in war, and as the Ottomans extended their conquests, slave labor increased correspondingly. Although girls and young women often became the concubines of their captors or buyers, many thousands of prisoner-slaves were settled as agricultural workers, or *ortaks,* on private or imperial domains, with the requirement that they furnish their masters half of their labor product.

But as the supply of slaves diminished once again after the middle of the sixteenth century, the *ortaks* often succeeded in improving their economic and social status. On the other hand, the pressures upon the "free" peasantry steadily increased. Thus, from the second half of the sixteenth to the early part of the nineteenth century, the intermediate categories between the "freemen" and the slaves again grew in number, giving rise to what is sometimes described as the "second serfdom."

PRICES, WAGES, AND SECOND SERFDOM

The "second serfdom" was aggravated, however, by a simultaneous long-term rise in prices, caused by the flow of American silver into the eastern Mediterranean and by a growing disparity between prices and wages. This price-wage disparity came about largely because the economy could not keep up with the rapid growth of a propertyless urban and rural population, and it was further aggravated by the technological stagnation of the seventeenth century and the technological backwardness of the eighteenth.

The customary wage of an unskilled worker in the second half of the eighteenth century could purchase only half as much grain as the customary wage of the mid-sixteenth century. For example, wages and prices in the Ottoman capital fluctuated in the following manner between 1550 and 1790:

TABLE 6

Years	Percentage of Rise in Grain Prices	Percentage of Rise in Wages of	
		SKILLED LABOR	UNSKILLED LABOR
1550–1585	40–60	0	0
1585–1605	25–33	100	80
1605–1700	200–250	100	40
1700–1790	80–100	100	25–50
1550–1790	700 or more	800	350

SOURCE: The documentation is given in Stoianovich, "Factors in the Decline of Ottoman Society," *Slavic Review*, XXI (December 1962), 625–27.

The decline in the real wages of unskilled labor made impoverished workers more willing to place their services at the disposal of powerful lords. If they were especially ambitious and able, they imposed themselves on the peasantry as second landlords or overseers.

As agents of the "second serfdom" or *çiftlik* regime, landlords and second landlords applied pressures on the government to allow the clandestine exportation of raw materials to the countries of Europe. Committed to exporting their own raw materials, they opposed the development of manufactures out of fear that this might deprive them of their cheap labor. European states similarly exerted pressures upon the Ottoman government to prevent it from aiding the growth of industry.

But if the government could not or would not stop the expansion of the "second serfdom," the Balkan peasantries eventually did. The means toward this end were the Rumanian peasant stirrings of the period 1793–1821 and the Serbian and Greek revolutions. By waging a struggle against domestic as well as foreign tyranny, the Balkan peoples were able to obtain between 1830 and the 1860's the abolition of the estates society and recognition of the principle of equality before the law.

The problems arising after 1860 stem from the fact that equality before the law does not abolish economic inequalities. Moreover, the latter inequalities were aggravated by a "population explosion" which left the peasantries with less and less land as they became "more and more equal."

POWER AND RHYTHM OF NUMBER

The population of the Balkans, like that of most of the rest of the world, has generally been growing since the "agricultural revolution" of the early neolithic period. Unfortunately, the present state of research is such that we can determine the average population density in the peninsula only for a very late period. But since a society of hunters can hardly exist if the population exceeds one person per square kilometer, we may assume that the population density in the fifth millennium, shortly after the establishment of the first Balkan agricultural communities, was approximately one person per square kilometer.

In Greece, the population density probably rose by 400 B.C. to 20 or 30 persons per square kilometer. In the Balkan interior, where cities were still nonexistent or in the process of initial formation, the density was much lower, probably no more than 5 persons. Demographic historians further estimate the population density of the nondesert portions of the Roman Empire in 14 A.D. at an overall average of 17 persons: 31 persons in the Asiatic, 27 in the African, and 10 in the European parts.

The population density in the Hellenic areas of the Balkans may have fallen between 400 B.C. and 200 A.D. In the northern regions, on the other hand, it continued to grow. Rising again between 300 or 350 and 540 A.D., the population of the Greek regions may have attained a density of 30 persons by the end of this period, as in antiquity. But as the southern zone became overpopulated, epidemics and famines mowed down the "surplus" population and facilitated the invasions of the Slavs.

A century or two after the Slavic invasions, the population of the Greek areas may have taken another upward turn, lasting until the close of the eleventh or until the twelfth century. In the northern areas, population growth characterized the period between the twelfth and fifteenth centuries.

The second half of the fifteenth century is chiefly a time of forced population transfers under the direction of the Ottoman government and of flights to Dalmatia, Italy, and Hungary. The western Balkan areas were seriously depopulated during this period, but the population density of the eastern areas, which generally profited from the Ottoman resettlement policies, either remained constant or went up. Taking the Balkans as a whole, however, the century from 1420 to 1520 was one of population decline.

Since 1520, the population density of the area south of the

Sava and Danube has varied from approximately 12 persons per square kilometer in 1520 to 17 in 1590, 12 in 1700, and 15 in 1800. The decades between 1520 and 1590 were a time of population expansion in the Ottoman Empire as in most of Europe, and in 1590 the population density of the Balkans was just about equal to that of Spain and Portugal, whereas the density of France was approximately 34, or twice as great, and that of Italy around 44.

During the second half of the nineteenth century the Balkan countries attained a population density that they had never previously known. By the middle of the twentieth century, the density was two, three, or four times as high as in any previous period. The following table shows how it increased in three of the Balkan countries:

TABLE 7

| Year | Population Density per Square Kilometer | | |
	SERBIA	GREECE	BULGARIA
1718	3.0	—	—
1735	5.0	—	—
1800	10.0	—	—
1821	—	19.8	—
1834	18.0	—	—
1838	—	15.8	—
1870	—	29.0	—
1874	36.0	—	—
1887	—	—	32.7
1889	—	34.4	—
1890	44.3	—	—
1900	51.3	—	38.9
1907	—	41.6	—
1910	59.9	—	45.0
1920	—	36.7	47.0
1950	—	56.9	—
1953	80.0	—	—
1956	—	—	53.1

From the close of the fifth century B.C. to the middle of the nineteenth century, the population history of the Balkans was characterized by the existence of a fairly uniform and unsurpassable point of saturation. In other words, a certain maximum population density simply could not be exceeded without a fundamental change in the existing social order and technology. The saturation point stood during this period at 20 to 30 persons per square kilometer. Finally, however, the "Western Revolution" allowed the Balkan countries to surpass the traditional maximum.

The upward readjustment of the saturation point was achieved in some measure by hygienic improvements and the control of epidemics through the institution of relatively well-regulated quarantine stations. Most of all, however, the accomplishment was a consequence of the systematic development of a cereal economy and of a change in the eating habits of the Balkan peoples: less meat, less cheese, and more maize, wheat, and other cereals. Since one pound of wheat releases between three and ten times as many calories as the same quantity of meat, a cereal diet, pound for pound, will sustain a larger population than a meat diet. That is why the growth of a cereal economy and the adoption of a cereal diet may explain much of the Balkan population growth of the nineteenth century. The cereal consumption of the Serbians, for example, grew by more than seven times between 1721 and 1890, while their consumption of meat was only one-third or one-fourth as great in 1905 as in 1830. Although the proportions are different for the other Balkan provinces, the trend was generally similar.

Let us note, however, that these changes were made possible by the revolution which brought an end to the "second serfdom," encouraging the peasant to put more land under cultivation because his production was now his own instead of going to a first or second lord. Finally, the readjustment was aided by the expansion of an urban economy.

The rise of Balkan cities has occurred, in fact, in several stages, each associated with a particular area or culture:

1. Minoan and Mycenaean cities of the Aegean during the second millennium B.C.
2. Greek Aegean cities after 800 B.C.
3. Greek colonies along the Black Sea and Adriatic littoral during and after the seventh century B.C.
4. Thracian cities during the fourth century B.C.
5. Celtic and Roman cities along the middle Danube, Sava, Morava, and their tributaries between the third century B.C. and the fourth century A.D.
6. Medieval cities, especially during the thirteenth and fourteenth centuries, in Serbia, Bulgaria, Bosnia, Croatia, Transylvania, Wallachia, and Moldavia.
7. Ottoman cities, such as Bosna Serai (Sarajevo) and Tirana, during the fifteenth and sixteenth centuries.

During this period, very few urban communities north of the Aegean had a population of more than 2,000 to 5,000. Thus, in Croatia (excluding Istria, Dalmatia, and Ragusa), the three largest towns—Varaždin, Zagreb, and Karlovac—each possessed a population of less than 5,000 as late as 1787. In the Balkan portions of the Ottoman Empire itself there were in 1520 only three towns with more than 20,000 inhabitants—Istanbul, Salonika, and Adrianople. In 1590, there were about ten such towns.

The great era of urban expansion, as in the rest of the world, has been the period since 1750, and particularly since 1850. Above all, this has been a period when great metropolitan centers, cities with a population of 100,000 or more, have grown. In no period of antiquity were there simultaneously more than two such cities. In 1450, moreover, there was no Balkan city with a population of 100,000, for Constantinople itself then numbered little more than 50,000. But a century later, when it was also known as Istanbul, its population once again exceeded 100,000. Not until 1850, however, did a second city reach such a size: Bucharest. By 1900, there were five such cities: Istanbul, Bucharest, Athens, Salonika, and Adrianople; and by 1910, Sofia joined the group. By 1920, there were nine such centers, the last three to join the group being Piraeus, Belgrade, and Zagreb.

Then came a period during which the existing large cities continued to expand but cities over 20,000 grew only very slowly, or stagnated, or even declined, and in 1930 and 1940 there were no more than ten cities with a population of 100,-000 or more, Pannonian Subotica being the newest addition. The birth rate was maintained at a high level and the death rate was arrested or reduced, but the city failed to absorb the population surpluses of the rural areas. A point of urban saturation had been reached.

As the rural population grew at a faster rate than the urban, clashes between city and country became sharper. Cities ceased to expand, but for the impoverished peasantry they were the enemy. They were doomed to feel the wrath of heaven. On the other hand, demagogues were quick to extol the "wholesome ignorance" of the peasant.

Without an alteration in the population pattern or without a more vigorous industrial program, the point of urban saturation could not be easily raised. For reasons explained elsewhere, however, the Balkan bourgeoisies failed to industrialize with sufficient confidence and energy. When the rural poverty and the generally very low standard of living were compounded in the 1930's and 1940's by fascist aggrandizement and a world war, the result was revolution. This revolution was homemade in Yugoslavia and Greece and partly homemade in the other Balkan countries.

Largely as a result of the rapid technological progress made since the Communist revolution, the number of cities with a population of 100,000 or more grew to 16 in 1950 and to 31 in 1960. Of the thirty-one, 13 are located south of the Danube and Sava, 6 are in Wallachia and Moldavia, 6 in Transylvania and the Rumanian Banat, and 6 in Yugoslavia north of the Danube and the Sava or along the Adriatic. In the Communist states, small and middle-sized cities also expanded during this period, and new industrialized towns came into being. On the other hand, in Greece, until a few years ago the most highly urbanized Balkan country, there are still only three cities with a population of more than 100,000 (Patras moved into the 100,000 catogory in 1960, but Athens and Piraeus are now generally counted as a single metropolitan area), but they are among the largest in the Balkans and are still growing very rapidly. Three Balkan cities—Athens, Bucharest, and Istanbul —today contain a population of more than a million each and two—Sofia and Belgrade—are not far from the million mark.

In all the Balkan states except Albania the peasantry today is no more than half the total population. Peasants have been organized into collective farms in Rumania and particularly in Bulgaria. In Yugoslavia, on the other hand, collectivization was largely abandoned after 1950 in favor of using the rural-urban commune (*komuna*) and socialist sector of society as devices to instill a socialist psychology in the peasantry. In Greece, no collectivization has occurred.

In terms of immediate human problems, the choice of one method or another was extremely important. In retrospect, however, the greatest change in the rural areas has not been collectivization so much as the shift of almost half the peasantry from the villages and hamlets to the cities.

VI

PERSONALITY and
CULTURE

❦

Besides the three value orientations described in our chapter
on biotechnics and social biology, we discover a fourth value
orientation in the Balkans today, one that first appeared
among the Greeks during the classical era and that came into
being among the South Slavs during the later Middle Ages. A
complex system of attitudes that ultimately strengthened the
notion of economic value and of individual as against group
responsibility, the new orientation, to which we may assign the
name of modern personality, was not fully elaborated in the
Balkans until the nineteenth and early part of the twentieth
century. It manifests itself most impressively in the development of a new conception of personality itself and of new attitudes toward space, time, work, and leisure.

WORK AND LEISURE

Social groups generally work well in terms of their own social and cultural requirements; indeed, they must do so in
order to preserve their own autonomy. Observations to the
effect that a particular people or culture is hostile to work thus

appear only when there is a cultural conflict between the observer and the observed as to what constitutes work and how and under what conditions one may perform "work" efficiently.

Within each society there is not just one but a variety of attitudes toward work. This is as true in the Balkans as it is in other societies. At the same time, we perceive in the Balkans—and we suspect this to be true in other areas—many regions in which one particular notion of work is more strongly emphasized or more widely prevalent than the others. Moreover, the various attitudes toward work possess a historical as well as a geographic basis, some being more archaic than others.

The anthropologist Dorothy Lee appropriately defines one of the most general contemporary Greek views of work:

> Diligence is an internal attitude; it rests on self-discipline and free incentive, it includes interest and enjoyment. It does not mean a valuation of work for its own sake; it is the personal quality of diligence, not work itself, which is good. To work compulsively is to be a slave to work; and what can be worse than slavery? Even to work under the compulsion of work as a virtue is to deny oneself prized freedom; all work under pressure, such as the pressure of a time limit or the dictates of an employer, means loss of freedom.[1]

In certain ways, the modern conception is Hesiodic, going back to the *Work and Days* of Hesiod or, rather, to the values current in Greece since 800 B.C. It is especially Hesiodic in embracing the notion that work is not *ipso facto* a virtue but acquires virtue only when it facilitates an accumulation of wealth and the latter in turn gives an actor a freedom to choose between the way of nobility and the way of wanton violence and overbearing pride.

---

[1] Dorothy Lee, "View of the Self in Greek Culture," in *Freedom and Culture* (Englewood Cliffs, N.J.: Prentice-Hall, 1959), pp. 150–51. This article is an adaptation from Mrs. Lee's "Greece," in Margaret Mead (ed.), *Cultural Patterns and Technical Change,* prepared for the World Federation of Mental Health (Paris: UNESCO, 1953), pp. 77–114. In the French edition of the latter work, published in the same year under the title *Sociétés, traditions et technologie,* the article appears on pp. 65–110.

Only in the post-Hesiodic classical era, however, did the Greeks modify and refine Hesiod's notions so that they begin to approximate the current Greek views of work. The new ingredient embodied a high regard for trade, precisely because trade was a way of acquiring great wealth and, through wealth, the freedom of the landed aristocrat. On the other hand, the cultivation of land that failed to result in the accumulation of wealth came to be regarded as dishonorable.

Obviously, in terms of their own ethic, most Greeks had to lead a dishonorable way of life, but their object was to flee that way of life whenever and as soon as possible. Except for a few, however, that moment did not come until the middle of the eighteenth century. Since that time the Greek aversion toward cultivating land has led to an increasingly persistent flight from the farm to the shop.

By the time of Napoleon, according to J. C. Hobhouse, the Greeks were "all traders in some degree. In the district of Athens, as well as in that of Livadia, and many parts of the Morea, the cultivation of the earth [was] left to the [Orthodox] Albanian colonists, and every Greek [had] either a shop or was employed in wholesale dealings." [2] Bulgarians, Vlachs, and Greeks from the island of Zante later supplemented the farm labor of the Albanians, whereas "the grand object" of most Greeks was "a place under Government, some authority with a little stipend, to enable them to live in idleness." If they were "of a more adventurous disposition," they tried their hand at revolution or took to the highway—"anything but work." [3]

Indeed, there was a form of work which they did not dis-

---

[2] John Cam Hobhouse [1st Baron Broughton], *A Journey through Albania, and Other Provinces of Turkey in Europe and Asia, to Constantinople, during the Years 1809 and 1810* (London: J. Cawthorn, 1813), Vol. I, p. 510.

[3] Edmund Spencer, *Travels in European Turkey in 1850, through Bosnia, Servia, Bulgaria, Macedonia, Thrace, Albania, and Epirus* (London: Colburn and Co., 1851), Vol. II, pp. 232, 235.

dain, *"l'activité de l'esprit."* Regarding the work of the culti-
vator as lowly, they were ambitious to become shopkeepers or
traders, but not so much out of a sheer desire to gain wealth as
"for the pleasure of selling." [4] In other words, they aspired to
demonstrate *ingenuity* in the acquisition of wealth.

A century later, in the 1950's, Greek attitudes toward work
were still very similar. An American historian and first-hand
observer, William H. McNeill, submits the following explanation:

> The disdain for manual labor is perhaps part of a more gen-
> eral social scheme of values which puts the rentier at or near the
> top of the social pyramid. To own land or buildings that will
> produce an income without personal effort is for most Greeks
> the pinnacle of ambition; and those who fall short of this ideal
> but still manage to escape the necessity of manual work some-
> times allow the nail of the little finger on one hand to grow long
> as public proof of their privileged status.[5]

While accepting this explanation as essentially correct, we
prefer another emphasis. Since Homeric and Hesiodic times,
Greeks have distinguished between the honorable and the demeaning on the basis of whether an activity allows or forbids
play and struggle, or *agon*. The honorable is the agonal. But
there can be free play and struggle only between approximate
equals; there cannot be a real game between a guardian and a
child, a freeman and a slave, a lord and a serf, a conqueror and
the conquered. One ought to distinguish, therefore, between
work that is agonal or competitive, a game that one may play
or forego, and work as an involuntary obligation.

In Hesiod, labor that neither originates in freedom nor culminates in wealth and aristocracy is *ponos,* burdensome toil.
While *ponos* demeans, voluntary works—*erga*—dignify precisely because they are freely given. In later times, and until

---

[4] Edmond About, *La Grèce contemporaine* (Paris: Librairie L. Hachette
et Cie, 1854), p. 64.

[5] William Hardy McNeill, *Greece: American Aid in Action, 1947–1956*
(New York: The Twentieth Century Fund, 1957), pp. 18–19.

the end of the nineteenth century, one of the most honorable forms of work, among Greeks and non-Greeks alike, was mutual aid—the *daneike ergasia* of the Theban countryside, the *xelasi* of the Peloponnesus and of Epirus, the *moba* of the Serbians, and even the *clacă* of the Wallacho-Moldavians before their lords changed it into compulsory labor during the seventeenth and eighteenth centuries.

Although a tacit understanding prevails that the family of a donor of such aid has a future claim to the labor of the recipient family, at the moment of the giving the labor is voluntary. Moreover, it is ennobling because it is agonal, taking the form of a contest among the donors to accomplish the greatest amount of work. Thus, at their *mobas,* the Serbians of the Morava used to engage in the singing of ritual songs, one of the most frequent of which was in honor of a contest between Marko Kraljević (Dionysos) and the Maid of the Morava (Persephone or Demeter), wherein victory accrued to the Maid:

> Marko gathered two hundred and two sheaves,
> Moravka reaped three hundred and three.

A second term used in classical Greece to denote honorable work was *ascholia*. Fundamentally, *ascholia* embodied a readiness to forego present leisure (*schole*) or freedom in order to win greater freedom and leisure in the future. Literally, however, the term signifies "un-leisure," much as the Latin *negotium* (from *nec* and *otium*), from which we obtain the English "negotiation" and French *négoce,* or trade. Un-leisure was honorable, however, only if the wealth so acquired was diverted in part to socially or politically desirable ends. In other words, it was honorable and a true creator of liberty only if it resulted in philanthropy. This definition of the purpose of *ascholia* was incorporated into the teachings of Orthodox Christianity.

but pious Serbian monk from the Banat, Dositej Obradović, a patriot as well as an admirer of the Greeks of the classical era and an advocate of the Enlightenment, issued a clear statement of the essence of *ascholia* without employing the term itself:

> Such is the law of the trader's profession. Whoever buys, is glad to buy cheap; and whoever sells, strives to sell dear. To acquire goods and money by honest trade and toil [in the original, the last term is *trud,* which we define below] depends on the one hand upon a man's capacity, and on the other upon the circumstances in which he finds himself. Wherever extensive trading is carried on, there a capable man can acquire money, and therein consists his capacity; but it is a virtue to employ for good ends what one has acquired, protecting the weak from the strong, aiding the wretched, freeing honorable families from poverty, furthering the advance of knowledge among one's own people.[6]

The South Slavs possess an abundance of terms to denote various kinds or conditions of work. For example, *delo* corresponds to the Greek *ergon* (pl., *erga*) and thus means a doing, especially a voluntary performance; it also contains the sense of an appropriate share of work. *Posao* refers to the exercise of a function; *trud* contains the sense of service dutifully or devotedly performed despite its difficult nature; *măka* (or *muka*) is the labor or torture of patiently endured martyrdom; *teg, tegota,* or *tegoba* is heavy, onerous labor.

At least four other words denote unfree, painful, compulsory, or difficult labor. Two—*ponos* and *angarija*—are taken directly from the Greek; one—*kuluk*—comes from Turkish; a fourth—*rabota*—is of Slavic origin. The last is the most common term for work among the Bulgarians and Macedonian Slavs, and among many Serbians of the Morava; it also occurs

[6] George Rapall Noyes (ed.), *The Life and Adventures of Dimitrije Obradović, Who as a Monk Was Given the Name Dositej, Written and Published by Himself* (Berkeley and Los Angeles: University of California Press, 1953), p. 170.

in many western South Slavic areas. Among the Rumanians of Wallachia and Moldavia, the terms for compulsory, heavy, and unfree labor are even more numerous: *angaria* and *rabot; povoz* and *slujbe; munci, lucru,* and ultimately, *clacă.*

A new word, absent in Old Slavonic or not employed to denote work or performance, entered into Serbian during the latter part of the Middle Ages. The new term—*rad*—was used to describe the performance of good works, the endowment or administration of a church, or employment in some higher capacity at a princely court. As time passed, the word was applied to many other activities that did not constitute wearisome toil or involuntary labor. In Ragusa, in addition to administration of an ecclesiastical or princely estate, noun (*rad*) and verb (*raditi*) acquired the sense of a business transaction (*negotium*) by a citizen or anyone not subject to corvée, that is, the obligation binding the peasant to the ignoble task of furnishing a certain amount of unrecompensed labor to his lord.[7]

Containing only the slightest element of pain, *rad* emphasizes the joy of creation, innovation, or management. But since there can be no joy in doing what is not voluntary, it was not at first applied to hard manual labor or to work symbolizing a lack of freedom or leisure. With the gradual abolition of compulsory labor obligations on private estates as a result of the Serbian (and Western) revolution, the fortune of *rad* was assured. As work in general began to acquire a new dignity, *rad* became in the new principality the commonest expression for work.

Until the end of the nineteenth century, the only kind of work acceptable to Montenegrin men was *nadžiranje,* the noble task of an overseer or a shepherd of men. Other work was

[7] A Slaveno-Italo-Latin dictionary published in Ragusa in 1806 thus defined the verb as "attendere, operare, cercare, procurare, trattare, dare operam, incumbere, vacare, operari, agere, efficere, facere, curare, tractare." See Joakim Stulli, *Rjecsoslòxje slovinsko-italiansko-latinsko,* 2 vols. (Dubrovnik: A. Martekini, 1806), Vol. II, under words in question.

relegated to women, beasts of burden like their mules and asses. In the new principality of Serbia, as late as 1844, according to a British traveler and later consul to Dubrovnik, the inhabitants were "haughty, warlike, and somewhat indolent," with a revulsion for most of the mechanical and manual arts and "very lazy in agricultural operations." [8] In other words, they entertained a conception of work and efficiency very different from that of the British observer.

Bulgarians, on the other hand, appeared to perform readily the "more humble and laborious services," [9] and in 1844 the Serbian statesman Ilija Garašanin ascribed the lack of a sufficiently widespread spirit of rebellion among them to the fact that work had become a tradition with them. Indeed, an apparently bourgeois-inspired nineteenth-century Bulgarian "folk" tale on "the share of each nation" relates that, on the occasion of the distribution of gifts to the peoples of the world, God granted lordship or the power of property to the Turks, the power of invention and imagination to the French, intrigue and negotiation to the Greeks, arithmetic to the Jews, misery to the Gypsies, and hard work—*rabota*—to the Bulgarians.

The attitude toward work, however, was not uniform in all Bulgarian areas. Where the geographic setting presented a challenge and a stimulus, as in many mountainous areas, the need for work often gave rise to ingenuity; where the work was imposed by men, as in the plains, the result was often an apparent submission. A Belgian consul general thus offered, in 1880, the following explanation for the enterprise of the inhabitants of the Sredna Gora or "Moderate Mountain," and notably of those of the towns of Elena, Tărnovo, Gabrovo, and Travna:

---

[8] Andrew Archibald Paton, *Servia, the Youngest Member of the European Family: or, A Residence in Belgrade, and Travels in the Highlands and Woodlands of the Interior, during the Years 1843 and 1844* (London: Longman, Brown, Green, and Longmans, 1845), pp. 232, 265.

The area is mountainous and its people are therefore more industrious, for it seems that they have had to find in their own enterprise what the soil, more ungrateful than that of the plain, refused to give them. . . .[10]

The impact of every mountain, moreover, is not exactly the same, and whether a geographic region produces one effect or another depends on the culture and society of its inhabitants. Furthermore, a rigid assignment of a single cluster of attitudes to each ethnic group is invariably misleading. The attitudes associated with *rabota* or hard work are not uniquely Bulgarian but are in fact proper to Serbians, Bulgarians, and Macedonian Slavs of the Morava, Marica, and Vardar valleys, and they extend from Old Serbia deep into Bosnia and beyond. The spirit of enterprise that has existed in the Sredna Gora since the latter part of the eighteenth century was a special manifestation of a more general pattern of attitudes and social organization that characterized a large area which surrounded and projected into the zone of *rabota* culture. Generally designated as *pečalba,* this pattern was intricately woven, in different colors, into the culture of Hercegovina, Old Serbia, Macedonia, southern Albania, Epirus, and Thessaly, and of the Bulgarian Sredna Gora and Bosnian Lika, as well as of Gorski Kotar and Primorje, or the region between northern Bosnia and the Adriatic.

Pečalba denoted two essential qualities, deriving perhaps from a double etymology: an attitude of patient endurance and a readiness to undertake a multitude of diverse tasks in order to accumulate a small sum of money, primarily for the needs of one's family. It normally involved a periodic migration in order to bring one's labor or to carry one's goods to a market where there was a demand for such "commodities." Like other regular movements, such migrations were originally

---

10 Nicholas V. Michoff [Nikola V. Mihov] (ed.), *Contribution à l'histoire du commerce bulgare,* Vol. I, *Rapports consulaires belges* (Sofia, 1941), p. 129. [Author's translation]

limited to the time between St. George's Day and St. Demetrius' Day. Although many *pečalbars* came from the zone of *rabota* culture, *pečalba* differed from *rabota* in entailing a self-imposition of hard work as a means of escaping hard labor imposed by others. It consequently possessed a greater degree of voluntariness. In fact, however, there were many variants of *pečalba,* the principal ones being *pečalba* that remains forever wearisome toil in spite of the fact that the *pečalbar* is free to move about, *pečalba* that leads to superintendence and management, *pečalba* as an un-leisure designed to secure freedom and leisure in the future, *pečalba* that develops into an art of negotiation and diplomacy and culminates in philanthropy.

An integral part of all of the attitudes toward work we have thus far described was either the notion that work is not an end in itself or the idea that there is a proper and improper time for work. Indeed, the Orthodox population of the Slavic Balkan areas used to celebrate about 120 religious and state holidays and 60 to 90 votive days, during which some or most kinds of work were considered taboo, and the workless days in the originally Greek zone of *ascholia* culture were almost as numerous. Integrated with the old attitudes toward work was thus the notion that work and leisure are complementary.

During the nineteenth century, however, a scheme of values emphasizing the virtue of production found expression in the region immediately south of the Sava and the Danube and began slowly to extend farther southward. A similar scheme penetrated to the maritime regions by way of the sea. This change demonstrates that some of the ideas of modern Europe were indeed extending into the Balkans. At the same time, the history of the new attitudes in Serbia suggests that the apparent diffusion of modern European values into the Balkans is in fact an example of historical convergence. In other words, the new valuation was an import for which there was a certain demand.

Under the influence of the European Enlightenment, as interpreted by Obradović and other early Balkan exponents of the rationalization of work, a body of opinion hostile to beggary began to emerge. In the Balkans, many medieval values persisted into the nineteenth century, including a tolerance, even a respect, for beggary by Muslim and Orthodox Christian alike. The Turks, indeed, looked upon fools and lunatics as persons assured of divine salvation. After 1850 or 1860, however, beggary became almost totally unrespectable among Greeks and Slavs, being thereafter largely confined to Gypsies. In the succeeding decades, certain members of the Turkish intelligentsia—among them Namik Kemal and Ahmed Midhat Efendi—similarly condemned laziness and sloth, urging sustained effort, diligence, and self-help; in short, "love of work."

Among the first to take concrete measures to encourage positive values toward production were Serbian political leaders. Miloš Obrenović, for example, issued an order in 1820 aiming to promote the immigration of industrious colonists. In 1837, a Serbian general assembly established the institution of *ekonom*, an appointed official whose task was to advise district subprefects on the best ways of achieving a more rational pattern of production. Immediately thereupon, Miloš issued instructions to the rural police to watch over the peasantry and see that they performed the right tasks at the right time and, in particular, that they refrained from distilling brandy when they should be harvesting.

In the 1840's, the "Constitutionalists" or "Progressists" continued to promote the immigration of colonists from the north (chiefly Vojvodina) to compensate for the influx of immigrants from the southwest (Hercegovina and Montenegro) who did not have a work ethic favorable to agricultural production. The Serbian policy of acquiring tillers of the soil in Hungary became serious enough to compel Metternich to write the following comment on July 16, 1847:

Ever since [it] has come to be persuaded that profits can be derived from agriculture, [the government of] Serbia has been more inclined to promote the cultivation of the soil. According to reports from the Royal-Imperial Consulate in Belgrade, it is attempting each year to put under cultivation stretches of land previously given over exclusively to cattle raising or forest life. In view of the fact that the natives have not yet decided to put their hand to the plow, [the government is pursuing a policy of making] welcome all immigrants who are ready to turn their energies to agriculture.[11]

After 1860, an entire Serbian literature developed around the theme of the value of work. Thus, in his *Précis of Political Economy,* published in 1867, the future Progressist Serbian minister and diplomat Čedomilj Mijatović defended work as an inspiring and refreshing source of individuality and civilization:

By working man grows morally stronger. Through his labor he lifts himself above nature and conquers it, and by this conquest, or discovery and elaboration of its laws, he becomes more independent of it, more autonomous, more of an individual. Civilization has developed most highly in those parts of the earth where man has been most obliged to work.[12]

In his provocative *Serbia in the East,* published in 1872, the young socialist Svetozar Marković sought to orient Serbian society around the goal of production (as against trade) and denounced the prevalence among bureaucrats and petty bourgeois of the idea that manual work was shameful. At the close of the introduction to his *Principality of Serbia* (1876), the anthropologist and political leader Milan Djuro Miličević concluded in didactic verse: "Knowledge is enlightenment, will is might; Let us learn, let us work day and night!" Twenty-five years later, he was more convinced than ever of the virtue

[11] Dj. Šurmin, "Dokumenti o Srbiji od 1842–1848," in Srpska Kraljevska Akademija, *Spomenik,* LXIX (1929), 57–58. [Author's translation]

[12] Čedomilj Mijatović, *Izvod iz politične ekonomike* (Belgrade: Državna Štamparija, 1867), pp. 47–48. [Author's translation]

of work: "Work (*rad*) is life while idleness (*nerad*) is virtual death." [13]

During the 1880's and 1890's, sentiment grew in favor of the notion of work as a virtue, a conception deriving from the late medieval view of work as the performance of good works or as administration, from the Ragusan view of work as trade and negotiation, and from the modern European view of work as a Positivist goal. The last two decades of the nineteenth century in the new Balkan states were, in fact, a period of canonization of Positivism with its triple slogan of progress, order, and modernism, defined in the Balkans as "European culture." A Serbian counterpart to the Latin American *científico* or exponent of Western culture and modern science and technology, the Progressist Vladan Djordjević—physician, historian, novelist, and organizer of the State Sanitary Service—would thus optimistically define his authoritarian government (1897–1900) as a regime of "Order and Work" (*Red i Rad*).

In many places, especially in the newly annexed (1878) districts of the Niš area, the non-Positivist conceptions of work continued to prevail nonetheless during most of the 1880's and 1890's. Indeed, a certain *baba* or "old woman" Mitra thwarted the efforts of the government to eradicate "superstition" and instill a Positivist work ethic by claiming to have experienced a vision in which St. Friday (*Sveta Petka*) had warned her that if the people worked on Fridays—in accordance with the new work ethic and in violation of the old—she would send hail, drought, and disease, and bring ruin to them and their crops. Rumors of the vision spread from village to village, and most villages and village priests decided to be idle on Fridays, prevent any violation of the taboo by members of their own communities, and turn back outsiders who might seek to cross their territories with their carts in order to engage in work. Only a

[13] M. Dj. Milićević, *Kneževina Srbija*, 2 vols. (Belgrade: Državna Štamparija, 1876), Vol. I, p. xiii; M. Dj. Milićević, *Dodatak pomeniku od 1888: Znameniti ljudi u srpskoga naroda koji su preminuli do kraja 1900 g.* (Belgrade: Čupićeva Zadužbina, 1901), p. 88. [Author's translation]

few villages and individuals failed to go along with the appeal to return to tradition, and it was many years before the government succeeded in diffusing the new work ethic.

Under the inspiration of the Serbian geographer and anthropologist Jovan Cvijić, efforts to institutionalize the new ethic became more systematic and were pursued with great diligence in the decade preceding World War I. Thus, in 1911, the Executive Committee of the Serbian Society of National Defense (*Narodna Odbrana*), a group sometimes accused of provoking war with Austria in 1914, issued a brochure in which it expressed its views on how to achieve Serbian national unification. The greatest need was to "transplant into our social order completely new methods of developing the work of private initiative." The theme of the pamphlet was consequently "the value of work on a small scale," the need to replace "big talk" with "modest small tasks" or "practical effort." "Small work" performed on a regular basis by everyone, implied the committee, was infinitely more important than gigantic strides by a few individuals, for "every great work is built of a number of smaller ones," as "the more civilized peoples of the world," especially the Germans and Czechs, "have long recognized." [14]

A further diffusion of the new work ethic continued in the interwar era, with an emphasis by the sociologist and agrarian leader Dragoljub Jovanović on the "heroism of work" and a criticism by the engineer Miodrag Novaković of Taylorism. Coined after the American efficiency engineer Frederick Winslow Taylor (1856–1915), Taylorism aimed at the "rationalization" of industry and business management, in part through the introduction of standard "time and motion" practices. Like critics in other lands, Novaković could thus maintain that Taylorism put too much stress on labor tempo. Holding

[14] Eugene N. Anderson, Stanley J. Pincetl, Jr., and Donald J. Ziegler (eds.), *Europe in the Nineteenth Century: A Documentary Analysis of Change and Conflict*, Vol. II, *1870–1914* (Indianapolis: Bobbs-Merrill Company, 1961), pp. 319, 326–27.

that the greatest capital in the world is human labor, he concluded that raising the tempo of labor would fail to ensure a higher labor productivity unless the purchasing power of workers was likewise augmented. He also urged that the science of "psychotechnics" be conceived henceforth in such a way that workers could be placed in occupations which would give them both personal satisfaction and an incentive to perform effectively. Until after World War II, however, these pleas went largely unheard.

In Rumania, Bulgaria, and Greece, the details were different. All Balkan countries, however, participated in the same general movement, the development of a new work ethic adaptable to either a capitalist or a socialist society. The fact that the new ethic took hold under socialism rather than capitalism in most of the Balkans is perhaps due to capitalism's reluctance to recognize that work and leisure are complementary; capitalism's special conception of time—time is chronometric and continuous, time is money and things—long prevented it from seeing man as a human being.

TIME AND SPACE

A Yugoslav anthropologist, Vladimir Dvorniković, distinguishes between the time system of a space-dominated people (*Raumvolk* or *narod prostora*) and that of a time-oriented people (*Zeitvolk* or *narod vremena*), between the time system of "historic" and that of "unhistoric" peoples. Indeed, he interprets the Yugoslav past, and inferentially the past of all the Balkan peoples and of mankind in general, as an unremitting struggle of a space-dominated people to nullify the compulsions of space or nature and transform itself into a historic nation, a time-oriented people.

This view of the time system of space-dominated peoples corresponds to that of the French geographer Pierre George. According to George, a space-dominated people and a time-oriented people may each have a time system that is exact and demanding. Each of these time systems, however, is based upon a different set of values; they are therefore exact and demanding in different ways. George even contends that the time system of nature (rural) peoples is more demanding than that of culture (urban) peoples: "the rhythms of the earth are not as flexible as those of the factory." [15] In other words, George and Dvorniković both reject the distinction made by Melville J. Herskovits between the "imprecise and relaxed" time system of societies in which man submits to nature and the "exact and demanding" time system of societies which refuse to submit to it without attempting to control it.[16]

While Herskovits' distinction is unacceptable, the terms "historic" and "unhistoric" are often misused. Let us, therefore, take note of the Bergsonian concept of the anthropologist Claude Lévi-Strauss, who recommends the term "cold societies" for societies that, in effect, ignore their own history, and "hot societies" for those that internalize their historical experiences for the purpose of mobilizing and bringing them to their aid whenever the need may arise.[17]

Accordingly, the "hottest" Balkan society before the mid-nineteenth century was the Greek, for Greeks were the inventors of historical writing and Greek society had preserved its historical tradition intact during the Byzantine and Ottoman eras. Among the South Slavs, on the other hand, historical scholarship was just emerging in the fourteenth and fifteenth centuries when the Ottoman conquest interrupted further progress in this new direction.

The notions of time and space of the non-Greeks of the pe-

[15] Pierre George, "Le Travail au village dans l'ancienne et dans la nouvelle Russie," *Revue des Etudes slaves*, XXVII (1951), 119.

[16] Melville J. Herskovits, "Economic Change and Cultural Dynamics," in Ralph Braibanti and Joseph J. Spengler (eds.), *Tradition, Values, and Socio-Economic Development* (Durham, N.C.: Durham University Press, 1961), pp. 127–31.

[17] Claude Lévi-Strauss, "Le Temps retrouvé," *Les Temps modernes*, XVII (April 1962), 1241.

ninsula were medieval Christian or resembled those of the pre-classical Greeks. Indeed, even most Greeks of the medieval and postmedieval era held views analogous to those of their neighbors, and there were fighters in the War of Greek Independence who had never heard of the hero Achilles. Moreover, a familiarity with culture heroes and an ability to trace kinship for six, nine, or ten generations, as was general among Albanians and Montenegrins, are far from being equivalent to the possession of a sense of historical time. They are rather manifestations of a kinship time.

For all the Balkan peasantries, time was a perpetual return of the seasons, of night and day, and of life and death; it was fate, an inexorable necessity. Conscious of the demands of time, peasants were also close to a timeless world, the way of life before the rise of farming and cities, a world in which time went unregulated, in which "the roosters did not crow." Although they were generally ready to submit to nature, they were prone to rebel when too many demands of human origin were imposed upon them. And then, as we have seen, the object was *re-volution,* a "golden age," an abolition of time.

While the "golden age" of the peasant was an earthly society, the "golden age" of the monk—or at least of some monks —was the "heavenly kingdom." This was similarly an abolition of time, but an abolition differently achieved—through work, meditation, and submission—and concerned with a wholly different "space." Preoccupied with the hereafter and devoted to the regular observance of liturgy, medieval Orthodox monasteries were freer of the time of nature but voluntarily yielded to an ecclesiastical time of hours (ὥαρ, *čas*) announced by the blows of a hammer against a plate of copper or iron, or against a wooden board. For pious Christian and Muslim alike, time was a moment of prayer.

A distinctly bourgeois time was late in coming, not because of the absence of a large bourgeoisie, but because bourgeois time was closely related to the time of religion. This had also been true in the West until the fourteenth century. But in the Balkans, the spread of Hesychasm and Islam acted to delay the laicization of time. Public clocks, which serve to call people to work, remind them of their civic duties, and diffuse a secular conception of time, were erected in the Balkans only long after they had been established in Western and Central Europe. In fact, the first such clocks did not appear there until two or three centuries after their appearance in the West. The Huguenot Philippe du Fresne-Canaye, who traversed the Balkans in 1573, maintains that the first public clock in any Ottoman-Balkan town was the clock of the wooden bell tower of Skoplje, brought there from Siget (Szigetvár) shortly after the Ottoman seizure of that Pannonian town in 1566. Sounding the hours "in the French manner," it could be heard by the entire city, and "in all of Turkey," he adds, there was "no other public clock, despite the liking and great esteem of the Turks for clocks." [18]

A century later, another French observer commented on the Turks of Istanbul:

> They esteem clockwork very much but they lack workers who understand it, wherefore some thirty clocksmiths of various nations, Frenchmen and Genevans among others, are drawn to Constantinople, where they perform a satisfactory business in time of peace.[19]

As late as the latter part of the eighteenth century, there was no public clock in Istanbul, and until 1850 there were still only a few Balkan towns with a clock tower, among them Skoplje, Gabrovo, Niš, Leskovac, and tiny Hercegovinian Nevesinje.

The scarcity of public clocks was as nothing, however, com-

---

[18] H.[enri] Hauser (ed.), *Le Voyage du Levant de Philippe du Fresne-Canaye (1573)*, Vol. XVI of *Recueil de voyages et de documents pour servir à l'histoire de la géographie depuis le XIIIe jusqu'à la fin du XVIe siècle*, Charles Schefer and Henri Cordier, eds. (Paris: Ernest Leroux, 1897), p. 34.

[19] *Bibliothèque Nationale* (Paris), Fonds Français 7176, t. I (Constantinople), "Estat des places que les princes mahométans possèdent sur les côtes de la mer Méditerranée," p. 22. [Author's translation]

pared to the inadequacy of illumination, or of a means of reducing the distinction between the order of day and the chaos of night. Past human efforts at illumination had been largely limited to special occasions, generally religious festivals and times of great rejoicing, and may have grown out of earlier fire festivals. By the fifth century, however, there were at least two Roman cities—Syrian Antioch and Edessa—in which streets were regularly lighted at night with oil lamps.

Efforts then flagged; the next successful attempt at street-lighting may have been made in Paris in 1524, when the occupants of houses fronting certain streets were ordered to keep lights burning in their windows. This was followed in 1558 by the establishment of large vases filled with pitch, resin, or some other combustible—and later of lanterns—at street corners. Even in Paris, however, the perfection of street-lighting was essentially an accomplishment of the period after 1667. But in Istanbul there was still no system of regular illumination at the end of the eighteenth century, although for the feast of Ramazan and other special occasions streets were brightened at night by the light of a red fire kindled by the burning of pinewood or tarred rags in irons raised high on pikes.

During the latter half of the nineteenth century, however, the Greeks emerge again as agents of visualism, bearers of oil from the petroleum fields of the Caucasus. The oil of the Caucasus, it is true, was inferior to the oil of Rumania, the best in the world for lamps and consequently reserved to the markets of Europe. Victor Bérard is nevertheless correct in describing modern Hellenism as

> . . . an agent of light, an illuminating power. It suffices to spend one day in Greece in order to know what place the petroleum of Batum and the tin cans—the *tenekes*—that contain it hold there. The number and the size of the lamps is the first luxury of the Greeks. During its life or after its death, full or empty, the *teneke* is the furniture, the instrument *par excellence:* buckets, basins, lamps, plates, watering-cans, everything comes from the *teneke.*

In Turkey, one might estimate the influence of Hellenism by each region's cubic consumption of petroleum. The Muslim and un-Hellenized Christian go to sleep with the sun or smoke and converse in obscurity; at the evening meal, in order to see themselves and show their guests the common plate into which the entire company fraternally plunges its fingers, they kindle only some small bits of wood if they are poor, or, when they are rich, great fires of resinous wood. Hellenism makes its appearance with the bringing of the *teneke,* as it formerly carried from Corinth and Athens terra cotta, lamps, goblets, and amphorae.[20]

A stronger influence was the formerly barbarian world, modern Europe. In 1857, according to the observations of a French consul, Belgrade established a street-lighting system and the obscurity of the night yielded, however partially, before the light of sixty lanterns set up at public expense and about a hundred more that wine shops and innkeepers were required to display. In the 1880's it began to study the lighting system of Vienna and Berlin and soon established modern gas and electric lighting, along with other municipal utilities. By the turn of the century, according to a Cairo newspaper, the capitals of Greece, Serbia, Bulgaria, and Rumania had been "illumined by the light of civilization," for they had acquired "straight and wide streets, public squares, theatres, museums, zoological and botanical gardens, electric light, tramways," while the great European and Asiatic cities of the shrinking Ottoman Empire—Istanbul, Adrianople, Brusa, Damascus, Aleppo, and Bagdad—had shamefully sunk into "darkness and ignorance," [21] or more correctly, had postponed to a later day their effort to annul or moderate the distinction between day and night.

[20] Victor Bérard, *La Turquie et l'hellénisme contemporain: La Macédoine* (Paris: Félix Alcan, 1893), pp. 53–54. Bérard writes *dénéke*. [Author's translation]

[21] Arminius Vambéry, *Western Culture in Eastern Lands* (London: J. Murray, 1906), pp. 343–44, cited by L. S. Stavrianos, "The Influence of the West on the Balkans," in Charles and Barbara Jelavich (eds.), *The Balkans in Transition* (Berkeley and Los Angeles: University of California Press, 1963), p. 212.

The search for the *white world* (enlightenment) had in fact never been totally abandoned, and in the eighteenth and early part of the nineteenth century it was resumed with more vigor and resolution than ever. For example, the Serbian archpriest Matija Nenadović reveals his sentiments—as he claims to remember them—upon embarking with his fellow envoys in 1804 to seek out Russia, bearer of the old light of Orthodoxy and of the new light of the Enlightenment:

> In the name of God we departed and when we sat down in the boat and set off, I said: "Columbus and his company set forth thus on the blue sea to find America and acquaint her with Europe. Today we have set forth on the pacific Danube [shortly, he would discover, not so pacific] to find Russia and acquaint Serbia with Russia, of whose location we know nothing but of whose existence we have heard in song." [22]

But raised for the most part in the *dark world* of the Šumadija forests, he lacked the visualism to appreciate in detail the magnificence of Moscow:

> When one has never before seen so many houses in one heap, will not one marvel in such a spacious town at whatever one sees first: the old imperial Kremlin, the churches, the wondrous palaces and shops? A child born and raised there may in its old age relate something about Moscow. Someone like me, virtually brought up in the mountain, who leaves a dark room at maturity to gaze at the [glittering] white world (*beli svet*) . . . sees only a fantasmagoria until he begins to rub his eyes. [23]

After having been space-dominated throughout their history, many of the inhabitants of the Balkans became space-oriented, conscious of space but thinking increasingly in terms of reorganizing it or regretting the particular reorganization that was being made. Villages became more compact, forests disappeared or grew thinner, roads were built, and after the roads, railroads.

[22] Matija Nenadović, *Memoari* (Belgrade: Prosveta, 1947), pp. 155–56. [Author's translation]
[23] *Ibid.*, p. 171.

This transformation of spatial horizons led to a change in temporal ones, and vice versa. Mijatović thus appropriately observed in his *Précis of Political Economy* that improvements of transportation result in a saving of time, and the saving of time results in turn in the saving of capital, including human capital or labor. The improvement of roads and transport may also result in a shifting of population because goods can be then transferred more rapidly and with greater certainty from the places where they are produced to the places where they may be needed, thus encouraging the growth of cities.

Even in such otherwise relatively isolated provincial towns as Bosnian Višegrad on the Drina, the advent of the railroad led to an acceleration of the rhythms of social time, a quickening of events, a craving for an everyday fare of sensations and exciting news, the *Reizsamkeit* of Karl Lamprecht. By the end of the century, even the idea that "time is money" (for Paul Valéry, the paragon of baseness)—attributed to Benjamin Franklin but actually older—began to be voiced occasionally. There was, on the other hand, some resistance to the notion of punctuality, and even today Greeks who are punctual, notably in their social relationships, are derisively called "Englishmen." The fact is, however, that the number of "Englishmen" in the Balkans has grown considerably during the last sixty years.

Whether capitalist or socialist, the new culture of the Balkans has not totally destroyed the old, and in many respects the old ways are more significant because they lie deep and rise to the surface in times of crisis. But the new ways are also a factor to contend with, and one day the new ways will become old and familiar.

INDIVIDUALITY

Some of the new ways have in fact a relatively long history. For example, the ideal of a large portion of the elite groups of classical Greece was *Sophrosyne*, a term that initially signified "sound midriff" but acquired after the seventh century B.C. the sense of "sound reason." Many Greeks doubtless preferred the Dionysian ideal of excess and rapture, but forever thereafter "sound reason" would remain as the goal of some Greeks. It was an especially vital force, however, during the period of its first emergence, during the European Enlightenment, and during the era of Positivism. If we were to define this Apollonian value in general terms, we should designate it as a striving for Order and Harmony—the Greek term was *eunomie*—or for Moderation and the Middle Way.

Among the other peoples of the Balkans, the first persistent call to *Sophrosyne* came during the second half of the eighteenth century, and one of its earliest South Slavic exponents was Dositej Obradović. Before fully discerning the European Enlightenment and becoming himself a minor European *philosophe*, Obradović discovered Hellenism by going from the writings of the Church Fathers to those of the classical and preclassical era. From the Greeks, along with other ideas, he borrowed the notion of *Sophrosyne*, which he translated into Serbian as *zdrav razum*, literally, "sound reason." Here commences an option among the South Slavs in favor of the Apollonian (and Hesiodic) value of measure and order as against the Dionysian ideal of frenzy and ecstasy. Other advocates of the Enlightenment and the exponents of Positivism continued the task of taking Serbians, Bulgarians, Bosnians, Montenegrins, Greeks, and Rumanians along a path that they thought would end in *eunomie* but that actually engendered discord.

The process of creating order is an interminable dialectic; each order leads to a new disorder, each harmony to a new discord. One of the consequences of enlightenment, order, progress, and European culture was the diffusion of the idea of land as private property. This was an idea that had been common among the Greeks since before the eighth century B.C., but it had been relatively weak in the rest of the Balkans and had become weakened to some degree even among the Greeks during the Byzantine and Ottoman eras. In the late Byzantine and late Ottoman eras, however, the idea of private ownership of land was reaffirmed, and benefices and other conditional properties were transformed into private property.

The "second serfdom" in particular represents a diversion of property from peasant families who regarded it as "ancestral" —that is, as belonging to a particular family rather than to a particular individual—to usurpers who regarded it as "theirs" —that is, as belonging to a particular individual. But legal recognition of the chief aim of the agents of the "second serfdom"—to transform the properties which they or their ancestors had stolen into private property—came late, in the era of reforms collectively known as the Tanzimat, 1826–1876.

In Rumania, the greatest spur to a further evolution of the notion of land as private property was the agrarian reform of 1864, which abolished corvée and allowed peasants to buy the land on which they had worked, generally below the current market value. This was another consequence of the Enlightenment, and of the Russian example and threat of revolution.

Along with the idea of private real property, the concept of "natural rights" soon won support. Thus, according to the manifesto of 1822 of the Greek National Assembly of Epidaurus, the object of the Greek revolution was to conquer, or reconquer, the rights of honor and of private property and individual liberty. The Serbian Civil Code of 1844 gave recognition to the idea that land was private property (although there were some restrictions on its sale or transfer) and asserted very specifically that "every man [this term did not include women] is considered a person," endowed with "natural rights" and entitled to "equality before the law."

The Serbian Civil Code also authorized the fission of the extended family into smaller family units and the subdivision of its land into smaller plots. Under the impact of a slowly evolving money and credit economy, this had been occurring in any case, especially after 1830. In spite of homestead laws, government policies were in general similarly favorable to the idea of the unrestricted sale and disposal of land. Under these circumstances, the notion of mine and thine slowly evolved. For example, in an article published in 1856, the anthropologist Milićević relates how his grandfather, a certain Milić who had migrated to Serbia from the unfree south, gathered together one day all his sons, grandsons, and older nephews, and told them that the family should separate, exculpating them of all blame for the exigencies of the time that were making of Serbians a *Zeitvolk,* or historical people:

> No one wants the division, my children, but I. More than any of you I regret that what was hitherto called *ours* will henceforth be called *ours* and *yours* and *theirs,* but it is better to separate now than when you too are of my age.[24]

Milić was then eighty-five. Unlike the grandfather, the pre-adolescent children experienced much difficulty in accommodating themselves to the new mentality, for after having been raised under one set of values they were told to operate according to another. Indeed, there is nothing unusual about this, for unlike adolescents and young persons in their twenties—who, in a changing society, often emerge as "nihilists"—children are essentially conservatives. They display this in their games, often reservoirs of the values of a bygone age, of an archaic mentality. Milićević comments appropriately on the problem:

> Accustomed to obey the old man in all things, they [the adults] separated. But their children were long unable to distinguish between one house and another and therefore always spent the day or night wherever day or dusk came upon them. They say that all sometimes started to cry vigorously when they were told: "Come, everyone to his own house; this is not your house." [25]

[24] M. Dj. Milićević, "Pregled zadružnog stanja Srba seljaka," in *Glasnik Društva Srbske Slovesnosti,* otdel 1, Vol. IX (1856), 157. [Author's translation]

[25] *Loc. cit.* [Author's translation]

All divisions were not as pacific as in the family of Milićević. Often there were quarrels, and sometimes disputes were taken to a court of law. But whether a division was achieved calmly or otherwise, the result was very largely the same, despite the games of children: a favoring of the idea of private and personal property, a transformation of attitudes toward space.

The extension of private property, however, did not allow an equally facile expansion of individuality. As the Serbian philosopher Božidar Knežević (1862–1905), who was receptive to some of the ideas of Macaulay, Comte, and Nietzsche, correctly observed in his two-volume *Principles of History* (1898–1901), men tend to separate into two categories, the "higher man" (*viši čovek*) and the "lower men" (*niži ljudi*). The first is endowed with ample resources to become almost a complete entity unto himself, rise to abstraction and achieve real autonomy; the "lower men," on the other hand, are prisoners of their senses and of the concrete and particular, complete only in society. Knežević freely acknowledged that the abstract is born of the concrete and that every great social goal should be formulated in terms of the needs and interests of the people; indeed, that civilization itself is a "glorification of labor." But innovation and abstraction, he insisted, are the work of individuals or higher men, whose blossoming society strives to prevent even though they are necessary to it if society itself is to bloom; that is, move away from tribal and nation-state systems toward the goal of a united humanity.

The very fact, however, that a Knežević could write in this manner in 1898 and that in 1899 a Rumanian disciple of Karl Lamprecht, Alexander D. Xenopol, could publish his *Principes fondamentaux de l'histoire,* is a demonstration of the appearance of the "higher man" in Balkan history. Turning to some of the same problems as Knežević, Xenopol devoted an entire chapter to "the constant factors in history." The constants, he observed, are biology, geography, and cultural conservatism, or the law of reaction against action, society vs. the individual, the past vs. the future: "Every modification of intellectual continuity, through the manifestation of evolutionary forces, provokes a movement of reaction which tends to preserve the acquisitions of continuity." [26]

For the first time in many centuries, "higher men" appeared in the Balkans in relatively great numbers. And as they appeared, they rebelled against what one writer called the "dead sea" of public opinion, which directs, meddles, and destroys, makes it difficult to rise above or fall below the "level line" of the crowd, forbids the *I*—this new factor, the *I*-factor—to ring out. The Spaniards call these "higher men" of their own country the generation of '98. But common opinion notwithstanding, the Spanish-American War was only incidental to their rise. The generation of the nineties was a European, not a narrowly national, phenomenon, and to the extent that this generation existed also in the Balkans, we may say that the Balkans—this "First Europe" and former "Asia in Europe"—were again *of* Europe as well as in it.

In the Balkans, as in Central Europe, the generation of the nineties and the prewar decade is sometimes called "Modernist." But some of its members rose above the quarrel that divided the "young" from the "old," the Modernists from the Traditionalists, or the Symbolists from the Realists, to bridge the gap between the two. Perhaps no one did this more brilliantly than the Serbian essayist and literary critic Bogdan Popović, especially in two essays entitled "On the Cultivation of Taste" and "Literary Leaves," published in 1896 and 1901, respectively.

In the first essay, Popović urged teachers to strive to develop in students an "independence of judgment," that is, judgment on the basis of facts that each individual is encouraged to find for himself through the creation of a milieu and atmosphere

[26] Alexandru Dimitrie Xenopol, *La Théorie de l'histoire: Deuxième édition des Principes fondamentaux de l'histoire* (Paris: Ernest Leroux, 1908), pp. 164–209. The definition of the law of reaction against action occurs on page 189. [Author's translation]

conducive to discovery. Independence of judgment, he recognized, does not necessarily result in correctness of judgment, but correct and sound judgments can be made more frequently through the exercise of the faculty of independent judgment, provided it grows out of knowledge and understanding. Indeed, one cannot know man—"Know thyself," said the ancient Greeks—without knowing oneself:

> A man will come to know himself if he learns, on every occasion, to be *conscious of what is happening within him.* There must be in him two men, one who will act, suffer, and live, a second who will observe and examine the first. This undoubling, this self-uncoupling aiming at self-understanding— *dédoublement,* as the French call it—is the key to our entire moral life.[27]

In his second essay, Popović drew again on psychology and invoked the principle of the economical use of energy in defense of the use of foreign models:

> From the psychology of creativity, it is well-known that every production is basically a reproduction; that every creation is more or less a new combination of attitudes and conceptions existing in the spirit previously, and without which neither the simplest image nor thing could be imagined. . . .
>
> It is indeed only too clear that we should be very poor economists if we refused to profit from what others have achieved before us in a misguided zeal to repeat every experience and error, to begin again the entire process of evolution.[28]

Borrowings, he continued, will never be made at the expense of autonomous creation; cultural imitation and innovation are complementary rather than contradictory:

> For original spirits, for spirits that have something of their own to tell, there is never a danger that foreign models will turn them into foreigners. The *"race" will always manifest itself* in the person who is original, precisely because he creates from

---

[27] Bogdan Popović, *Ogledi iz književnosti i umetnosti* (Belgrade: S. B. Cvijanović, 1914), pp. 43–44. [Author's translation]

[28] *Ibid.,* pp. 77, 81–82. [Author's translation]

his own special fund of resources; such an artist will always be national. Where originality is lacking, there is generally nothing anyhow, with or without models.[29]

The old Balkan values and personality types did not disappear; indeed, in modified form, they continue to dominate. But a new type of personality was added to the others by the 1890's. To understand the Balkans today, one must bring together all these types and be ready for all kinds of combinations and confusions.

The rise of communism has not fundamentally altered the direction of movement except to some degree in regard to property. Communism differs from capitalism, however, in a very important respect: It looks back to a more distant past and forward to a more distant future. In so doing, it may be able to effect a reconciliation between the older values and the new personality and culture, but precisely how remains a question. Moreover, with new experiences, there may arise new sets of "new men." No, human personality is not unchanging, although the old Chaos remains in the Balkans, as in us all.

[29] *Ibid.*, pp. 83–85. [Author's translation]

BIBLIOGRAPHY

◦—◦◦◦—◦

A good portion of this study in Balkan civilization is based on publications in languages other than English. Since, however, spatial and pedagogical considerations prohibit the citation of all important works, the bibliography is confined to books and articles in English and to a few studies of special merit in French or German.

General Studies. Apart from some of the books listed below under "Civilization," very few studies consider the Balkans as a unit and attempt at the same time to probe into the many diverse aspects of Balkan society and culture. Among the oldest of such works are the very useful and almost irreplaceable multivolume studies of the Ottoman Empire by Josef von Hammer-Purgstall, Johann Wilhelm Zinkeisen, and Nicolas (or Nicolae) Iorga, all in German, with the Hammer study translated into an even better edition in French. Among the most recent works, aimed primarily at an American college public, are two short studies, one by Wayne S. Vucinich, *The Ottoman Empire: Its Record and Legacy* (Princeton, N.J.: Van Nostrand, 1965), and the other by Barbara and Charles Jelavich, *The Balkans* (Englewood Cliffs, N.J.: Prentice-Hall, 1965), a view of this area in modern times. Finally, general studies of the Balkans and neighboring areas of special value include the following:

Jelavich, Charles, and Barbara Jelavich (eds.): *The Balkans in Transition: Essays on the Development of Balkan Life and Politics since the Eighteenth Century.* Berkeley and Los Angeles: University of California Press, 1963. Useful collection of essays by thirteen different scholars on geopolitics, Ottoman views of the Balkans and the Ottoman legacy, religion and nationalism, Russia and the Balkans, the influence of the West on the Balkans, Greek and South Slavic literatures, the social foundations of Balkan politics, the bipolar nature of politics in small states, Balkan heritage and continuity, and Balkan historiography.
McNeill, William H.: *Europe's Steppe Frontier, 1500–1800.* Chicago: University of Chicago Press, 1964. A challenging interpretative study of the European steppe or zone of civilization at the edges of which the Russian, Ottoman, and Habsburg empires met or failed to meet.

Oliva, Pavel: *Pannonia and the Onset of Crisis in the Roman Empire*. Prague: Czechoslovak Academy of Sciences, 1962. Good political, social, and economic history of Roman Pannonia, that is, of the northern fringes of the Balkans and of the area beyond.

Ostrogorsky, George: *History of the Byzantine State*, translated from the German by John Hussey, with a foreword by Peter Charanis. New Brunswick, N.J.: Rutgers University Press, 1957. Invaluable political, social, and economic history of Byzantium.

Stavrianos, Leften S.: *The Balkans since 1453*. New York: Holt, Rinehart and Winston, 1958. Excellent. Indeed, the best general study of the Balkans from the Ottoman era to the end of World War II. See also his study, *The Balkans, 1815–1914* (New York: Holt, Rinehart and Winston, 1963).

National Histories. Studies in English of individual Balkan states or peoples include a history of Rumania by Nicolas Iorga, translated by Joseph McCabe (1925), and another of that country by R. W. Seton-Watson (1934); a one-volume history of Greece from 1821 to 1921 by William Miller (1922), and an old but still valuable seven-volume study of Greece from the Roman conquest to the 1860's by George Finlay; a collection of essays on Serbia by Serbian scholars and other specialists, edited by Alfred Stead (1909); and a history of Serbia by Harold W. Temperley (1917). In addition, a collective work on Yugoslavia, edited by Robert J. Kerner (University of California Press, 1949), examines various aspects of Yugoslav history until World War II. During the 1950's, Frederick A. Praeger published a series of collective studies on Yugoslavia, Bulgaria, Albania, and Rumania, edited respectively by Robert F. Byrnes, L. A. D. Dellin, Stavro Skendi, and Stephen Fischer-Galati. They carry the history of the countries in question to the first decade of the Communist era, on which they generally also put their primary emphasis. In a recent study edited by Stephen Clissold, *A Short History of Yugoslavia from Early Times to 1966* (Cambridge, Eng.: University Press, 1966), H. C. Darby provides a good introduction to the political history of Slovenia, Croatia, Dalmatia, Bosnia-Hercegovina, Montenegro, Serbia, and Macedonia. R. W. Seton-Watson, R. G. D. Laffan, Stephen Clissold, and Phyllis Auty complete the remaining two-fifths of the book with chapters on the formation of a Yugoslav state, the insoluble problems of the new political entity during the interwar era, occupation and resistance during World War II, and the creation of a socialist Yugoslavia. The most serious shortcoming of this compact study is its inadequate grasp of some of the problems of economic history. The best synthesis of a national history is a short study in French by Nicolas G. Svoronos, *Histoire de la Grèce moderne* (Paris: Presses Universitaires de France, 1953), a political, social, and economic history of Greece from the decline of Byzantium to our own time.

Geography. For an easy introduction to the manifold problems of Balkan physical and human geography, readers may turn to:

Blanc, André: *Géographie des Balkans*. Paris: Presses Universitaires de France, 1965. Excellent introduction to the natural milieu, the human mosaic of the Balkans, and to the creation of an industrial and urban society. Rumania is not included in the study.

Hoffman, George W.: *The Balkans in Transition*. Princeton, N.J.: Van Nostrand, 1963. Good introduction to the transformation of the Balkan milieu as a result of industrialization, urbanization, and political, economic, and social change since World War II.

Newbegin, Marion I.: *Geographical Aspects of Balkan Problems*. New York: Putnam, 1915. Useful introduction to the relationship between Balkan geography and European politics on the eve of World War I.

Prehistory. Much of the material on prehistory is published in the form of articles in such reviews as *Antiquity* or the *American Journal of Archaeology*. Individually, and especially to the untrained reader, such contributions may appear to be of little significance. Collectively, however, they result in a rapid expansion of our knowledge of the paleolithic, neolithic, and preliterary or early literary eras. Among books and articles pointing to significant recent archeological research or consciously subscribing to a specific theory of human development, we recommend in particular the following:

Braidwood, Robert J.: *Prehistoric Men*, enlarged 3rd ed. Chicago: Chicago Natural Museum, 1957. Lucid. By far the best synthesis of prehistory. See also Robert W. Ehrich (ed.), *Chronologies in Old World Archaeology*. Chicago and London: University of Chicago Press, 1965.

Childe, V. Gordon: *The Prehistory of European Society*. Baltimore, Md.: Penguin Books, 1958. Excellent on prehistoric cultures of the Danube.

Fewkes, Vladimir J.: "Neolithic Sites in the Moravo-Danubian Area (Eastern Yugoslavia)." *American School of Prehistoric Research Bulletin*, No. 12 (1936), 5–81. Defense of the theory of the rise of a Balkan neolithic culture through the process of "primary diffusion."

Pittioni, Richard: "Southern Middle Europe and Southeastern Europe," in *Courses toward Urban Life: Archeological Considerations of Some Cultural Alternates*, Robert J. Braidwood and Gordon R. Wiley (eds.). New York: Wenner-Gren Foundation for Anthropological Research, 1962, pp. 211–26. Defense of the theory of "historical convergences" explained in Chapter I of this book.

Rodden, Robert J.: "An Early Neolithic Village in Greece." *Scientific American*, CCXII (April 1965), 83–92. Important comments on the earliest Balkan neolithic. For specialist and cultivated public alike.

Civilization. Some readers may have chosen our book because it copes with the problem of civilization, others because it is a study of the Balkans. We hope that the first group will continue its interest in the Balkans and that the second will extend its concern to the comparative study of civilizations. Apart from the article by Fernand Braudel and the book by Anthony F. C. Wallace cited in the footnotes to the Introduction, studies that clarify various aspects of the problem of cultures and civilizations include:

Bagby, Philip: *Culture and History: Prolegomena to the Comparative Study of Civilizations.* London, New York, Toronto: Longmans, Green, and Co., 1958. An introduction to the chief identifying characteristics of civilizations.

Braudel, Fernand: *La Méditerranée et le monde méditerranéen à l'époque de Philippe II.* Paris: Armand Colin, 1949. A work of art, a work of science. Theoretically significant. Thorough probing into the environmental, economic, and demographic structures of the empires, civilizations, and societies of the sixteenth-century Mediterranean. Valuable data on the Balkans. A revised and enlarged two-volume edition of this study appeared in 1966. Routledge & Kegan Paul, Ltd., London, is publishing an English edition.

Kroeber, Alfred Louis, and Clyde Kluckhohn, with the assistance of Wayne Untereiner: *Culture: A Critical Review of Concepts and Definitions,* appendices by Alfred G. Meyer. Cambridge, Mass.: Peabody Museum, 1952. Collection of many different definitions of culture with pertinent comments.

Redfield, Robert: *Peasant Society and Culture: An Anthropological Approach to Civilization.* Chicago: University of Chicago Press, 1956. Valuable for its discussion of the "little tradition of the largely unreflective many" as against the "great tradition of the reflective few."

Our own study represents one of the first attempts ever made to describe and analyze continuity and change in Balkan societies and cultures from neolithic to modern times. As essays on special questions of culture, or for more restricted periods and for individual Balkan civilizations, the following are useful aids:

Actes du Colloque International de Civilisations Balkaniques. International colloquium organized for UNESCO and for the Académie de la République Populaire Roumaine, under the auspices and with the aid of UNESCO, by the Commission Nationale Roumaine, at Sinaïa, July 8–14, 1962. Colloquium participants dealt with many different expressions of Balkan culture, but the general emphasis was on the simultaneous plurality and interpenetration of Balkan civilizations.

Burn, Andrew Robert: *The Lyric Age of Greece.* London: Edward Arnold, 1960. Fine study of Greek culture in post-Hesiodic era. Some Greeks, but not all, discover the sense of sin or guilt.

Cvijić, Jovan: "The Zones of Civilization of the Balkan Peninsula." *Geographical Review,* V (1918), 470–82. A summary of portions of Cvijić's *La Péninsule balkanique* (Paris: Armand Colin, 1918). Geologist, geographer, and anthropologist, Cvijić examines in the larger study the geographic milieu, South Slav migratory movements since the fifteenth century, the geohistorical basis of Balkan societies and cultures, and the psychic qualities of the members of each of these societies. Now dated in some respects, but there is no comparable work to replace it.

Dodds, Eric Robertson: *The Greeks and the Irrational.* Berkeley and Los Angeles: University of California Press, 1963. Presents thesis of the passage of Greek society in the post-Hesiodic era from a "shame" to a "guilt" culture. A corrective to conventional histories that emphasize the rational aspects of Greek historical evolution.

Dvornik, Francis: *The Slavs in European History and Civilization.* New Brunswick, N.J.: Rutgers University Press, 1962. A specialist in the religious history of Byzantium and the Slavs, Father Dvornik here provides a valuable history of Slavic societies from medieval times to the close of the eighteenth century.

Gibb, Hamilton Alexander Rosskeen, and Harold Bowen: *Islamic Society and the West,* Vol. I, *Islamic Society in the Eighteenth Century,* 2 parts. London: Oxford University Press, 1950–1957. Excellent on Muslim sectors of Ottoman society. Also recommended is Bernard Lewis, *Istanbul and the Civilization of the Ottoman Empire.* Norman, Okla.: University of Oklahoma Press, 1963.

Iorga, Nicolas: *Le caractère commun des institutions du Sud-Est de l'Europe.* Paris: Gamber, 1929. The most prolific Balkan (Rumanian) historian develops thesis of the persistence and unity of Balkan folk culture from pre-Roman times to the nineteenth century. Little known, this short survey is one of Iorga's best studies.

Jireček, Constantin J.: *Staat und Gesellschaft im mittelalterlichen Serbien.* Vienna: Kais. Akademie der Wissenschaften, 1912–1914. Political, social, and economic history of medieval Serbia, with good sections on Serbian medieval civilization. Under the direction of Louis Eisenmann, the latter have been translated into French under the title *La civilisation serbe au Moyen âge* (Paris: Bossard, 1920).

Niederle, Lubor: *Manuel de l'Antiquité slave,* 2 vols. Paris: Librairie Ancienne Honoré Champion, 1923–1926. The first volume is on the "history" or origins and migrations of the Slavs. The second, on Slavic civilization in prehistory and during the early Middle Ages, is still the best study of its kind. Emphasis is on material culture but there are good sections on religion and social values. Based on a larger Czech study. Niederle's first volume ought to be modified in the light of an important article by Vladimir Georgiev, "The Genesis of the Balkan Peoples," in *The Slavonic and East European Review*, XLIV (July 1966), 285–97.

Starr, Chester G.: *The Origins of Greek Civilization, 1100–650 B.C.* New York: Alfred A. Knopf, 1961. Modifying the gradualistic view of social and cultural evolution, Starr emphasizes the importance of evolution in spurts and appropriately points to the mutation of Greek civilization during the eighth century B.C.

Thomson, George: *Studies in Ancient Greek Society: The Prehistoric Aegean*. London: Lawrence & Wishart, 1949. A profound study of the material and social foundations of prehistoric Greek values and psychology.

Folk Culture. Many of the books cited in the footnotes to Chapters I and II of this book are studies that probe into some aspects of folk culture or Robert Redfield's "little tradition." For readers who wish to penetrate more deeply into this subject, the following are of value:

Blum, Richard, and Eva Blum, assisted by Anna Amera and Sophie Kallifatidou: *Health and Healing in Rural Greece: A Study of Three Communities*. Stanford, Calif.: Stanford University Press, 1965. Good analysis, based on a survey made in 1962, of the health practices, beliefs, social organization, and values of three rural communities in Attica.

Brkić, Jovan: *Moral Concepts in Traditional Serbian Epic Poetry*. 's-Gravenhage: Mouton, 1961. Valuable analysis of the qualities held in esteem by Serbian and Montenegrin patriarchal societies as exemplified in their epic poetry.

Campbell, John Kennedy: *Honour, Family, and Patronage: A Study of Institutions and Moral Values in a Greek Mountain Community*. Oxford: Clarendon Press, 1964. Excellent study of the society and values of the Sarakatsan shepherd communities of the district of Zagori to the northeast of Janina during the mid-1950's. Discussion of changes in Sarakatsan way of life since 1930.

Friedl, Ernestine: *Vasilika: A Village in Modern Greece*. New York: Holt, Rinehart and Winston, 1962. Good description and fine analysis of the family, dowry system, views of the world, and patterns of production and consumption in the Boeotian village of Vasilika.

Halpern, Joel Martin: *A Serbian Village*. New York: Columbia University Press, 1958. An anthropological study of the community of Orašac during the 1950's. Good historical introduction, valuable observations on the relationships between Orašac culture and the larger cultures of Serbia and the other Yugoslav lands.

Hasluck, Margaret M.: *The Unwritten Law in Albania*. Cambridge, Eng.: University Press, 1954. Albanian rural and tribal society before Communist leadership came to power. Useful exposition of the interpenetration of values and social structures.

Kemp, P.: *Healing Ritual: Studies in the Technique and Tradition of the Southern Slavs*. London: Faber and Faber, 1935. Excellent study of the medical folk tradition and healing rituals, techniques, and practices of the South Slavs, particularly during the nineteenth and early part of the twentieth century.

Kunst, Jaap: *Cultural Relations between the Balkans and Indonesia*. Amsterdam: Royal Tropical Institute, 1954. A short study of some of the musicological, choreographical, and thematic traits common to the folk cultures of the Balkans and Indonesia. Good illustrations.

Lawson, Cuthbert John: *Modern Greek Folklore and Ancient Greek Religion: A Study in Survivals*. Cambridge, Eng.: University Press, 1910. A highly readable scholarly study of the survival of ancient Greek religion in modern folklore.

Onians, Richard Broxton: *The Origins of European Thought: About the Body, the Mind, the Soul, the World, Time, and Fate*. Cambridge, Eng.: University Press, 1951. Both interesting and remarkably profound. Deals extensively with the subjects of the title, giving due attention to the biotechnics, attitudes toward various parts of the body, and views of the world of the ancient Greeks, Romans, and other Mediterranean and European peoples.

Sanders, Irwin T.: *Balkan Village*. Lexington, Ky.: University of Kentucky Press, 1949. A good study of the Bulgarian village of Dragalevtsy (near Sofia) during the 1930's, with a description of the changes observable a decade later.

Skendi, Stavro: *Albanian and South Slavic Oral Epic Poetry*. Philadelphia: American Folklore Society, 1954. Albanian and South Slavic cultural patterns, interpenetration of North Albanian (Gheg) and Serbian cultures. For more detailed studies of Balkan oral epic poetry, readers may refer to the excellent studies of Albert B. Lord and Milman Parry.

Wace, Alan John Bayard, and M. S. Thompson: *The Nomads of the Balkans: An Account of Life and Customs among the Vlachs of Northern Pindus*. New York: Dutton, 1913. Excellent study of a declining way of life.

Religion: Folk and Elite. Many of the books listed under our headings "Civilization" and "Folk Culture" provide an introduction to the problem of folk and elite religions. We also recommend the following book-length studies:

Hadrovics, Ladislas: *Le peuple serbe et son Eglise sous la domination turque*. Paris: Presses Universitaires de France, 1947. Serbian folk and elite religion under Ottoman rule.

Harrison, Jane Ellen: *Themis: A Study of the Social Origins of Greek Religion*. Cambridge, Eng.: University Press, 1912. A classic.

Hasluck, Frederick William: *Christianity and Islam under the Turks*, Margaret M. Hasluck (ed.), 2 vols. Oxford: Clarendon Press, 1929. A wealth of fact and interpretation relating to problems of Christian and Muslim folk religion and practices in the Ottoman Empire.

Mousset, Jean: *La Serbie et son Eglise (1830–1904)*. Paris: Institut d'Etudes Slaves de l'Université de Paris, 1938. Serbian folk and elite religion, with sections on Jews, Roman Catholics, and Nazarenes in nineteenth-century Serbia.

Obolensky, Dmitri: *The Bogomils: A Study in Balkan Neo-Manichaeism*. Cambridge, Eng.: University Press, 1948. A good study of Bogomilism.

Papadopoullos, Theodore: *Studies and Documents Relating to the History of the Greek Church and People under Turkish Domination*. Brussels: Wetteren, 1952. One of the best studies of the Greek Orthodox Church under Ottoman rule, with useful discussions of the Phanariots and lay administrators of the finances of the Church.

Technology. Scholars have unfortunately largely neglected one very important manifestation of civilization: technology. True enough, much is known about ancient Greek, Hellenistic, and Roman, some information is available on Byzantine technology, and scholars have explored some aspects of medieval and preindustrial Balkan technology. But many of the latter studies are in one of the Balkan languages and thus largely inaccessible to most of our readers. On Balkan technology of the industrial era, there is hardly anything in English except in studies devoted more particularly to problems of geography and social and economic history. In view of these handicaps and considering the fact that our own study is not oriented around ancient Greek or Byzantine inventions and applications of inventions, it should be obvious why the few studies cited below refer mainly to mining enterprise and common farming implements.

Alexander, John: "Greeks, Italians, and the Earliest Balkan Iron Age." *Antiquity*, XXXVI (1962), 123–30. Author holds that iron-using developed west of the Neretva and Bosna and south of the Sava rivers under Italic influences.

Beckmann, Johann: *A History of Inventions, Discoveries, and Origins*, 4th ed., revised and enlarged by William Francis and J. W. Griffith, 2 vols. London: Henry G. Bohn, 1846. Dated but still a very good study of technology, especially in regard to Central Europe.

Haudricourt, André G., and Mariel Jean-Brunhes Delamarre: *L'Homme et la charrue à travers le monde.* Paris: Editions Gallimard, 1955. Best general study of ards and plows throughout the world, with good sections on the Balkans.

Kovačević, Desanka: "Dans la Serbie et la Bosnie médiévales: Les mines d'or et d'argent." *Annales (Economies, Sociétés, Civilisations),* XV (1960), 248–58. Excellent. Geographic distribution and productivity of Serbian and Bosnian gold, silver, and other mines between the mid-thirteenth and mid-fifteenth centuries.

Lefebvre des Noëttes, Richard (Commandant): *L'Attelage: Le cheval de selle à travers les âges, contribution à l'histoire de l'esclavage,* 2 vols. Paris: A. Picard, 1931. Important contribution to our knowledge of harnessing techniques and horsepower deployment of ancient and medieval societies. Second volume consists of illustrations.

Vryonis, Speros: "The Question of the Byzantine Mines." *Speculum,* XXXVII (January 1962), 1–17. Good study of mining activity in Anatolia and the Balkans during the Byzantine era. Author holds the view that Slavic and Arab invasions did not provoke a complete cessation of Byzantine mining enterprise.

"Western Revolution." The footnotes to Chapter IV provide an introduction to the old tripartite structure of society (on which one of the foremost authorities, particularly in regard to Indo-European societies, is Georges Dumézil), the modification of the estates structures, and the ultimate rise of a society based on the principle of individual liberty and equality before the law through national and social revolution. Robert R. Palmer contends that the last decades of the eighteenth and first decades of the nineteenth century witness in Europe and the Americas a series of political and social revolutions that may jointly be described as the "Western Revolution." The Rumanian historian Nicolas Iorga has expressed a similar view in some of his studies. For other conceptions and for a further exposition of the notion of the interpenetration of the Balkan and "Western" revolutions, see:

Botzaris, Notis: *Visions balkaniques dans la préparation de la Révolution grecque (1789–1821).* Geneva: Droz; Paris: Minard, 1962. A good study of Balkan cooperation in secret societies, Greek participation in the Serbian revolution, the Balkan-wide appeal of the revolutionary ideology of Rhigas Pheraios, and of other inter-Balkan aspects of the Balkan revolutions.

Djordjević, Dimitrije: *Révolutions nationales des peuples balkaniques, 1804–1914,* Margita Ristić, trans. Belgrade: Institut d'histoire, 1965. A good comparative study of Balkan national movements from the end of the eighteenth century to World War I, with an abundant bibliography in the footnotes and good sections on the social and economic foundations and inter-Balkan character of the national movements.

Fischer-Galati, Stephen: "The Peasantry as a Revolutionary Force in the Balkans." *Journal of Central European Affairs*, XXIII (1963), 12–22. Author holds that the Balkan peasantries were often wary of the leaders of anti-Turkish rebellions—priests, klephts, *hajduks*, notables, and boyars.

Lebel, Germaine: *La France et les Principautés danubiennes (Du XVIe siècle à la chute de Napoléon I-er)*. Paris: Presses Universitaires de France, 1955. French contributions to a Rumanian Enlightenment and to the expression of a revolutionary ideology among urban and aristocratic Rumanian youth.

Ranke, Leopold: *The History of Servia, and the Servian Revolution, with a Sketch of the Insurrection in Bosnia*, translated from the German by Mrs. Alexander Kerr. London: Henry G. Bohn, 1853. Written by the famous Ranke on the basis of data provided by the Serbian lexicographer, grammarian, cultural anthropologist, and historian Vuk Karadžić, this study provides a vivid and generally good introduction to Serbia during the last decades of Ottoman rule. Basically a study of the Serbian revolution and of the political and social transformation of Serbia during the early decades of the nineteenth century, it fails to place the Serbian revolution in a general European framework.

Stavrianos, Leften S.: "Antecedents to the Balkan Revolutions of the Nineteenth Century." *Journal of Modern History*, XXIX (December 1957), 335–48. Balkan commercial links with Europe and intellectual links with the European Enlightenment and French Revolution as stages in the preparation of the Balkan revolutions, and Balkan national rivalries as obstacles to a concerted Balkan revolution.

Vucinich, Wayne S.: "Marxian Interpretations of the First Serbian Revolution." *Journal of Central European Affairs*, XXI (April 1961), 3–14. Marxist interpretations of the Serbian revolution as a social as well as national movement and as an expression of general South Slavic and Balkan inclinations in both the Ottoman and Habsburg empires. Yugoslav Marxists disagree on the relative importance of "bourgeois" and "peasant" contributions to the revolution.

Woodhouse, Christopher Montague: *The Greek War of Independence*. London, New York, Melbourne, Sydney, and Capetown: Hutchinson's University Library, 1952. A good study of the Greek war of independence, but with a stress on political and a negligence of economic factors.

Nationalism and Power Politics. A partial bibliography on Balkan nationalism has been presented under the previous heading and under the heading "National Histories." Below we add a few more studies. Readers should note, however, that the literature on nationalism and power politics is enormous. We have consequently excluded any reference to books dealing with very short periods—partly for reasons of space, but chiefly because studies of longer periods generally furnish a better perspective.

Barker, Elisabeth: *Macedonia: Its Place in Balkan Power Politics.* London: Royal Institute of International Affairs, 1950. Political rivalries in Macedonia, with a useful section on Communist views of the Macedonian problem.

Bérard, Victor: *La Turquie et l'hellénisme contemporain: La Macédoine.* Paris: Félix Alcan, 1893. As stimulating as Brailsford's study below. Sensitive to the thesis of Macedonia as an area of Greek culture.

Black, Cyril Edwin: *The Establishment of Constitutional Government in Bulgaria.* Princeton, N.J.: Princeton University Press, 1943. Introduction to Bulgarian society during the last decades of Ottoman rule and excellent sections on Russian policy, Bulgarian nationalism, the Bulgarian intelligentsia, and the formation of Bulgarian political parties.

Brailsford, Henry Noel: *Macedonia: Its Races and Their Future.* London: Methuen, 1906. In spite of almost inevitable biases, the best study of Macedonian society and economy in the framework of Ottoman bureaucracy and landlordism on the one hand and power politics on the other. Good sections on the nationalities of Macedonia. Regards Macedonian Slavs as closer to Bulgarians than to Serbians.

Jardé, Auguste François Victor: *The Formation of the Greek People,* M. R. Dobie, trans. New York: Alfred A. Knopf, 1926. Excellent study of the process of formation of Greek nationality in antiquity.

Jelavich, Charles: *Tsarist Russia and Balkan Nationalism: Russian Influence in the Internal Affairs of Bulgaria and Serbia, 1879–1886.* Berkeley and Los Angeles: University of California Press, 1958. A good continuation of the Sumner study cited below, it deals with some of the same problems as the Black study.

Lederer, Ivo J.: *Yugoslavia at the Paris Peace Conference: A Study in Frontiermaking.* New Haven, Conn.: Yale University Press, 1963. Excellent study of diplomacy, politics, and national aims of individual Yugoslav political leaders and of the Yugoslav government and peoples at the close of World War I. See also: Sherman David Spector, *Rumania at the Paris Peace Conference: A Study of the Diplomacy of Ioan I. C. Brătianu.* New York: Bookman Associates, 1962.

Pavlowitch, Stevan K.: *Anglo-Russian Rivalry in Serbia, 1837–1839: The Mission of Colonel Hodges.* Paris, The Hague: Mouton, 1961. Far from limiting himself to questions of diplomacy and power politics, the author provides a good political and social history of the autonomous principality of Serbia during the 1830's.

Stavrianos, Leften S.: *Balkan Federation: A History of the Movement toward Balkan Unity in Modern Times,* Smith College Studies in History, XXVII (October 1941–July 1942). Menasha, Wis.: George Banta Publishing Co., 1944. A good study of the ideology and social and political foundations of movements of Balkan federation, especially since the nineteenth century, by an author who has oriented his research increasingly toward problems of world history.

Sugar, Peter F.: "The Roots of Eastern European Nationalism," in *Premier Congrès International des Etudes Balkaniques et Sud-est Européennes, Sofia, 26 août-1-er septembre 1966: Résumés des communications, Histoire moderne et contemporaine,* ed. Association Internationale d'Etudes du Sud-est Européen. Sofia, 1966, pp. 162–94. Stresses German contributions to East European conceptions of nationalism, examines relationship between religion and nationality, and distinguishes among five types of nationalism: popular (Serbia and Bulgaria), aristocratic (Hungary), bourgeois (Slovenia), bureaucratic (Greece and Turkey), and bureaucratic-aristocratic (Croatia). For a description of Albanian nationalism, we must await Stavro Skendi, *The Albanian National Awakening, 1878–1912.* Princeton, N.J.: Princeton University Press, 1967.

Sumner, Benedict Humphrey: *Russia and the Balkans, 1870–1880.* Oxford: Clarendon Press, 1937. A good study of Russian policy and Balkan national ambitions.

Vucinich, Wayne S.: *Serbia between East and West: The Events of 1903–1908.* Stanford, Calif.: Stanford University Press, 1954. Good introduction to the political, social, and economic history of Serbia, 1875–1903, as well as an excellent discussion of the "events" of 1903–1908: regicide, Serbo-Bulgarian customs union, political parties and ideologies, Austria-Hungary's "pig war" against Serbia, and the Austro-Hungarian annexation of Bosnia-Hercegovina.

Societies: Colonialist, Peasant, Bourgeois, and Communist. Virtually every other work cited in this bibliography deals with some aspect of society. Hardly any, however, is primarily concerned with the problem of the creation of a Communist society. We shall consequently indicate below some studies pertaining to Ottoman colonialism, the Balkan peasantries, and the "middle" or "bourgeois" sectors of Balkan society, but most of the items will relate to the rise of Communist ideologies and the formation of Communist societies.

Avakumović, Ivan: *History of the Communist Party of Yugoslavia,* Vol. I. Aberdeen: Aberdeen University Press, 1964. A useful work of reference on the Communist Party of Yugoslavia from the Russian Revolution to 1940.

Burks, Richard V.: *The Dynamics of Communism in Eastern Europe.* Princeton, N.J.: Princeton University Press, 1961. A valuable study of the social foundations of communism in the Balkans as well as in other parts of Eastern Europe.

Dedijer, Vladimir: *Tito*. New York: Simon and Schuster, 1953. Primary source. Valuable discussion of the differences between the Soviet and Yugoslav Communist revolutions by one of the leaders of the Yugoslav Partisan movement.

Dicey, Edward: *The Peasant State: An Account of Bulgaria in 1894*. London: John Murray, 1894. A description of Bulgarian politics, society, and economy.

Djilas, Milovan: *The New Class: An Analysis of the Communist System*. New York: Praeger, 1957. A study of communism as a device of economically underdeveloped countries to speed up industrialization and a discussion of the phenomenon of national communism. By a former Yugoslav Communist leader, now a liberal Hegelian.

McClellan, Woodford D.: *Svetozar Marković and the Origins of Balkan Socialism*. Princeton, N. J.: Princeton University Press, 1964. Very good study of one of the earliest Serbian socialists, his experiences in Russia and Switzerland, and his views on Marx, Bakunin, and other socialist or radical ideologists. Good picture of Serbian society in the period 1868–1875 and useful introduction to Serbian society since the Napoleonic era.

MacLean, Fitzroy: *The Heretic: The Life and Times of Josip Broz-Tito*. New York: Harper, 1957. Primary source. A picture of Tito as leader of the Yugoslav Partisans and commander of the Yugoslav Army of National Liberation during World War II.

McVicker, Charles P.: *Titoism, Pattern for International Communism*. New York: St. Martin's Press, 1957. Objective analysis of Yugoslav communism and of the potentialities of national communism.

Mitrany, David: *The Land and the Peasant in Rumania: The War and Agrarian Reform (1917–1921)*. London: H. Milford, 1930. Land reform as an ethnic, political, social, and economic problem.

Roberts, Henry L.: *Rumania: Political Problems of an Agrarian State*. New Haven, Conn.: Yale University Press, 1951. Excellent study of society and politics in interwar Rumania, with an introduction to problems of the peasantry and agrarian structure of Rumanian society and the threats and realities of authoritarianism and fascism.

Rothschild, Joseph: *The Communist Party of Bulgaria: Origins and Development, 1883–1936*. New York: Columbia University Press, 1959. Not only a valuable analytical study of communism but of Bulgarian political and social structures in general.

Roucek, Joseph S.: *The Politics of the Balkans*. New York and London: McGraw-Hill, 1939. Sociological study of interwar domestic politics.

Smothers, Frank, William Hardy McNeill, and Elizabeth Darbishire McNeill: *Report on the Greeks: Findings of a Twentieth Century Fund Team Which Surveyed Conditions in Greece in 1947*. New York: The Twentieth Century Fund, 1948. The Greek Civil War and the "complex pattern of fear" that it generated. There are other studies of the

Greek Civil War and of Greek postwar problems by William H. McNeill, Leften S. Stavrianos, and C. M. Woodhouse.

Stoianovich, Traian: "The Social Foundations of Balkan Politics, 1750–1941," in *The Balkans in Transition: Essays on the Development of Balkan Life and Politics since the Eighteenth Century*, Charles and Barbara Jelavich (eds.). Berkeley and Los Angeles: University of California Press, 1963, pp. 297–345. Analysis of the transformations of Balkan social structures over a period of two centuries.

Vucinich, Wayne S.: "The Nature of Balkan Society under Ottoman Rule." *Slavic Review*, XXI (December 1962), 597–638, with comments by Stanford J. Shaw and Traian Stoianovich. Three different views of the dominant and dominated sectors of Balkan society under Ottoman rule.

Yovanovitch, Dragolioub (Dragoljub Jovanović): "Les classes moyennes chez les Slaves du Sud." *Inventaires III. Classes moyennes*, publ. of the Centre de Documentation sociale de l'Ecole Normale Supérieure. Paris: Félix Alcan, 1939, pp. 217–50. Excellent study by an Agrarian leader of the South Slav middle classes in the interwar era.

Economy. Many of the studies under "Societies" cope with some manifestation of Balkan economic life. Works more specifically devoted to this subject include:

Bolkestein, Hendrik: *Economic Life in Greece's Golden Age*, revised and annotated by E. J. Jonkers. Leiden: E. J. Brill, 1958. Social basis of business activity in ancient Greece.

Busch-Zantner, Richard: *Agrarverfassung, Gesellschaft und Siedlung in Südosteuropa in besonderer Berücksichtigung der Türkenzeit*. Leipzig: Otto Harrassowitz, 1938. Fine study of the pastoral and agrarian economy and of the aggravation of peasant servitude in the Balkans during the intermediate centuries of Ottoman rule.

Gerschenkron, Alexander: "Some Aspects of Industrialization in Bulgaria, 1878–1939," in *Economic Backwardness in Historical Perspective*. Cambridge, Mass.: Belknap Press of Harvard University Press, 1962, pp. 198–234. Excellent study by a specialist of economic change in economically underdeveloped societies.

May, Jacques Meyer: *The Ecology of Malnutrition in Five Countries of Eastern and Central Europe (East Germany, Poland, Yugoslavia, Albania, Greece)*, Studies in Medical Geography, No. 4. New York: Hafner, 1963. Patterns of consumption.

Sakazov, Ivan: *Bulgarische Wirtschaftsgeschichte*. Berlin and Leipzig: Walter de Gruyter, 1929. Excellent economic history of Bulgaria since the medieval era.

Spulber, Nicolas: "Changes in the Economic Structures of the Balkans, 1860–1960," in *The Balkans in Transition: Essays on the Development of Balkan Life and Politics since the Eighteenth Century*, Charles and

Barbara Jelavich (eds.). Berkeley and Los Angeles: University of California Press, 1963, pp. 346–75. Very good discussion of long-term changes in employment capacity, in patterns of industrial activity, and in size groups of plants.

Stoianovich, Traian: "The Conquering Balkan Orthodox Merchant." *Journal of Economic History*, XX (June 1960), 234–313. Rise and growth of a Balkan merchant class from the fourteenth century to the Napoleonic era, with emphasis on the importance of eighteenth-century developments.

Stoianovich, Traian: "Land Tenure and Related Sectors of the Balkan Economy, 1600–1800." *Journal of Economic History*, XIII (Fall 1953), 398–411. Relationship between the expansion of an export economy and of cereal and cotton production, and the aggravation of serfdom.

Stoianovich, Traian: "Le Maïs dans les Balkans." *Annales* (*Economies, Sociétés, Civilisations*), XXI (1966), 1026–40. Balkan popular tradition as a force in the diffusion of maize cultivation.

Sugar, Peter F.: *The Industrialization of Bosnia-Hercegovina, 1878–1918.* Seattle: University of Washington Press, 1963. Austro-Hungarian industrialization policies in an economically underdeveloped area.

Svoronos, Nicolas G.: *Le commerce de Salonique au XVIIIe siècle.* Paris: Presses Universitaires de France, 1956. Excellent study of Greek merchantry and of the trade of Salonika and Macedonia during the eighteenth century.

Sweet-Escott, Bickham: *Greece: A Political and Economic Survey, 1939–1953.* London and New York: Royal Institute of International Affairs, 1954. Good on economic problems, politically very conservative.

Tomasevich, Jozo: *Peasants, Politics, and Economic Change in Yugoslavia.* Stanford, Calif.: Stanford University Press; London: Geoffrey Cumberlege, Oxford University Press, 1955. Excellent social and economic history of the various Yugoslav provinces from the Middle Ages to the end of World War II. No comparable study for any of the other Balkan countries. Abundant bibliography.

Warriner, Doreen (ed.): *Contrasts in Emerging Societies: Readings in the Social and Economic History of South-Eastern Europe in the Nineteenth Century,* selected and translated by G. F. Cushing, E. D. Tappe, V. de S. Pinto, and Phyllis Auty. Bloomington: Indiana University Press, 1965. On Hungary, Rumania, Bulgaria, and Yugoslavia. Good selections.

Zagoroff, Slavtcho D., Jenö Végh, and Alexander D. Bilimovich: *The Agricultural Economy of the Danubian Countries, 1935–45,* Publication of the Food Research Institute, Stanford University. Stanford, Calif.: Stanford University Press, 1955. Survey of the agricultural economy of Hungary, Rumania, Bulgaria, and Yugoslavia, with useful sections on consumption, production, land tenure since the nineteenth century, interwar economy, war and economics, and UNRRA measures of relief.

Demography. For the economic and political consequences of population growth and for the political and economic origins of territorial shifts of population in Eastern Europe during the present century, readers may turn to the studies of Eugene M. Kulischer, Wilbert E. Moore, and Joseph B. Schechtman. On other aspects of Balkan demography, especially for antiquity and for the twentieth century, there are important articles in the French review *Population*. Finally, readers may profit from the following:

Antoniadis-Bibicou, Hélène: "Villages désertés en Grèce: Un bilan provisoire," in *Villages désertés et histoire économique, XIe–XVIIIe siècle*, ed. Ecole Pratique des Hautes Etudes, VIe Section, Centre de Recherches Historiques (Les Hommes et la Terre, XI), preface by Fernand Braudel. Paris: S.E.V.P.E.N., 1965, pp. 343–417. Good introduction to the problem of lost or abandoned villages in Greek-Balkan areas from the Middle Ages to the nineteenth century.

Barkan, Ömer Lûtfi: "Les déportations comme méthode de peuplement et de colonisation dans l'Empire ottoman." *Revue de la Faculté des Sciences Economiques de l'Université d'Istanbul*, XI (October 1949–July 1950), 67–131. Population transfer policies in the Ottoman Empire. Should be read along with the Charanis article indicated below.

Barkan, Ömer Lûtfi: "La 'Méditerranée' de Fernand Braudel vue d'Istamboul." *Annales (Economies, Sociétés, Civilisations)*, IX (1954), 189–200. A critique of Fernand Braudel's *Méditerranée*, including an evaluation of Ottoman demographic growth during the sixteenth century.

Baxevanis, John: "Population, Internal Migration, and Urbanization in Greece." *Balkan Studies*, VI (1965), 83–98. Greek demographic situation in 1961. Should be read along with an article by Richard Kayser in *Annales (Economies, Sociétés, Civilisations)*, XX (March–April 1965), 301–08.

Charanis, Peter: "The Transfer of Population as a Policy in the Byzantine Empire." *Comparative Studies in Society and History*, III (January 1961), 140–54. Charanis has also published important articles on Byzantine towns and on the Jews of Byzantium.

Polyzos, Nicos J.: *Essai sur l'émigration grecque*. Paris: Librairie du Recueil Sirey, 1946. Greek demography and problems of emigration, 1821–1940.

Russell, Josiah C.: "The Medieval Balkan and Asia Minor Population." *Journal of the Economic and Social History of the Orient*, III (October 1960), 265–74. Actually a numerical estimate of the Balkan and Asia Minor populations, based on the studies of Ömer Lûtfi Barkan.

Valaoras, Vasilios G.: "A Reconstruction of the Demographic History of Modern Greece." *Milbank Memorial Fund Quarterly*, XXXVIII (April 1960), 115–39. A good study of a hundred years of population history, 1860–1960.

Personality and Culture. American cultural anthropologists in general and the French anthropologist Marcel Mauss in particular have contributed substantially to the development of a theory (or theories) of culture and personality. The footnotes to Chapter VI provide an introduction to some of the literature directly pertinent to the problem of culture and personality in the Balkans. For a view of personality in Greek antiquity, the following are recommended:

Jaeger, Werner: *Paideia: The Ideals of Greek Culture*, 3 vols., translated from the 2nd German edition by Gilbert Highet. New York: Oxford University Press, 1945. Greek values in antiquity and the processes of their communication.

Kluckhohn, Clyde: *Anthropology and the Classics* (The Colver Lectures in Brown University, 1960). Providence, R.I.: Brown University Press, 1961. Cultural values and personality of the ancient Greeks as seen through their literature.

Wassermann, Felix M.: "Thucydides and the Disintegration of the Polis." *Transactions and Proceedings of the American Philological Association,* LXXXV (1954), 46–54. Suicide of the *polis* through a shift from a spirit of restraint and conservation (*Sophrosyne*) to one of recklessness and love of honors (as against honor).

INDEX

A NOTE ON THE TYPE

This book was set on the Linotype in "Baskerville," a fac-
simile of the type designed, in 1754, by John Baskerville, a
writing-master of Birmingham, England. This type was one
of the forerunners of the "modern" style of type faces. The
Linotype copy was cut under the supervision of George W.
Jones of London.

*Printed by Halliday Lithograph Corp., Inc.,
West Hanover, Mass. Bound by
H. Wolff Book Manufacturing, Inc., New York.
Typography by Leon Bolognese.*